MEXICAN ROAD RACE
Carrera Pan-Americana Mexico

1950 BORDER TO BORDER

By ROLAND GOODMAN

●

IN APPRECIATION

The photographs which appear in this book were furnished by many persons and firms who are interested in auto racing. With so many different sizes and shapes, it would have complicated matters to have given credit for each individual photo, for in many instances, photos by different photographers appear on the same page.

We desire to thank all those who contributed the interesting shots which are included. They are: the Government of Mexico, the Mexican Pan-American Race Committee, Mexican newspapers "Excelsior" and "Novedades" — and the magazine, "Impacto," various American newspapers, Foto Mayo (Mexico City), Nash-Kelvinator Corporation, Oldsmobile Division of General Motors Corporation, Speed Age Magazine, Pemex Travel Club of Mexico, Sr. Antonio Cornejo, Jack Cansler, Bill Martin, Hershel McGriff, Jack McAfee, Bud Sennett, T. E. (Ted) MacDonald (Crown Film Productions), Rudolfo Dressel, Humberto Estudio, and El Automovil Mexicano & Carlos Lazo de la Vega, of Mexico City. Thanks also to any others whom we might have unintentionally overlooked.—FLOYD CLYMER.

●

This edition published by:
www.VelocePress.com
2009

Originally published by:

FLOYD CLYMER

America's Largest Publisher of Books Pertaining to Automobiles, Motorcycles and Motor Racing

1268 SOUTH ALVARADO STREET, LOS ANGELES 6, CALIFORNIA

Copyright 1950 by Floyd Clymer

The Prize Winners with many of the 80 trophies taken in a group at Victory Banquet in Mexico City after the race.

Sr. Antonio Cornejo C., Director General (general manager) for the race and his assistant, Sr. Arnoldo Baeza, go over plans for the race in the former's office before the start from Ciudad Juarez.

An Announcement

This book is dedicated to the motor racing enthusiasts of the world.

Surely no more colorful or unique automobile road race ever has been held than the Carrera Panamericana of 1950. This is especially true when we consider the large number of entries from so many different countries, the vast length of the race, and the manner in which it was conducted.

The result was a great tribute to the sportsmanship and courage of our good neighbor, the Republic of Mexico.

If I had foreseen the importance the contest eventually was to attain, I most certainly would have made the journey to see it, but to my sorrow I did not. I imagine thousands of other North American race followers will feel the same way after reading this book.

In order to present the complete story of the 1950 Mexican Road Race, I asked Sr. Antonio Cornejo C., Director General of the event, to suggest the name of a newspaperman closely connected with it, and he proposed a widely-known U. S. newsman, Mr. Roland Goodman, who was then living in Mexico. I am happy to have secured his services. Mr. Goodman wrote most of this book and sent complete details such as statistics, maps and accurate lists which are such a necessity in a record of this kind.

In addition, I have included other articles by famous authorities, some of the leading drivers themselves . . . including the winner, Hershel McGriff — and still and newsreel photographers who covered every aspect of the huge undertaking. Thus the reader may see the race from several different viewpoints and in a truly complete way.

Last but far from least, I wish to salute the government of Mexico and all race officials for their excellent efforts to publicize their new Panamerican Highway which extends the full length of the nation from north to south. Every report we received from returning drivers and others connected with the race agreed that, particularly for a first-time undertaking, the many details of such a complex operation were smoothly handled. I am sure that the goodwill created can be measured in far more than dollars and pesos.

More "horsepower" to Mexico in her future plans!

Sincerely,

Floyd Clymer

Top Officials of the Famous Race

Attorney Miguel Aleman, President of the Republic of Mexico, and honorary chairman of the organizing committee of the Mexican Pan-American Race.

Agustin Garcia Lopez, Secretary of Communications and Public Works, and chairman of the central executive committee of the race.

Antonio Cornejo, general manger of the race.

Arnoldo Baeza, assistant general manager of Mexican Pan-American Race.

Foreword
by the Race Director

Looking back on the Mexican Pan-American Race, I have a natural feeling of pride to have been associated with it as general manager.

The race was more than a personal triumph for those of us who were associated directly with it. It was a victory for Mexico, a proof that we could stage an event of this magnitude.

Of course there were faults, as no one knows better than I do, but I remember that Bob Estes said after it was over: "You should have seen the first Indianapolis Speedway race." The best proof that our event was a success is the generous compliments which the foreign entrants paid to our committee and our highway, and the statements of many of them that they'll be back next year if we have another race.

I want to take this opportunity to express my appreciation for the backing I had throughout from President Miguel Aleman and Secretary Agustin Garcia Lopez, as well as for the unselfish cooperation of the numerous members of the race committee.

Roland Goodman, the author of this book, was closely connected with the preparations for the race. I have read his manuscript, and he has told a good story.

ANTONIO CORNEJO C.
General Manager,
Mexican Pan-American Race.

Officials and Sportsmen discuss the Race

Gen. Leandro Sanchez Salazar, army commander in State of Chihuahua, who did fine job of safety preparations for first two legs of race, chats with Antonio Cornejo.

Antonio Cornejo (gesturing) explains a point to Secretary Agustin Garcia Lopez at pre-race meeting. Between them is Enrique Martin Moreno.

Bob Estes and Sr. Cornejo talk it over during the party, as another guest listens in.

Enrique Martin Moreno, Control Chief of the race, speaks to the drivers and guests at one of the many receptions in Mexico City.

Gen. Francisco Grajales, governor of the State of Chiapas (left), shakes hands at Tuxtla Gutierrez with Enrique Martin Moreno, race control chief. Between them is Attorney Pedro Viyao, race official.

6

Introduction

THE biggest and most exciting highway race of 1950 was a result of the imagination and energy of Mexico. Known as the **Carrera Panamericana Mexico** — the Mexican Pan-American Race — it was staged in six days, from May 5 through May 10, and attracted an entry list of 132 to compete for $38,610.40 (334,000 pesos) in prize money.

Only 58 cars crossed the finish line in the run across the entire country of Mexico from north to south. And although the top prizes and positions went to United States and European competitors, the comparatively inexperienced Mexican drivers came out of the 2,135-mile speed contest with plenty of credit for courage and nerve.

The big cash prizes were for the first three positions, and these went to U. S. entries — the first, of 150,000 pesos ($17,341.04), to a 1950 Oldsmobile entered by Roy Sundstrom, of Portland, Ore., and piloted by young Hershel McGriff and experienced Ray Elliott, of the same city. Second prize of 100,000 pesos ($11,560.69) was carried off by Thomas A. Deal of El Paso, Tex., who entered and drove his own 1950 Cadillac with Sam Cresap of El Paso as his copilot. It was Deal's first race, but he knew Mexican highways well. And third prize, 50,000 pesos ($5,780.35), went to a 1949 Cadillac inscribed by Eugene Barry, of Colorado Springs, Colo., and driven by Al Rogers, a three-time winner of the Pikes Peak Hill Climb, and Al's brother Roy, both of Colorado Springs.

RACE ATTRACTS 132 ENTRIES

Honors also went to three teams of courageous European professionals, two from Italy and one from France, who showed their stick-to-it-iveness and faith in their cars by finishing in the first twelve places after being outrun on the early level-country stages by their U. S. and Mexican rivals.

Of the 132 entries attracted by the race, 59 were from the United States, 57 from Mexico, and 16 were in the names of eight other foreign countries—four each from Colombia and Venezuela, two each from Italy and Peru, and one each from France, Guatemala, the Republic of China and El Salvador.

It was a stock-car race, so every car was of a standard make, with the overwhelming majority bearing familiar U. S. names, whether from factories in the United States or from assembly plants in Mexico. There were 132 entries, but one of these never designated a car or crew, and of course did not start in the race. Of the other 131, only six were of European makes—two Alfa Romeos; a Delahaye, a Jaguar, a Lago Talbot and a Hotchkiss.

Since not a single car was listed as being entered or sponsored by a manufacturer, it must be concluded that the choice of makes represented the preferences of the individual entrants. On that basis, products of General Motors and the Ford Motor Co. came out as overwhelming favorites, though it may be pointed out that the long strike which made it more difficult to obtain Chrysler Corp. new models was a factor in this situation.

Anyway, regardless of the reasons, here's the way the 125 cars of U. S. makes were divided up:

General Motors, 56, including 22 Cadillacs, 17 Buicks, 13 Oldsmobiles and 4 Chevrolets.

Ford Motor Co., 35, including 16 Lincolns, 11 Mercurys and 8 Fords.

Chrysler Corp., 5, including 3 Chryslers and 2 De Sotos.

Others, 29, including 9 Hudsons, 8 Nashes, 7 Packards, 4 Studebakers and one Cord.

There were so many factors in addition to the cars themselves, that it would hardly be fair to go into the matter of what proportion of each make was able to finish the race, until some of the other aspects have been discussed.

The chief point is that this was a race that tested men as well as autos, and in which luck certainly played a part, along with skill and strength.

All of which brings us to the highway itself, the reason for the race and the central fact behind everything that happened. The highway is one of the world's great road-building achievements, and as such it deserves a chapter all to itself, which is what it shall have.

In this introductory chapter, it's sufficient to say that Mexico staged the race in order to tell the world about its accomplishment in throwing a magnificent road across its varied terrain from its northern to its southern border.

The highway, designed as an artery for both commercial transportation and pleasure travel, proved to be a grueling test for the drivers and their cars. Those who crossed the finish line—27 Mexicans, 20 from the U. S., three each from Colombia and Venezuela, two from Italy, and one each from France, China and Peru—knew they had been in a battle. The satisfaction of having completed the run was almost as good as having won a prize.

POLICE AND ARMY PRAISED

Along with the excitement there was tragedy. One driver and one spectator met their deaths, and a number of drivers were injured in crackups. Really superior policing by Mexico's Army and various police forces kept down the accidents, as literally millions of Mexicans lined the hundreds of miles of unfenced road to watch the speed drivers whiz past.

With men dying and being injured, it would hardly be correct to say that the race was run in a picnic atmosphere, but it certainly was different from the rigidly formal competition of the Indianapolis type. This was a national celebration, and Mexico wanted everyone in on it. There was an air of fiesta over the whole affair.

The terms of entry were made deliberately easy in order to attract a large list. The experienced drivers, professional and amateur, carried off the top honors, of course, but the conditions were such that numerous persons entered as much for the excitement as for the chance of winning a prize.

An example of this was the number of woman entrants. No less than nine of the cars had women in their crews. Seven of these were from the United States, including the one all-girl crew. The other two women in the race were British-born, one the wife of a Mexican bullfighter, the other married to one of the Colombian drivers. The bullfighter, who learned at the last minute that his wife wasn't joking about the race, stayed home and listened nervously to the radio while the missus triumphantly piloted her car the entire distance.

None of the cars with women in them won prizes—the best was the Colombian, which finished 33rd—but they had a better record than the all-male crews. No less than five out of the nine crossed the finish line, including both of those in which the girls did the driving the whole way.

Accepting the judgment of its own people and its foreign guests, Mexico has decided that the race was such a success that it should be an annual affair. Whether this can be achieved is not certain at this writing, but a committee is at work on the problem.

ROLAND GOODMAN

Two notices, one in Spanish about Mantz' record run and an ad for the race. Also an ad in a Los Angeles paper advising drivers of the race situation by a committee who made the journey over the course before the race was run. Bottom: Car that broke record from Mexico City to Los Angeles.

Left to right: Les Viland, Johnny Fisher and Bill Martin before leaving Los Angeles for the race.

CHAPTER I

The Pre-Race Story

AUTO racing has a long history in Mexico, going back to the first speed contest, from Mexico City to Puebla, on Christmas Day in 1908. But there hadn't been a major race there, on either track or highway, since 1939 until the great Mexican Pan-American Race was staged in 1950.

Numerous persons share credit for the idea of putting on a race over the new border-to-border route to celebrate its opening. It wasn't a thing that sprang full-grown from any single individual, but a casual notion that gradually gathered force until it reached the attention of President Miguel Aleman and his Secretary of Communications and Public Works, Agustin Garcia Lopez, who gave it not only approval, but also the forceful backing which turned a dream into reality.

Eventually involving the volunteer efforts of more than 15,000 persons, as well as numerous government offices and private organizations, the idea for the race can be traced back to the major Mexican automobile and road associations.

Even before 1949, various leaders of the Mexican Automobile Association (the Asociacion Mexicana Automovilistica, or AMA for short) and the National Automobile Association (the Asociacion Nacional Automovilistica, or ANA) had mentioned the possibility of holding a major road race.

In early 1949 the magazine Panorama, official organ of the ANA, published a series of articles on the Pan-American Highway system, and about auto races which had been held in Europe and the Americas. It went into some of the preliminary steps which would be necessary for putting on such a race in Mexico, reviewing the regulations of the International Automobile Federation (FIA), of which the ANA is the Mexican affiliate. The FIA, while not the only international organization connected with auto racing, includes among its member groups (one to a country) those which sanction the greater part of the world's major races. Among these is the AAA, under whose auspices is held the Indianapolis Speedway race. Unless the FIA places a race on its international sports calendar, drivers licensed by member groups run the risk of being penalized for taking part in it.

The Mexican Highway Association (the Asociacion Mexicana de Caminos, or AMC), organized in early 1949, added its voice to those talking about a race.

COURSE TOTALS 2,135 MILES

Finally, in March, 1949, high officials of the Secretariat of Communications and Public Works, with the active backing of Secretary Lopez, announced definitely that a major race would be staged in Mexico. Not even a tentative date was fixed for it, but the route was defined for the first time—it would run from north to south, border to border, along the section of the Pan-American Highway system which, when completed, would link Ciudad Juarez in the north with El Ocotal in the south. It was a staggering distance for a highway race, because it is 2,135 miles from Ciudad Juarez, which is across the Rio Grande from El Paso, Tex., to El Ocotal, a tiny village on the mountainous frontier of Guatemala.

After the March announcement, matters were allowed to simmer for awhile. In view of the total lack of precedents in Mexico for a race of this magnitude, to say nothing of the fact that such a competition had rarely (one could almost say "never") been held elsewhere, it was wise to take things slowly. Besides, in early 1949 it wasn't possible to set a date for the race, since this would depend on when the highways were completed. On this last point, U. S. friends of Mexico were more optimistic than some Mexicans. The northerners, mindful of the country's amazing road-building progress, felt that the job was going well; their gloomier Mexican friends, said, "Sure, our grandchildren will be able to use this road." In 1950 the answer was given—the highways are open for today's generation as well as those of the future.

In June, 1949, however, the work of setting up committees was begun, and on August 5, 1949, the complete list was announced, with the chief race officials formally taking over their duties on that date.

The basic organization was known as the Organizing Committee for the Mexican Pan-American Race. So that government and private enterprise might cooperate freely, the committee was set up as a separate organization outside the government, though federal and state officials and offices were active in it, and of course there was full government approval.

This last was demonstrated by the fact that President Aleman, who had been enthusiastic about the project from the moment it was first discussed, accepted the honorary presidency of the Organizing Committee.

Active direction of the race was in the hands of the central executive committee, made up of four members: Secretary Garcia Lopez as president; Carlos Novoa, head of the official Bank of Mexico, as vice president and treasurer; Romulo O'Farrill, Jr., son and active associate of a leading newspaper publisher and auto industrialist, as a member, and Antonio Cornejo C. as general manager of the race.

AN IDEAL RACE MANAGER

Tony Cornejo deserves several paragraphs to himself. An energetic, compactly built man of 55, he is still youthful in spite of his graying hair. Cordial and never ruffled, yet quick in action and never hesitant about making a decision, he was an ideal choice for the full-time manager of the race.

Proudly a Mexican, Cornejo nevertheless fitted in well as chief of this international event, for he was educated at Stanford University, Palo Alto, Calif., and is almost as much at home in English as in Spanish. Though he came from a family situated safely beyond the danger of poverty, Tony Cornejo could be called a self-made man. Always interested in things mechanical, he even did a little auto racing as a youth, which of course was an important basis for his activity in the big competition he managed.

It was natural, then, for Cornejo to start in business with a service station. Over the years his activities have expanded until he now operates a large garage, has the only Pontiac agency in Mexico City, and runs radio station XELA, which specializes in fine music.

But business is not enough to keep Cornejo occupied. In his home he has a completely equipped workshop in which he turns out delicately accurate models of sailing ships, and a full array of photographic equipment plus darkroom with which he produces professional-standard portraits.

As if all this weren't enough, he started growing orchids as a hobby a few years ago, and his greenhouses have been so productive that, to his surprise, the sale of the surplus has enabled this avocation to pay for itself.

Cornejo worked day and night for long months as general manager, without receiving a centavo of salary. The same was true of the man he selected as assistant general manager, quiet bachelor Arnold Baeza. Baeza is Cornejo's partner and right-hand man in all his business enterprises, and together they make a perfect team. Retiring and yet friendly, Baeza is the picture of precision and efficiency. He supervised all the office work of the race—the bookkeeping, the inscriptions, the myriad of details with which Cornejo, busy with committee meetings and tours of inspection, had no time to concern himself.

THE COMMITTEES

In addition to the committee group, six committees and a commission were set up, as follows:

Control Committee, in charge of timing, enforcement of the rules, and, in general, the actual running of the race. Its president was Gen. Ignacio M. Beteta, president of the ANA and vice president Manuel E. Razo, with Julio Brunet, Ezequiel Godinez, Vicente Luengas and Enrique Martin Moreno as members. Martin Moreno, manager of the ANA, was named control chief for the race. In this position the slender, quick-speaking 33-year-old auto-club executive was the third member of the hard-working trio whose labors made the race a success. Along with Cornejo and Baeza, Martin Moreno knew few hours of rest for long months, and like them, he refused to accept any compensation for his services.

Safety Committee, concerned with protection of both racers and spectators. Its members were Ricardo Estrada Berg, executive vice president of the ANA, as committee president; Alfonso Villaseñor as vice-president, and Robert W. LaMontagne and Guillermo Trevino.

Service Committee, responsible for arranging lodging and hospitality for contestants and officials. Armando Herrerias, then manager of the Mexican Tourist Association, was president, with Pedro Viyao de la Prida as vice president and Manuel G. Leyva and Mario Cabrera as members.

Publicity Committee, also in charge of advertising, with Tomas Marentes, assistant chief of the National Lottery, as president, Jose J. March as vice-president, and Jose Luis Fernandez, Walter Glass and Robert W. LaMontagne as members.

Finance Committee, headed by industrialist Aaron Saenz, president, and Gen. Beteta, vice president, and including Cornejo, Estrada Berg, Alfredo Guijarro, Ramon Llano, George B. Manning, J. J. McIntyre, Vernon A. Moore, Novoa, George B. Olbert, Henry G. Paasch, Edmundo Phelan, Fraine B. Rhuberry and Edmundo Stierle.

Race Commission, in charge of certain legal details, with Gen. Carlos Real as president, Horacio Casasus as vice president, and Pablo Macedo and Jose Rivera as members.

Public Relations Committee, for international ceremonial contacts. Francisco del Rio Cañedo, director general of the federal tourist bureau, president; Col. Jose Garcia Valseca, vice-president, and Raul Mitchel, Luis Ochoa and Guillermo Palmieri.

In addition to these active committees, there was a list of patrons which included two cabinet members, the governors of the 12 Mexican states through which the race passed, U. S. Ambassador Walter Thurston, and a number of leading businessmen and editors.

The committees set up, there was just two jobs ahead, but they were big ones: To finish the highways, and to organize and publicize the race.

In mid-December the engineers of the Secretariat of Communications and Public Works were able to forecast that the highways would not only be open to transit by early 1950, but that all river crossings would have either permanent or temporary bridges or fords proper to permit a high-speed race.

February was set as the termination date, but the Central Executive Committee, allowing the minimum time for its own preparations, selected May 5, 1950, as the day the race would start. This is one of Mexico's important national holidays, the anniversary of a victory over invading French imperial troops at Puebla in 1862. It also was about as late as the race could be held in 1950 if it was to serve as effective publicity for the summer tourist season, which begins in June.

It happened that the later date was fortunate for another reason. The highways were open to ordinary travel by February, but the U. S. steel strike delayed the delivery of material for bridges, so that if the race had been held earlier, cars would have been forced to wait for ferries to take them across some of the wider northern rivers.

FINANCING THE RACE

The committee was aware that the date would make it difficult for drivers to compete in both Mexico and the Indianapolis Speedway race on Memorial Day, but this handicap had to be accepted.

Financing was partly a matter for the private backers of the race, but the federal government provided 250,000 pesos in addition to invaluable services. Eventually about 750,000 pesos—$84,000—was spent on all aspects of the race, about half for prizes and a quarter for advertising inside Mexico. This money came from four principal sources besides the government: 2,000 pesos from each entry fee (the rest of the 2,300 went for insurance), and gifts from the Mexican states through which the race passed, from the contractors who built the highway, and from Mexican importers, assemblers and manufacturers of autos, accessories and tires.

The decision to concentrate most of the prize money on 300,000 pesos (about $34,700) in premiums for the first three places seemed for a while to have been an error. Experienced racing men pointed out that, although the prizes were attractive, they put the competition pretty much on an everything-or-nothing basis. Thus, said these experts, the realistic professional, weighing his chances to finish among the first three, would hestitate to enter. Nor did the budget have room for guarantees, appearance money or payments to all who finished.

The results showed that the gloom-casters were overly pessimistic. The total of 132 entires included sufficient foreign professionals to insure high-quality competition, though doubtlessly many more of the men who drive for a living would have been attracted if the prizes had been arranged differently. The entry list is believed to be one of the greatest ever achieved for an international auto event of this size, so that the race was the reverse of a failure in this aspect. A few U. S. competitors dropped out when it became apparent, after half the race had been run, that they had no chance for the big prizes, but 20 of the 59 entered from north of the border stuck it out right to the finish line. Mechanical trouble and accidents accounted for

They came by Air, Sea and Land

Right: Felice Bonetto and Bruno Bonini brought their Alfa Romeo No. 103 over from Milan, Italy, for the event.

Joel Thorne, of Las Vegas, Nevada, an Indianapolis driver (right), is greeted at Ciudad Juarez by Alfonso Villasenor (left) and Armando Herrerias (center), of the race committee, after arriving at Juarez in his own plane. Thorne, in car No. 47, was wrecked in first day of racing.

Mr. and Mrs. Juan Riu of Colombia, pose beside their car No. 104.

Right: Jean Trevoux and Andre Mariotti finished creditably in their French Delahaye.

11

$38,000 Stock Car Race Will Open Mexican Central Highway Tomorrow

EL PASO, Tex., May 3.—(Special to Los Angeles Examiner)—The door to a modern land of Arabian Nights will be opened here to United States travelers when Mexico says "open, sesame" Friday on completion of the Mexican Central Highway from El Paso through Mexico City to Guatemala.

The 2174-mile route from the U. S. border to the Guatemalan border will be inaugurated formally on that date by a stock car race with more than 100 drivers from a dozen nations vieing for 330,500 pesos (about $38,000) in prizes.

President Miguel Aleman of Mexico is scheduled to officiate at the start of the highway race in Juarez.

ANCIENT CITIES—

The highway opens the way to some of the most colorful Mexican cities which heretofore have been virtually inaccessible.

Ruined cities, primitive Indian villages, ancient state capitals, a land of Amazons, pyramids, mysterious tunnels, jungle, desert, volcanoes and mountains are part of the kaleidoscopic picture along the new route.

It was in 1596 that Juan de Onate first worked his way north through Mexico to the pass of the North at the future site of El Paso.

But over 350 years passed until today, in the middle of the 20th Century, El Paso has begun to gain fame among Americans as the pass of the South.

This inaccessibility of cities along the route in Mexico has kept them unspoiled, native and quaint. The highway's opening is virtually a magic carpet to a world of ancient wonders.

CHIHUAHUA—

Moving south from Juarez along the highway, the traveler encounters Chihuahua, for which the diminutive Chihuahua dogs are named. Just beyond is Boquilla Lake, famous for its fishing, and the hot sulphur springs of Camargo.

At Durango, a 387-year-old city, is a mountain composed almost totally of iron.

The highway then climbs through rugged mountains to Zacatecas at 8112 feet and continues on to Aguascalientes with its mineral baths and mysterious tunnels of pre-historic origin.

Next is the mile-high Bajio plateau, a tremendous fertile plain rimmed by mountains, rich in silver and gold and dotted with beautiful towns.

At Silao a 15-mile paved side road leads to Guanajuato, one of Mexico's chief showplaces, a colonial city built on sides of a steep canyon.

10,000-FT. CLIMB—

Mexico City, with its Aztec ruins, pyramids and hundreds of attractions, and Puebla beyond are well known.

After climbing 10,000 feet to reach Puebla, the highway continues south past volcanoes and through sugarcane fields to Huajuapan, then winds through brilliantly colored mountains to Oaxaca with its perfect climate, near-by Indian villages, and amazing ruined cities.

A land of handsome costumed women is on the highway on the Isthmus of Tehuantepec, almost at sea level. The state of Chiapas is a country of jungle, mountains and primitive Indians.

The new highway is part of the Pan-American highway system of Mexico and makes it possible for the traveler to drive on a complete loop through Mexico, entering at either Laredo, Tex., or El Paso.

The Mexican government is so optimistic about travel along the new route that it has installed a travel office in El Paso to assist tourists.

This special license plate and armband were issued to the entrants.

Alexis Rovzar (right), Eastern Air Lines representative in Mexico, presents the Rickenbacker trophy to Cornejo before the race.

most of the eliminations.

It wasn't until the end of January that the rules were ready in definitive form, making it possible to begin a twofold international promotional campaign aimed at attracting entrants and gaining attention for the new highway route.

The closing date for entires was set at first for April 5, allowing only two months—February and March—to put the race over, in contrast to the year or more usually necessary for such a job. Even though this time eventually was extended by 20 days to April 25, the labor faced was truly Herculean.

Inside Mexico, the promotion took the form of an intensive advertising and publicity campaign which blanketed the country with posters, billboards, and notices in every publication, plus countless personal contacts. The governments of the states and territories responded to appeals to local pride, and no less than 18 of the 32 Mexican territorial divisions were represented eventually in the entry list.

The best Mexican drivers found sponsors, led by the veteran Jose Estrada Menocal, known by the affectionate nickname of "Che," a tall, lean man whose youthful face belies his 48 years. "Che" began his racing career as a boy mechanic in 1917 on the old Condesa racetrack in Mexico City. In 1930 he set a record of 1:09:21.40 over the then-recently paved Mexico City-Puebla highway, and in 1939, in Mexico's last important road race until 1950, he cut this time to 1:07:34.60. This last race, by the way, was won by Romulo O'Farrill, now publisher of the Mexico City daily newspaper Novedades, in 1:05:47, a record that stood until it was bettered by 11 of the 1950 competitors. The winner of this leg in 1950, Fernando Razo Maciel, did it in 1:03:05, and Estrada Menocal was second with 1:03:26.

Other experienced Mexican drivers in the 1950 race were Gregorio Pirez G. of Puebla, Spanish-born Jose Antonio Solana, Javier Razo Maciel, and Jesus Valezzi. Dogged by bad luck and accidents, only one of this group, Valezzi, reached the finish line, and he had a battle to work back up to 20th place after reaching Mexico City in 49th.

THE YOUNGER GENERATION

It was a younger generation of Mexican drivers, without competitive experience, but with plenty of nerve and, the know-how gained in handling trucks as well as passenger cars on mountain roads, who eventually gained the principal honors for their country. Chief among these was Luis Leal Solares, who learned his driving on the Mexico City-Tampico bus route, and finished seventh to be the only Mexican among the first 10 cars in the race.

A proper campaign of paid advertising in the U. S. would have required as much money as the entire budget for the race. Anything less would have meant slighting numerous publications which have proved themselves good friends of Mexico. so the executive committee decided to depend instead on the news value of the race, and seek attention in the U. S. strictly on the basis of providing information to foreign correspondents in Mexico, as well as directly to newspapers and magazines.

Press releases began pouring out to U. S. and Canadian publications, eventually reaching 300 sports editors, 300 auto editors, 175 travel editors, and the news editors of all the important daily papers of the border states of Texas, New Mexico, Arizona and California. Special releases went to 50 auto and racing magazines, and compilations of travel information to a number of editors who asked for additional data.

In addition, copies of the rules book went to all AAA affiliates. Most important, the AAA Contest Board cooperatively made available its mailing list of some 600 registered racing-car owners, drivers and mechanics, and these men received direct invitations to compete.

The news was received with interest, and soon replies and queries began pouring in, until more than 300 potential U. S. entrants had been heard from.

Even before the publicity campaign began, however, the race committee had gained an enthusiastic volunteer collaborator from across the frontier. He was C. D. Evans, of El Paso, who said he was a six-time Indianapolis race entrant who carried off sixth prize there in 1933. Known as "the world's safest driver," Evans has a record of 3,700,000 highway miles, including 191 New York-Los Angeles round trips, without an accident. Recently he had devoted himself to safety lecturing and to campaigning for uniform highway laws, but the Mexican Pan-American Race lured him out of retirement.

Evans heard of the race in November, 1949, and immediately wrote to Tony Cornejo for information, which was quite scant at the time. As soon as the rules book was ready, copies were rushed to Evans, and he wrote about the race to no less than 42 other drivers. He also determined to enter himself, and in late March, 1950, he made a trial run over the highway with Ramiro Aguilar, Jr., his assistant, in the 1950 Oldsmobile he was to drive in the race.

Deserving better luck in the competition, Evans was forced out on the sixth leg, between Mexico City and Puebla, when his steering apparatus broke.

The first paid entrant was Conrad Barrett, a Ford dealer of Anthony, on the New Mexico-Texas line just north of El Paso. He enlisted Rafael and Luis Almodovar, two brothers from Ciudad Juarez, as his drivers, and they piloted Barrett's 1950 Ford across the finish line in 31st place.

U. S. DOUBTS DISPELLED

Inquiries from U. S. drivers revealed two major worries—possible competition from European sports cars, and whether there would be Mexican taxes or currency-export control on prize money. The second was the easiest to answer; Mexico levied no taxes whatsoever on prizes, and the winners changed their checks to dollars and took them home with no difficulty.

Cornejo stuck to his guns on the matter of European cars. Any auto from across the Atlantic which met the specifications—closed body, five seats, standard factory model—would be permitted to compete. The size of the entry list proved that not many U. S. drivers were frightened by possible European competition. And in the end it was the entrants of European cars who complained about the U. S. makes. Not one of the four entries with "sports" reputations—a U. S. Cord and European Jaguar, Hotchkiss and Lago Talbot—was still in the race at the end of the fourth leg. The three touring-type European cars, two Alfa Romeos and a Delahaye, finished in the first 12, however.

Incidentally, the experiences of these last three entries proves that nothing is certain in auto racing. The entry for the Delahaye was cabled from France on March 17, and the car itself, accompanied by copilot Andre Mariotti, reached Veracruz by ship in mid-April, followed shortly by driver Jean Trevoux. This 1950 model, a beautiful, sleek gray two-door sedan, was valued at $10,000, making it the most valuable car in the race. It was a six-cylinder job with three carburetors. Trevoux and Mariotti went through days of road-testing, but they had constant carburetor trouble, and lost so much ground in the early legs of the race that it took all their skill to finish twelfth.

In contrast, the Italian cars were entered less than a week before the deadline, and reached New York barely in

Preparations for the Race

Final preparation of No. 38 back in Long Beach, California.

Les Viland putting final touches to No. 38 at Long Beach.

Stopping to change jets for better mileage.

time for shipment to Ciudad Juarez for the start of the race. But their crews, Piero Taruffi and Isidoro Ceroli, and Felice Bonetto and Bruno Bonini, maintained a respectable pace in the first legs and moved up rapidly toward the end to capture fourth and eighth positions, respectively.

Nor did experience have everything to do with it, because Trevoux, Taruffi and Bonetto are all veterans of professional racing, over European roads.

Many foreign drivers besides Evans and Trevoux tried out the highways in advance. When they reached Mexico City, they would drop into headquarters, which was in the Cornejo auto agency on the beautiful Paseo de la Reforma, the capital's widest and handsomest boulevard. Earnest discussions were always going there, under the huge map of the race route which was painted on the wall, in Spanish, English or French, but the subject was always the same—autos and racing. But there was almost no betting and very little predicting, because no one had enough information to go on to guess with any confidence as to the outcome of this unprecedented competition.

Al Rogers, of Colorado Springs, who was to take third place in the race, greeted Trevoux as an old friend when the Frenchman arrived. They had met each other at pre-war contests. Ed Kasold and Geano Contessotto, of Huntington Park, Calif., 26th at the finish line, also dropped in, as did George Nelson Ashley and Alfredo Saucedo, of El Paso, Tex., who were eliminated by engine trouble in the eighth leg.

The most productive visit, however, was paid in mid-April by two groups from the Los Angeles area who happened to hit town on the same day. One group was headed by Bob Estes, Inglewood Lincoln-Mercury dealer, backer of cars in the Indianapolis and other races. With him were Johnny Mantz, who took seventh prize at Indianapolis in 1949, and their friends Les Viland and John Fisher. The other pair were Tommy Francis, nephew of famed driver-car designer Lou Moore, and Bob Sommer.

Both groups had the same idea in mind—not only to try out the highways before deciding whether to enter the race, but to get some definite answers to questions. Their queries revealed to Cornejo that a lot of rumors about his race had been floating about the Southern California area. He met the situation squarely, "opened the books" for his visitors, and ended up not only by gaining two more entries but also by clearing the atmosphere considerably.

THE QUESTION OF PRIZE MONEY

There was the old question about the prize money. There was a report that the highway would never be finished. There was gossip that Pemex gasoline was no good. There were reports that the race preparations were disorganized, and that the rules were constantly being changed.

The men had seen the highway and tried the gasoline by then, so no argument was necessary on those points. Cornejo showed that the money was in the bank, how the race was being organized and that there had been only one set of rules changes, which he reviewed in detail, with the reasons for them.

Not only were the visitors convinced, so that Estes decided to enter a Lincoln with Mantz as driver, and Francis reported back favorably to his sponsor, Frank Carroll, a Ford dealer, but they put their signatures on a statement which was published immediately as a paid advertisement in the Los Angeles Times:

"To the auto-racing fraternity of California:

"We have come to Mexico to see for ourselves about the Mexican Pan-American Race. We have driven over the highway, we have used Mexican gasoline, we have talked with the general manager of the race, Mr. Antonio Cornejo, and we have been shown the records.

"We are now satisfied about the following points:

"The highway is a good one, in good condition.

"The prize money is on deposit.

"The rules have been changed only once, and for the benefit of the drivers.

"Super-Mexolina 80-octane gasoline is a good fuel, proper for use in such a race.

"The Race Committee has properly organized all matters of timing, lodging, refueling and other technical details.

"We are entering the race and recommend it to our friends in California.

"The entry deadline is now midnight April 25.

"We'd like to see 50 more Californians send their entries to the Race Committee."

California entries did reach 20, all but a couple from the southern part, and more than from any other U. S. state.

Further, both Mantz, who had Bill Stroppe as copilot, and Francis, who drove with Jimmie Crum, emerged as favorites of Mexico as a result of the race. Johnny won six leg prizes—a first, three seconds and two thirds—which was more than any other driver. He held second position in the race through the second, third and fourth legs, and climbed up to first during the fifth and sixth. But hard luck hit him in the seventh and ninth legs, and he ended up in ninth position.

Tommy Francis, already a hero of the Kathy Fiscus tragedy for his efforts in the fruitless attempts to rescue the little California girl from a well won new respect when he nearly cracked up his car in the ninth leg of the Mexican Pan-American Race in order to avoid hitting a child who ran in front of him. He had started the day in 15th position, but was so badly hurt when his car turned over completely that he was unable to continue, even though it righted itself. While Crum limped across the finish line hours later with the Ford, Tommy was taken to a hospital with the applause of the Mexicans for his sacrifice that saved a life.

Cornejo was able to show results to his visitors because he and his committees had been hard at work. The general manager personally made two survey trips to check on the condition of the highways and on the efforts of local committees at each stopping point along the route. Martin Moreno had been traveling up and down the road to train local control officials in timing and rules enforcement.

Perhaps the most spectacular achievement, to those who know Mexican roads, was the work of the safety committees, headed in each state by the commander of the military zone. The policing problem was literally tremendous, for, as every tourist knows, there are few fences along the highways, and one of the chief driving hazards is the livestock which wander about at will.

Mindful of the cows (and bulls), horses, mules, burros, sheep and goats which so often block the motorist's way, the wiseacres would ask Cornejo, "And what do you think you're going to do about the cattle?" He'd tell them, "Don't worry, everything's under control," and it turned out he was right.

Putting to work every soldier in their commands, the zone generals really did a job of making the race route safe. Aided during the race itself by federal and local police, plus numerous private volunteers, the Mexican Army rang up this record: Not a single accident on the open road was caused by spectators or stray animals. The very few incidents involving spectators—one of which was fatal to one person—occurred inside towns and cities.

THE SYSTEM IN OPERATION

Here's an example of how it was done, in the state of Chihuahua, which included the entire first two legs of the race and part of the third leg.

Cavalry started patrolling to a depth of a mile and a half on each side of the highway a day before the race, making sure that all domestic animals were tied up, and that no strays wandered into the area. After proper warning to farmers, loose animals were shot, though this was rarely necessary.

On the day of the race, all traffic was halted an hour before starting time, and all cross-traffic was forbidden. In the country spectators were required to stay 50 yards from the highway; in villages and towns, they were required wherever possible to watch from the flat rooftops.

Besides the cavalry, there were federal motorcycle police in motion along the highway until the racers actually started to pass, and overhead six light planes kept up a constant patrol. The planes were linked to the ground command post by short-wave radio, as were the chief secondary guard points along the highway.

Every six miles or so, depending on road conditions, there was a stationary group of soldiers ready to render immediate aid. Additionally, ambulances and tow trucks were placed at greater intervals, their positions determined by where the danger was greatest.

Not only regular soldiers but the reserves who drill each Sunday were put to work on the safety job. The results already have been told.

Entries, slow to come in at first, began to pour in faster and faster as the final deadline neared. When the first of April arrived with only a handful of cars entered, Gloomy Gusses around headquarters said that the committee would be lucky to have 50 drivers in the race. "We'll do all right," Cornejo told them, but even he admitted he was surprised at the final total.

One of the earliest U. S. entrants was Roy Pat Connor of Corsicana, Tex., whose Nash finished in third place, but later was disqualified. On April 17 was received the entry form for the Cadillac in which Al Rogers finally carried off third-place money for owner Charles Barry. The first- and second-place winners, Roy Sundstrom's Oldsmobile and Thomas Deal's Cadillac, weren't signed up until just before the April 25 deadline, however.

On April 15 the entry list had reached 66, with 33 from the U. S., 32 from Mexico and one from France. Definite word also had been received that the two Italian Alfa Romeos and two Venezuelan teams would be in the race.

And then, in the final 10 days, entries really began pouring in, with U. S. and Mexican inscriptions remaining neck and neck right to the end. Three more of the first 10 finishers—the entries of Tony Parravano of Manhattan Beach, Calif.; H. G. (Joe) Littlejohn of Spartanburg, S. Car., and the James Motor Co. of Los Angeles—signed up at about this time.

Bill France, of Daytona Beach, Fla., chairman of the National Stock Car Racing Commission, got his entry in, and it was generally understood that he'd be unofficially representing Nash interests in the race. Through no fault of France's, the Nashes bumped into a lot of hard luck; he himself had to drop out in the middle of the last leg, and the Connor car ran into a disqualification. To top it off, Oscar Fraley, United Press sports columnist, had to give up his plans to ride with France as copilot.

Both the president, Jack Gaynor, and the vice-president, Fred J. Steinbroner, Jr., of the Stock Car Racing Association of Los Angeles, entered cars in the race, but both Gaynor's Hudsons and Steinbroner's 1939 Ford were forced out before Oaxaca.

Women drivers and assistants also began appearing, until there were eight cars with half-female crews, and one piloted by two girls.

The two oldest cars in the race were 1937 models. One was the Cord, entered by Hugh J. Reilly, of Chicago, who had serious hopes of getting somewhere—hopes which were doomed to disappointment. The other was a 1937 Hudson with a more romantic story.

THE SAGA OF THE HUDSON

The old Hudson was entered in the name of El Nacional, semi-official Mexico City daily newspaper, but the initiative came from its driver, Ismael Alvarez, a resident of the capital who was born in the town of Altotonga, Veracruz. Always fascinated by automobiles, he learned to drive at the age of 12, but never could get together enough money to buy his own car.

When he heard of the Mexican Pan-American Race he determined to enter, and got leave from his humble job in Mexico City to return to Altotonga to seek help. There his family and neighbors not only lent a sympathetic ear, but took up a collection. All their modest resources came to a little less than 5,000 pesos—under $600—and cars cost more in Mexico than in the U. S.

The deadline was near, and no more money was in sight, so Ismael did the best he could under the circumstances. He bought the most car possible for the money, a 1937 Hudson, and set out to put it into condition and to raise the entry fee. El Nacional heard of his plight and took over sponsorship of Ismael, arranging for him to be inscribed in the race.

Alvarez drew No. 4 starting position, but that was the end of his luck. Driving north in early May, he reached Chihuahua safely, but there the Hudson's wiring caught fire, and Ismael and his copilot, Eliseo Cruz, were scorched putting out the blaze. They hastily installed new wires, but the clutch collapsed as they reached Ciudad Juarez, and they had to spend the entire night before the race making repairs.

No. 4 required five hours, 32 minutes and three seconds for the first leg, while the winner took less than half that time—but even though he finished in 113th position among the 113 cars to cross the line at Chihuahua, he was still in the race while 19 others had dropped out.

In the second leg, from Chihuahua to Parral, Ismael did better. His four hours, 32 minutes, gave him next-to-last place in the leg, though he was still last in the race as a whole. But then, on the third leg, from Parral to Durango, the final disaster struck; the transmission fell to bits, and the frantic efforts of Ismael and Eliseo to repair it with wire were fruitless. They had to call for a tow truck to take them into Durango, and the race was over for No. 4. Alvarez took his exit with a modest statement:

"I did what I could, raced at the best speed the car was capable of, and overcame many obstacles. I would have arrived at El Ocotal in the name of El Nacional if the transmission hadn't broken. All that's left for me is to say to my sponsor and my friends who helped me that I'm eternally grateful to them."

Getting back to the pre-deadline days, it was in the final week before April 25 that the South Americans began to arrive. First to appear was Henry Bradley, native of England who had lived in Peru for 27 years. A solid, silent sort, he had competed in various South American races. Like the other Peruvian entry, Luis Astengo Albizuri, a customs official from Lima, Bradley had to find both a car and a copilot in Mexico, and had little time for training. This

Drivers who helped make Race History

Ismael Alvarez and his '37 Hudson leave the starting line at Juarez. Clutch and transmission trouble put the car out after the second leg.

Below: Jacqueline Evans de Lopez, actress who drove No. 17 in race.

Above: Mexican hero Rodolfo Castañeda signs his autograph for some spectators.

17

The Field Marshal of the Battle

A close up of one of the short wave radio stations, operated by Mexican Army Signal men, which were used for communication with the spotter planes, flying over the racers, notifying officials of the arrival of the cars.

The Field Marshal of the Battle — Sr. Antonio Cornejo C., General Manager and Director of the race was everywhere to supervise the organization of this great enterprise. Here he is seen at Leon during the race.

told in the final results; Bradley cracked up in the fourth leg and Astengo, after a bad start, finished the race in 32nd place, just twice as far back as the 16th he had captured in the 1948 Buenos Aires-Caracas run.

The first two Colombian entries, Gabriel Herrera R. of Bogota, who came alone, and the brothers Samuel and Arturo Marin of Pereira, found a 1950 Ford and a 1950 Mercury in Mexico City, but the others, Juan Riu, of Bogota, and his pretty British wife, Jean Mott, and Artesio Paz P., had to hurry north to pick up autos.

The four Venezuelan teams reached Mexico so late that they went directly to Ciudad Juarez to buy cars and complete preparations, leaving Rito Giorgio, one of the copilots, to sign them up in Mexico City.

On the final day another "foreign" entry appeared. Manuel Luz Meneses is a Mexican citizen, son of a Chinese father and a Mexican mother, who changed his name from "Loo" to "Luz" to make it easier for Latin tongues to pronounce. When he signed up, he said, "Put me down as running in the name of the Republic of China." The entries from Guatemala and El Salvador also came in on the last day.

DRAWING FOR POSITIONS

A large batch of U. S. entries were reported in by telephone from Ciudad Juarez and Los Angeles, where they were being accepted on the night of April 25. These included the Cadillacs from El Paso which William W. Sterling drove to early honors in the race, and which Tom Deal piloted to second position at the finish.

Headquarters' work was complicated that evening of April 25 by the sudden decision of Secretary Garcia Lopez that, as a shot in the arm for Mexican public interest in the race, it would be better to hold the drawing for starting positions on the night of April 29 in Mexico City, rather than on May 2 in Ciudad Juarez, as specified by the Rules Book.

Telegrams were quickly sent to all entrants informing them of the change, and offering to have their ambassadors represent them at the ceremony if they were unable to be present in person, as proved to be true for nearly all of them.

The drawing was held in the auditorium of the National Lottery Building, under the supervision of Guillermo Ostos, executive officer of the Secretariat of Communications and Public Works, and Antonio Cornejo, Arnold Baeza, Enrique Martin Moreno and Gen. Ignacio Beteta. Handled by the personnel of the National Lottery, famed in Mexico for their absolute probity and impartiality, the luck of the draw gave the first places to Mexicans, with Tommy Francis as No. 6 and Henry Bradley as No. 7. These numbers affected the start for the first leg only, after which the cars were to begin each day in the order of their finish the previous day.

Other events of the final month before the race included the flying trip of three members of the race committees— Gen. Beteta, Horacio Casasus, attorney for the Mexican Hotel Association, and Alfonso Villaseñor, head of the Pemex Travel Club—to the United States to promote the tourist aspects of the new highways. Among other cities, they visited Los Angeles, San Francisco, Houston and New Orleans, and although they set out too late to recruit any entries for the race, they made many new friends for Mexico.

A week or so before the race, Secretary Lopez named Engineer Octavio Trias Aduna as its technical director, and he issued a booklet of regulations which appeared only in Spanish and reiterated the instructions which the U. S. drivers received in English.

On May 1 the officials who were to supervise the actual race, including Cornejo and Martin Moreno, headed north for Ciudad Juarez, leaving Baeza in charge in Mexico City. And the rest of the story is of the competition itself.

At drawing for starting numbers in Mexico City on April 29, before start of race. L. to R., seated at table: The Colombian ambassador; Guillermo Ostos, aide to Secretary Garcia Lopez; Gen. Ignacio Beteta; Antonio Cornejo; and Governor of Mexican Territory of Lower California (Southern half).

A view of the Santa Fe Bridge across the Rio Grande between El Paso, Texas, and Ciudad Juarez, Chihuahua. The new north-south route the length of Mexico starts here and extends 2,178 miles to the Guatemalan border.

CHAPTER II
The Highways of Mexico

THE highways—two of them—over which the Pan-American Race was run are among the greatest prides of Mexico, and with reason.

First of all, they represent the fulfillment of an obligation, a promise to the other countries of the Western Hemisphere that Mexico would complete her share of the Pan-American Highway system, a promise that has been more than kept.

Second, they add up to one of the most difficult road-building jobs in the world, across a variety of terrain that challenged the ingenuity of highway engineers.

Third, the highways were built entirely from Mexican funds, without a penny of outside aid.

And finally, perhaps of most lasting importance to U. S. travelers, the route is one of the finest anywhere from the tourist point of view—scenically beautiful and fascinating for the varied glimpses it affords of a country which is both colorful and quite different from the United States.

The race traversed the Central Highway, 1,288 miles from Ciudad Juarez on the Rio Grande to Mexico City, the nation's capital; and the Cristobal Colon Highway, 847 miles from Mexico City to El Ocotal, a village of fewer than 300 persons on the Guatemalan border. Cristobal Colon, by the way, is the Spanish name of Christopher Columbus, and El Ocotal has since been renamed Ciudad Cuauhtemoc, in honor of the last Aztec emperor, a national hero because of his brave resistance to conqueror Hernan Cortez.

These are properly known as "part of the Pan-American highway system in Mexico," because the country has in operation and under construction more than one road linking its northern and southern borders. The race route's 2,135 miles are only part of the 8,500 miles of paved and 5,000 miles of all-weather highway now in existence in Mexico.

Another part of Mexico's share of the Pan-American system is the well-known highway from Laredo to Mexico City, and a third north-south route, now about half paved, is being built between Nogales, on the Arizona border, and Mexico City via Guadalajara.

Mexico has a population of 25,000,000, about a sixth of that of the U.S., spread across an area a quarter the size of the nation to the north. Further, its economic development is much behind its neighbor's, though advanced in comparison to most other Latin American countries. In terms of highways, this means that Mexico has much greater comparative distances to span than the U. S., and much less money to do it with. To this must be added the fact that Mexico is so criss-crossed by mountains that per-mile costs for a long road are comparatively high.

ACHIEVEMENT OF CONSTRUCTION

All the foregoing adds luster to the Mexican highway-construction achievement. More glory is supplied by the fact that Mexico now builds her roads with her own engineers, most of them trained inside the country, and using her own construction materials, chiefly stone from the immediate countryside, plus asphalt from the national oilfields and domestically produced concrete. Heavy machinery and bridge steel are the chief imports. Her first highway engineers were U. S.-educated, and U. S. experts helped at first, but now Mexican universities are training all the personnel needed.

The Central and Cristobal Colon Highways have been 25 years in the building, slowly at first, when the first short stretches near Mexico City were completed, and with a concentrated effort in the last five years or so. They represent a cost of 500,000,000 pesos, perhaps a little more, a sum that can't be accurately translated into dollars because the exchange rate during the 25 years fluctuated from about 3.5 to the present 8.65 pesos per dollar. Make it $100,000,000 and you won't be far off.

One aspect of the new highways that hasn't been mentioned is of tremendous importance to Mexico, and incidentally to the United States. This is their service in providing direct and quick transportation to areas which have been isolated, except by horseback, for centuries from the rest of Mexico and the world, or have had so-so train connections.

This is going to mean—in fact, it's already happening—the awakening economically of great areas which have produced barely enough for local needs, and have imported only a scant minimum of products from other areas. Now that the output can get to market, a large-scale growth of agriculture and industry is expected everywhere the highways pass. And steady building of feeder roads is enlarging the areas affected.

To the tourist, all this may be beside the point. Let's get down to "business" for him, then, and take a look at what there is to be seen along the highway, traveling from north to south. This is what the racers saw when they were returning the opposite way, because they didn't have time to lift their eyes off the highway itself on the way down.

In general, all the distance from the U. S. border to San Cristobal Las Casas, 107 miles from El Octoal, 1950's motorist will be driving over an asphalt-surfaced road 33 feet wide, with a maximum grade of 6 per cent, and curves that have a minimum radius of 134.5 feet. Permanent steel or concrete bridges are quickly replacing the temporary wooden structures over which the racers crossed a few of the rivers in the north, and 29 grade separations are on the construction list. The final stretch near Guatemala was gravel-surfaced for the race, and will remain that way until Guatemala finishes her connecting road, because at present there isn't enough traffic to make paving worth while.

This is no place go into matters like hotels and filling stations; there are information offices at the border, in El Paso and Ciudad Juarez, and for the race it was simple—the officials reserved every hotel room in every overnight stop except Mexico City, and special fueling stations were designated.

EN ROUTE TO CHIHUAHUA

For most of the racers from the U. S., their first glimpse of Mexico was from the international bridge between El Paso and Ciudad Juarez, a modern city of more than 100,000. Catering to tourists who wander across the border for the day, Juarez won't appeal to those looking for more "Mexican" atmosphere.

The first leg of the race took the drivers from Ciudad

Some Cameramen took to the Air

This camera plane was used for some of Bill Martin's pictures shown in this book.

Highway near Mexico Ciy was conducive to speed. Tom Deal, winner of second place, repares to take turn.

Fancy stepping could be attained on this long, straight stretch.

Typical small Mexican village along the Pan American Highway.

22

Along Mexico's new Border-to-Border Highway

Ever-changing, but always distinctively Mexican, the scenery along the country's thousands of miles of paved highways is one of the chief attractions for tourists. These pictures were taken between Durango and Torreon on a branch of the new 2,178 mile border-to-border route which leads from El Paso to the Guatemalan frontier by way of Mexico City.

This up-to-date filling station in Aguascalientes is typical of the facilities available for motorists using the new highway through Mexico to Guatemala —all paved except the last few miles.

Juarez, 3,117 feet above sea level, to Chihuahua, 4,600 feet high. This is probably the dullest stretch of the road. There are almost no hills, and most of the 233 miles is through semi-desert. It is hot in the daytime, especially during the summer, and during the race tires were popping along here like balloons at a party as cars whizzed along at top speeds. Hunting is good in this part of Mexico, incidentally.

Chihuahua, state capital with some 80,000 people, is where the sightseeing begins. A progressive city with many modern buildings—its sports center, with a huge diving tower, is right out of Hollywood—is also full of fine old colonial structures. From here Benito Juarez carried on his long battle against Emperor Maximilian; here Pancho Villa had his headquarters; here the father of Mexican independence, Miguel Hidalgo, was killed by the Spaniards.

The next two legs of the race were to Parral, 186 miles past Chihuahua, and from Parral to Durango, another 251 miles. The road descends to about 3,500 feet altitude, then climbs gradually through rolling country until shortly before it reaches 6,207-foot-high Durango.

Along this stretch, the chief interest at first is in the great irrigation projects which are transforming arid acres into rich farms. Cotton, wheat and fruit grow in this warm region, fed by several huge and beautiful dams which may be seen by driving a few miles up various side roads.

At Parral, a town with about 25,000 population, is the famous Prieta silver mine. This is the beginning of the north-south Mexican mineral region which over the centuries has produced fortunes in gold, silver, copper, lead and zinc. Mines are dotted through the mountains all the way from Parral to Guanajuato along the Central Highway. And with them go hot and mineral springs, many of which have led to the construction of resort hotels.

Durango, besides being a mining center, is the capital of a state famous for its great forests and its cattle, and now beginning to acquire industries as well. It has some 40,000 people. Coming into Durango and on south to Leon, the motorist gets his first real experience of Mexican mountain roads which curve in and out interminably as they reveal one breathtaking view after another, never two alike.

Past Durango 180 miles is another state capital, Zacatecas, which at 8,112 feet is the highest and coldest place along the northern part of the route. Mexicans say that only the richness of its silver mines keeps its 25,000 inhabitants in chilly Zacatecas, but the tourist will want to linger awhile to see the fine old cathedral and the lovely parks from which there are striking views of the surrounding hills. Also of interest are the ruins of Chicomoztoc, ancient Aztec site at least 800 years old, with great stone structures, and the Hacienda Troncoso, where stand a score of incredible tall cone-shaped buildings used to store grain.

Aguascalientes, 90 miles further, is a city of almost 100,000 that is 6,280 feet high. As its name indicates, it has famous hot springs. It also is undermined with an extensive network of tunnels, of mysterious manmade prehistoric origin. Though Aguascalientes is chiefly a railroad and weaving town, it has many fine old colonial buildings, and is known for its perfect mild climate.

Onward through Lagos de Moreno, a pretty agricultural center, the highway leads another 70 miles to Leon, where begins the great mile-high plateau of the Bajio, the lush farming region of central Mexico. Leon itself is a modern boom town, a manufacturing city which specializes in shoes and other leather goods, and has doubled its population to about 150,000 within a decade. Its huge cathedral is worth a visit, and its town square is handsome with carefully shaped trees.

At Silao, 19 miles past Leon, the traveler should do something which the racers couldn't—turn off the main highway for a half-hour paved drive to Guanajuato, perhaps the most interesting city in Mexico. Built in a steep mountain valley, Guanajuato is a maze of twisting narrow streets, most of which are really cobbled stairways. Its old houses are beautiful, and it contains sights like the cemetery with coffins stacked in "filing cabinets" above ground, and mummified corpses standing along the walls of a tunnel beneath.

Back on the main road, its 137 miles of easy going over the level Bajio plain from Silao to a highway fork known as Palmillas. Along the way are the busy cities of Irapuato, Salamanca, where a big new oil refinery has just gone into operation, Celaya, Queretaro and San Juan del Rio. Celaya and Queretaro are noted for their superb architecture, and the latter is historically important as the place where the Mexican independence movement was sparked into action, and where Maximilian was captured and executed.

THEN TO MEXICO CITY

At Palmillas one road leads east to Ixmiquilpan, where this branch of the Central Highway joins the Laredo-Mexico City route. The race was sent over the alternate, more sporting branch which leads south to the city of Toluca and then east to Mexico City. The Ixmiquilpan branch slopes gradually upward to an altitude of about 9,000 feet, then back down to Mexico City's 7,340 feet. Via Toluca, 8,760 feet high, there is another slow climb over a distance of 82 miles until that city is reached, then a sharp ascent over a 10,006-foot mountain pass on the final 40 miles to Mexico City.

In the race, the distance from Durango to Mexico City was run in two legs divided at Leon.

Mexico City, a metropolis of almost 3,000,000, is not only the capital of the country, but one of the world's great cities. It has everything—luxury hotels, thousands of shops, good night clubs, magnificent modern and older architecture, great factories and tiny handicraft workshops, and a population that varies from barefoot Indians to elegant millionaires. Here the racers paused overnight before beginning the last three days of their six-day competition.

The first leg along the Cristobal Colon Highway, the sixth of the entire race, was also the shortest. It took the cars over miles of curving highway built along mountain precipices, past the highest point on the entire route, 10,485 feet above sea level. Just before completing the 84-mile run, the road passes through the town of Cholula, said to have a church for every day in the year. Cholula's most interesting church is built atop an enormous Aztec pyramid which is said to be the world's largest in volume, though there are others higher. The mountains on this leg, by the way, used to be the haunt of bandits who preyed on horseback and stagecoach travelers.

Puebla itself, a city of 220,000 which is a textile center, is amazingly beautiful. Nearly every building is decorated profusely with multicolored tiles, and its churches and many other structures are masterpieces of the elaborate art of past centuries.

The altitude on the 256-mile stretch from Puebla to Oaxaca, the next leg of the race, varies only between Puebla's 7,010 feet, the 3,550 feet at the midway low point, and Oaxaca's 5,067. But this proved to be one of the toughest parts of the race, because there are few straight or level sections. Curve follows curve, and the road always is climbing or descending.

Nevertheless the Puebla-Oaxaca drive is one of the most pleasant of the entire trip. Here may be seen nearly every

Scenery and Facility

This picture was taken between Delicias and Chihuahua.

"AGUA, AIRE, GASOLINA, ACEITE . . . A SU SERVICIO." At your service with water, air, gasoline and oil—and a comfortable room for the night. That's what the motor traveler is offered in this super-filling-station-and-tourist-courts in Chihuahua, on the brand-new highway.

Scenery Galore

The winding turns of the Panamerican Highway near El Ocotal.

The drivers' impression of the highway in the mountains of South Mexico.

Typical mountain road near the Mexican-Guatemalan border.

type of the varied vegetation with fascinates visitors from the north. There are huge cultivated fields of sugar cane and rice, as well as the more familiar corn and wheat. Mixed in with pine forests are every type of Mexican cactus, including the cultivated maguey or century plant which provides such drinks as pulque and mescal as well as fibers and roofing material, and the towering wild organ cactus. And the rocks rival the Grand Canyon in color, at least— deep red, light pink, purple, and a wide selection of greens.

Oaxaca is a favorite little city among those who know Mexico well. With only 40,000 people, it is an easy-going state capital that boasts of a perfect mild climate. Linked with it are the names of two of Mexico's most important presidents, liberator Benito Juarez and dictator Porfirio Diaz, both of whom called it home. Handsome ironwork decorates its old buildings, its Santo Domingo Church is the leading example of Mexican religious art, and its market is full of fine pottery and weaving.

Just outside Oaxaca are the pre-Spanish ruins of Mitla, with walls that are a mosaic of separately carved little stones that form beautiful friezes, and Monte Alban, a great mountain-top agglomeration of ancient pyramids. Marvelous gold jewelry found in a Monte Alban tomb is on display in the Oaxaca museum.

The next leg was the second longest of the race, 336 miles from Oaxaca to Tuxtla Gutierrez. The highway continues about 27 miles through the long, mountain-girt Valley of Oaxaca, then winds into the sierras again, passing through wild, green scenic territory until it descends to the fabled Isthmus of Tehuantepec.

ON AND ON SOUTHWARD

This is the low point on the route, 155 miles past Oaxaca and 100 to 300 feet above the level of the near-by Pacific. It is also one of the most colorful regions, full of tropical fruits and the home of the handsome Tehuana women, famous for their bright and sumptuous costumes, and known as "Amazons" because they carry on most of the trade.

The road goes on through rolling warm country with little of interest, angling inland to Tuxtla Gutierrez, 1,770-foot-high little capital city of Chiapas, Mexico's southernmost state. Though it has only 25,000 people, Tuxtla has concrete-paved streets that are kept spotless, and nice little parks, one of which includes a zoo.

It was the last leg, from Tuxtla Gutierrez to the border, that was the toughest, because of the unpaved surface of the last 107 miles out of the 171-mile total on this run. Even the paved part isn't easy. There's a brief level stretch from Tuxtla to the interesting village of Chiapa del Corzo, and then the road begins to climb fast. It goes up 5,480 feet—more than a mile—in the 42 miles from Chiapa del Corzo (1,452 feet) to San Cristobal Las Casas (6,932 feet).

Las Casas, end of the pavement, is another richly historic town. With scarcely a modern building, it is almost unchanged from the days, dating back to the 1500s, when it was the trading and governing center for inland Chiapas. Until less than 10 years ago it could be reached only by horseback trails, and its market is still full of primitive Indians in strange costumes.

The only town of any size past Las Casas is Comitan, backward for all its 20,000 population, but boasting a pleasant climate, for it is 5,020 feet above the sea. In the neighborhood are lakes which may soon be vacation spots. At present Comitan is the entry "port" for mule-train trade with near-by Guatemala, but the new highway brings promise that before long trucks will be roaring through on their way to Central America.

It's hard to say when this last will happen. For now it is possible to drive only to the border, where Ciudad Cuauhtemoc, the former El Ocotal, is still only a cluster of thatched huts. Guatemala has just 25 miles of road to complete in order to link up Mexico with all of Central America, but they are difficult mountain miles, and Guatemala hasn't very much money.

It'll be a great day for Mexico and for the tourist, too, when Guatemala opens the door.

Through the Windshield...

A driver's view of a straight stretch through the plains.

Skid marks on a sharp turn.

Part of the unpaved road on the last 100 miles up to the Guatemalan Border.

CARRERA PANAMERICANA México

OFICINAS EN: AUTOMOTRIZ CORNEJO, S.A. VERSALLES Y REFORMA TELS. 18-43-29, 35-15-18, 36-38-43 MEXICO, D.F.

DE FRONTERA A FRONTERA

PRESIDENTE HONORARIO DEL PATRONATO
Sr. Lic. Miguel Alemán,
Presidente de la República

COMITE CENTRAL EJECUTIVO
Presidente:
Sr. Lic. Agustín García López,
Secretario de Comunicaciones y Obras Públicas.

Vice-Presidente y Tesorero:
Sr. Lic. Carlos Novoa,
Director General del Banco de México, S.A.

Vocal:
Rómulo O'Farrill Jr.,
Asociación Mexicana de Caminos

Gerente General:
Sr. Antonio Cornejo C.,
Automotriz Cornejo, S.A.

MIEMBROS DEL PATRONATO:
Sr. Adolfo Ruiz Cortines
Sr. Manuel Tello
Sr. Lic. Fernando Casas Alemán
Sr. Gral. Francisco J. Grajales
Sr. Lic. Eduardo Vasconcelos
Sr. Ing. Carlos I. Betancourt
Sr. Alfredo del Mazo
Sr. Lic. Vicente Aguirre del Castillo
Sr. Lic. Eduardo Luque Loyola
Sr. Lic. José Aguilar y Maya
Sr. Lic. J. Jesús González Gallo
Sr. Ing. Jesús M. Rodríguez Flores
Sr. Leobardo Reynoso
Sr. José Ramón Valdés
Sr. Ing. Fernando Foglio Miramontes
Sr. Walter Thurston
Sr. Adolfo M. Monsanto
Sr. Senador Antonio J. Bermúdez
Sr. Pedro A. Chiapas
Sr. Guillermo Guajardo Davis
Sr. Mariano Suárez
Sr. Luis de la Rosa
Sr. Martín Ruiz
Sr. Lic. Miguel Lanz Duret
Sr. Gilberto Figueroa
Sr. Luis Novaro
Sr. Lic. Guillermo Ibarra
Sr. Rómulo O'Farrill
Sr. Lic. Aarón Sáenz
Sr. Clemente Serna Martínez
Sr. Dr. Enrique Ruiz Hurtado
Sr. Lic. Alejandro Quijano

April 20th, 1950

To U.S. Entrants:

This bulletin will bring you up to date on a number of details connected with the Mexican Pan-American Race.

First, here are some specific interpretations of the rules which we have made at the request of various entrants, and which all of you should be acquainted with:

Apart from the right to use any tires, automobiles must be stock. Standard parts may be replaced where needed, if they are within factory specifications for the make and year model of the car entered.

Cylinders may be rebored on 1949 and 1950 models up to 30/1000ths. (.030) of an inch, and the pistons may be replaced with other pistons manufactured for that particular car.

On earlier models, cylinders may be rebored up to 60/1000ths (.060) of an inch.

Shock absorbers may be replaced as a safety factor.

Stronger horns may be substituted, but sirens are barred.

It is optional to remove the rear seat and back cushion to install the extra gasoline tank or to carry spare parts or tools.

Open exhaust is forbidden; direct exhaust pipe must have silencer. Cutout valve is forbidden.

Hubcaps and rear fender shields may be removed (this supersedes any previous ruling).

One more prize has been offered--the A.N.A., a Mexican automobile association, will give a 2,000-peso prize to the <u>last</u> car to finish within the time limit.

Yours sincerely,

ANTONIO CORNEJO C.
General Manager

A Few of the Drivers Instruction Books

CHAPTER III

Rules and Regulations

DRAWING up a rules book for the Mexican Pan-American Race was a serious problem for the officials. There were examples to draw from, as used in other countries, but the Mexican race presented a special situation without precedent.

The race would have to be run over a long, open course which would be not only impractical, but actually impossible, to police mile for mile. At least it would be impossible to have trained officials, conversant with every word of the rules book and competent to spot every possible violation, posted along the entire route. And even if there had been the funds and the time available for training, there was the language question. Half the entrants would be non-Spanish-speaking, so that even if the officials could have been posted, the foreigners would have been unfairly handicapped by the inability to make themselves understood.

The practical answer to this question was two-fold: To make minor time losses part of the luck of the race, and to depend on the sportsmanship of the contestants to live up to the rules in unsupervised stretches.

As a matter of fact, the first part of this worked out quite well. The only situation which might have made a change in the final standings was the three minutes which Thomas A. Deal, driving Car 113, claimed he lost in the first leg, when he said he stopped 19 miles from the starting line to see if he could help after the crackup which cost the life of Enrique F. Hachmeister of Guatemala, driving Car 112. Deal said that he tried to find Enrique Martin Moreno, control chief, in Chihuahua at the end of the leg in order to reclaim the time, as required by the rules, but couldn't locate him. Instead, said Deal, he told his story to Antonio Cornejo, general manager of the race. He didn't present his claim again until the end of the race, when three minutes would have given him first place instead of second. It was not allowed, and Deal accepted the situation without further complaint.

In a similar situation, William W. Sterling, driver of Car 68, the early leader in the race, lost 32 minutes when a bridge was blocked by the smashup of Car 7 in the fourth leg. Sterling got a notation to this effect by a policeman and a Mexican Red Cross doctor who were present, and submitted his claim as soon as he arrived in Mexico City. Martin Moreno okayed the subtraction of the time, which gave Sterling second place in the fourth leg. Since Sterling's car was knocked out by brake trouble before the end of the race, this didn't affect the final standings.

The sportsmanship angle worked out well, too. Except for a couple of formal complaints that certain drivers had not permitted others to pass them, everyone agreed that the spirit of fair play ruled the race, regardless of the nationality of contestants.

Those were the big problems. There were a host of smaller ones in connection with formulating the rules, however. These will be mentioned in the following detailed discussion. In general, it may be said that in spite of possible refinements which came to everyone's mind after the race had been run, the officials came up with a rules book which made it possible to send more than 100 cars over 2,135 miles of highway in fair competition.

As a base for the rules-writing, Martin Moreno had a single copy, in proof form, of the latest revision of the rules of the F.I.A., which are the initials of the French or Spanish name of the International Automobile Federation, the world auto-racing organization under whose sanction the Mexican race was held.

In addition, of course, there were the rules of the AAA Contest Board, which are designed basically for closed-course professional racing, as well as the regulations of the Buenos Aires-Caracas races, which came closest to the conditions of the Mexican race.

One bit of hard luck kept the race committee from getting some valuable additional advice. General Manager Cornejo made a trip to the United States in December, 1949, on various matters connected with the race, and stopped off in Washington to confer with AAA Contest Board officials. Before he could talk to them, however, a microbe nipped him, and Cornejo spent all his limited time in Washington in a hotel bed. Later the board officials evidently were unwilling to comment on another's country's rules by mail, as requested, although they co-operated in many other ways. Thus one fount of wisdom remained closed to the race committee.

Doing the best they could, the officials had a rules book ready at the beginning of February, 1950. With a single group of revisions issued on March 15, these rules stood for the race, although interpretations were made as necessary, and various minor technical details as to actual day-by-day procedure were added in an instruction leaflet handed to competitors before the start.

Let's go over them point by point, starting with the rules book as it stood after the March 15 revisions:

PREAMBLE AND ARTICLES 1 AND 2

These state that the race is "an open test of speed" across Mexico, and say frankly that it is organized to draw international attention to the new highway route, especially from the tourist aspect. They further point out that the race is patronized by Mexico's President Miguel Aleman, and that the Organizing Committee is headed by the Secretary of Communications and Public Works, Agustin Garcia Lopez, and includes the governors of the 12 states through which the route passes.

ARTICLE 3

This defined the eligibility of automobiles. The basic idea was that the race was open to any five-seat closed-body passenger automobile, as long as it had factory equipment without changes or special added equipment. At first "sports," coupe and convertible types were excluded, but it proved so hard to draw the line on five-seat models that the word "coupe" was eliminated. Also, in what was intended as a safety measure, and turned out to be a very wise precaution in view of the curving mountainous route, all restrictions on tires and tubes were dropped in the March 15 revision.

ARTICLES 4 AND 5

Everyone was required to use 80-octane Ethyl Super-Mexolina, a gasoline produced by Petroleos Mexicanos, the national petroleum corporation, but was permitted to use any lubricants preferred.

ARTICLE 6

This gave competitors liberty to carry whatever standard spare parts and repair equipment they wanted, as well as spare tires.

ARTICLES 7 AND 8

These listed the nine legs into which the six-day race was divided (at first eight legs in five days), and gave the maximum time for each leg, based on a minimum speed of 60 kilometers (37.2 miles) an hour—reduced from 80 kilometers after a survey of the final stretch of the highway. It explained that a car which exceeded the maximum time on any leg could continue competing for leg prizes, a provision which a handful of drivers took advantage of. It gave permission to control officials to make allowances for time lost in circumstances not the fault of the driver—a provision which, for reasons given previously, was applied sparingly.

ARTICLES 9 THROUGH 16

These governed entries. A deadline of April 5, 1950, was set originally, then extended to April 15, and finally to April 25 as South American contestants appealed for more time. As it was, nearly all the South Americans barely got under the wire by flying to Mexico, where they bought cars, after trying until the last minute to arrange for shipping them. The entry fee, originally 2,500 pesos ($289.02), was cut to 2,300 pesos ($265.88) as a result of a reduced rate on the public-liability insurance which was included in the fee. These articles also covered the right to refuse entries, postpone the race, etc.

ARTICLES 17, 18 AND 19

These governed entrants, making the race open to organizations and business firms as well as individuals, and granting the right to change crews before the race, but not during it. It was under this last rule that Car 49 was disqualified for third place because of a change of crew which was officially ruled to have been unauthorized. A similar change of crew was officially permitted for Car 9, entered by Mexico's presidential offices, but with the understanding that this car, while being classified in each leg and for the race as a whole, was out of the competition for prize money.

ARTICLES 20 AND 21

The first of these required that Mexican participants have licenses from the Mexican Automobile Sport Commission, and that foreigners have similar credentials from organizations affiliated with the F.I.A. A difficulty developed when the race committee discovered suddenly that many U. S. entrants, particularly the strict amateurs who never had driven in any other race and probably never would enter another, lacked information about the AAA Contest Board, which is the U. S. affiliate of the F.I.A., and were moving too slowly in obtaining credentials. In order to insure the success of the Mexican race, the AAA generously granted permission to the Mexican commission to issue licenses to U. S. participants, good only for this one race, and with the Contest Board absolved of all responsibility for participants thus licensed. The board was given no reason to regret its action, as all went off smoothly. Entrant and driver were made jointly responsible for observing the rules.

ARTICLES 22, 23, 24 AND 25

These provided for all cars' being in Ciudad Juarez three days ahead of the race for examination and other preparations. There was to be a drawing on May 2 for numbers which the cars were to carry, and which were to govern the order of their start in the first leg. (Thereafter they were to start each day in the order in which they finished the previous day. In order to drum up more public attention for the race, Secretary Lopez, ordered the drawing to be held instead on April 29 in Mexico City, where it could be broadcast nationally. Telegrams were sent to all entrants, and their ambassadors were invited to represent the foreign entrants who could not be present. Numbers were painted on the roofs as well as the sides of the cars so that the race could be monitored from the air. Special metal license plates also were provided. Each car was provided with a route book which the crew carried through the race; it included photos for identification, and space for entering times as recorded by the synchronized chronometers of the timekeepers.

ARTICLES 26 AND 27

The manner of start was defined, cars taking off from the line at one-minute intervals, each in turn taking a standing position with engine running. The size of the entry list permitted extension of this interval to five minutes after every 20th car, giving the drivers more road room.

ARTICLES 28 THROUGH 39

These defined the road rules for the race. The right to pass was to be granted on a single signal of the horn. On two-leg days, cars were to start the second leg half an hour after they finished the first, thus leaving the mid-point in the order of arrival. An extra 120-liter (31.7-gallon) gasoline tank had to be installed to avert the need for intermediate refueling stations. Crews were forbidden to accept help for repairs along the road. In certain towns, drivers were required to cut their speed to 25 miles an hour while passing through, as directed by flag signals.

ARTICLE 40

This listed the prizes. Besides the prizes of 150,000, 100,000 and 50,000 pesos for the first three finishers in the entire race, there were three speed prizes for each leg. For eight of the legs, the prizes were 2,000, 1,000 and 500 pesos. For the fifth leg, from Leon to Mexico City, the prizes were 3,000, 2,000, and 1,000 pesos. Prizes were to be split in the event of ties.

ARTICLE 41

The Organizing Committee did not take responsibility for accidents involving competitors.

ARTICLE 42

Timing was to be done by three officials, with their times averaged in the event of discrepancies.

ARTICLES 43, 44 AND 45

Governing advertising on competing cars and regarding race results.

ARTICLES 46 AND 47

These set a one-hour limit for making protests, and covered identification of contestants and officials.

Those were the basic rules of the race. But application of Article 3 did not prove to be simple. The intention was to keep the competition strictly among stock cars.

Almost immediately it was necessary to pin down the question of what was a "standard" factory model. For this, the AAA Contest Board's definition of a stock car was adopted—at least 50 must have been produced of any one model, with another 500 on order. Further, the car must have been offered for sale to the general public through authorized dealers.

Intermezzo

Right: All drivers were given ample supply of food for each race leg.

Left: Mexican boy at the famous fountain at Taxaco.

Mexican girl serving iced drinks for the drivers and spectators.

One of the native Indians near San Cristobal in the southern part.

The Interesting Log Book of Car 118

Every car had a log book for checking purposes signed by control authorities.

On this basis, entries of at least three each of two particular models were refused: The "police Ford," a Ford with a Mercury engine, produced by the factory, but only on special order from law-enforcement agencies and others having legitimate need for such cars; and the Fordillac, a combination of Ford chassis and Cadillac engine. The latter is the invention of Philip F. Walters, of Baldwin, N. Y., widely-known as a racing driver under the name of Ted Tappett. Although more than 50 Fordillacs had been produced, it was clearly a special job, and the entry fees were returned.

More complex was the question of what reconditioning could be permitted on older stock cars, since there eventually were 42 1949 models entered, and 25 from earlier years, dating back as far as 1937. The race committee adopted three criteria:

1. Essentially, reconditioning and repairs must be limited to restoring cars to the condition in which they left the factory.

2. Certain changes would be allowed in the interests of safety, although in one instance it was recognized that this would have the secondary effect of affecting speed.

3. Lenience would be shown toward minor changes that could not affect speed.

As formalized, usually in writing, here's how these points worked out in a number of instances:

1. Cylinder reboring was allowed up to .030 inch on 1949 and 1950 models, and up to .060 inch on earlier cars, with pistons replaced by other factory-made pistons. For a couple of pre-war cars, permission was given to replace engines with identical others made a year or two later than the original ones. On the other hand, open exhausts and cutout valves were forbidden, and silencers were required on direct exhaust pipes.

2. Although it was recognized that cars could achieve greater speed on the many curves if stronger shock absorbers were installed, the committee decided that the safety factor was so important that this substitution should be permitted. A similar decision was reached regarding tires and tubes. Because of the danger to spectators if hubcaps and rear fender shields came loose at high speed, drivers were permitted to remove these parts, even though this would save them a few precious seconds in making tire changes.

3. Installation of chronometers, r.p.m. indicators and other special instruments were not interfered with. Safety belts were encouraged, and stronger horns were allowed (but no sirens). And rear seats and back cushions could be taken out to make space for the extra gasoline tank and spare parts.

The more important of these points were repeated to all entrants in a circular letter airmailed on April 20, in time for everyone to be able to take advantage of them.

It is important to emphasize that these were neither changes nor additions to the rules, but rather definitions and clarifications of an article which needed to be applied to specific problems which everyone knew would be sure to arise.

The final document for general distribution was the mimeographed instructions, in Spanish and English, delivered to all contestants on their arrival in Ciudad Juarez. In 13 double-spaced pages, it gave minute details of the manner of running the race.

At each overnight stop a parking enclosure was established where cars were to remain under guard from arrival until departure, with the exception of time allowed for fueling at designated stations, plus two hours for repairs (the time consumed in going to and returning from the garage was not counted). Engines were sealed before the start, and the presence of a control official was required if repair work called for the breaking of the seal. Actually this two-hour limit proved extremely difficult to enforce, especially in the smaller towns, where repair facilities were not numerous. At least, everyone got the same break in the loose enforcement of this regulation.

THE TIMING PROCESS

This was the routine for timing: At the start of each leg, the time was entered in the route book at the starting line and the book was handed back to the driver. The finish line was passed at full speed, of course, with cars required to stop at a designated point thereafter, where the books were handed in. When there were two legs in one day, there was a half-hour stop between legs. During this stop the arrival time was noted in the route book, which was returned to the driver before he started the day's second leg. At the end of each day the books were retained by the officials until the classification of cars' positions had been completed, and the positions were entered in the books before they were returned.

The Ciudad Juarez inspection of cars was frankly superficial, because of the number entered. The chief point was to spot any obvious deviations from stock specifications, and to seal the engines against changes during the race. The first 15 (actually reduced to 11 later) cars in the race were to be put under strict guard at the finish line at El Ocotal, until they could be inspected by factory technicians, and each car being gone over closely by an expert from an assembly plant not connected with that make.

Under the topic of "Rules of the Road," Mexican Federal Highway Police were designated as "judges of transit," to spot violations of the rule forbidding any competitor to bar the passing of another car. Flag signals also were described.

Garages were required to make detailed reports on all repair work done.

Not only were crews strictly forbidden to carry alcoholic beverages, but also the slightest degree of intoxication was sufficient basis to eliminate both crew and car from the race. It was never necessary to enforce this regulation.

Finally, either driver or assistant was permitted to continue the race alone if, because of sickness or injury, the other member of the crew had to drop out.

At the start, Old Dodge fixed up with wings and all.

Complete Entry List of Entrants, Drivers and Co-Pilots

CAR NO.	MAKE & YEAR	ENTRANT	DRIVER	ASSISTANT
1	Hudson 1950	Luis Iglesias Davalos Mexico, D.F.	Entrant	Tomas Iglesias Davalos
2	Packard 1949	State of Guerrero Chilpancingo, Guerrero	Oscar Lopez de Llergo	Cesar Peinado
3	Cadillac 1949	State of Guanajuato Guanajuato, Gto.	Jose Soto Beltran	Arturo Monreal T.
4	Hudson 1937	El Nacional (newspaper) Mexico, D.F.	Ismael Alvarez	Eliseo Cruz Carballo
5	Oldsmobile 1950	Firez y Haces, S.A. Puebla, Pue.	Gregorio Pirez Granier	Roberto Vargas
6	Ford 1950	Frank Carroll Los Angeles, Calif.	Tommy L. Francis	Jimmie Crum
7	Nash 1950	Automovil Club de Peru Lima, Peru	Henry Bradley	Jesus Reyes Molina
8	Packard 1949	Industrias 1-2-3, S.A. Mexico, D.F.	Jose Estrada Menocal	Miguel Gonzalez
9	Cadillac 1950	"Mexico" car, entered by President's offices	Lt. Rodolfo Castaneda G.	Florencio Estrada C.
10	Buick 1948	Mrs. H.R. Lammons Jacksonville, Texas.	Entrant	Merryl Bedford
11	Mercury 1949	Earl Allen San Antonio, Texas.	B.A. Hemesby	Margie Allen
12	Oldsmobile 1950	James Motor Co.	Bud Sennett	John C. Balch
13	Lincoln 1950	Cerveceria Modelo, S.A. Mexico, D.F.	Antonio Alzua Echaiz	Ramon Diaz Fernandez
14	Hudson 1950	Jack Gaynor Inglewood, Calif.	Lou Figaro	Dempsey Wilson
15	Mercury 1950	Henry S. Dabdoub, S.A. Mexico, D.F.	Rafael Montes de Oca P.	Francisco Gasca A.
16	Cadillac 1947	Alberto Pedro Rojas, Jr. Mexico, D.F.	Entrant	Luis Gomez Barrera
17	Chrysler 1947	Jacqueline Evans de Lopez Mexico, D.F.	Entrant	Arturo Medina
18	Ford 1939	Fred J. Steinbroner, Jr. Los Angeles, Calif.	Entrant	Harry Nicklin
19	Delahaye 1950	Republic of France	Jean Trevoux Paris, France	Andre Mariotti
20	Hudson 1948	Charles Fraley Columbus, Ohio	Entrant	Regi (Speed) McFee
21	Cadillac 1949	Eugene Barry Colorado Springs, Colo.	Al Rogers	Ralph Rogers
22	Buick 1948	Pete Goedhart Norwalk, Calif.	Ralph J. Hop	Entrant
23	Cadillac 1948	State of San Luis Potosi San Luis Potosi, S.L.P.	Jose Sanchez Ruiz	Severiano Carrillo T.
24	Oldsmobile 1949	State of Nuevo Leon Monterrey, N.L.	Ireneo Rojas Garza	Ignacio Arellano S.
25	Lincoln 1949	David C. Aprezza Broderick, Calif.	Entrant	Willie Earl Wooders
26	Lincoln 1949	Raymond D. Parks Atlanta, Ga.	Entrant	Robert N. Byron
27	Cadillac 1941	Alfonso Oviedo y O. Mexico, D.F.	Entrant	Eulalio Rodriguez O.
28	Chrysler 1950	Olivetti Mexicana S.A. Mexico, D.F.	Gutierre Tibon	....
29	Nash 1950	Jose Paullada Escalante Mexico, D.F.	Jose Antonio Solana	Javier Solana
30	Lago Talbot 1947	Otto Francis Foster N. Hollywood, Calif.	Edward Walker	Entrant
31	Lincoln 1949	Ray Crawford Alhambra, Calif.	Entrant	Frank Valdez
32	Mercury 1950	State of Morelos Cuernavaca, Mor.	Olegario Perez P.	Arnulfo Manjarrez T.
33	Nash 1949	State of Queretaro Queretaro, Que.	Salvador Santoyo	Manuel Lopez R.
34	Lincoln 1949	State of Chiapas Tuxtla Gutierrez, Chis.	Octavio Anza Esquivel	Rogelio Anza Esquivel
35	Packard 1949	State of Zacatecas Zacatecas, Zac.	Javier Razo Maciel	Jose Collia
36	Cadillac 1950	John and Andrew Moran Chicago Ill.	Anthony Musto	John Moran
37	Nash 1950	William (Bill) France Daytona Beach, Fla.	Entrant	Curtis Turner
38	Lincoln 1949	Bob Estes Inglewood, Calif.	John Mantz	Bill Stroppe
39	Mercury 1950	Raul Arguelles Salgado Mexico, D.F.	Entrant	Enrique Paredes H.
40	Lincoln 1949	Marie H. Brookreson Willcox, Arizona	Ross Barton	Entrant
41	Ford 1950	Edmund A. Kasold Huntington Park, Calif.	Entrant	Geano Contessotto
42	Lincoln 1949	Teodoro Schultz Guadalajara, Jalisco	Jesus Nava Gonzalez	Guillermo Parada
43	Cord 1937	Hugh J. Reilly Chicago, Ill.	Entrant	Walter E. Dorsey
44	Packard 1949	Techo Eterno Eureka, S.A. Mexico, D.F.	Fernando Razo Maciel	Luis Solorio
45	Packard 1948	John N. Stewart Clovis, N. Mex.	Entrant	James I. Massey
46	Oldsmobile 1949	Transportes Tampico, S.A. Mexico, D.F.	Luis Leal Solares	Damaso de la Concha
47	Cadillac 1949	Joel Wolfe Thorne Las Vegas, Nev.	Entrant	....
48	Buick 1950	Lyle McKinley Warren Inglewood, Calif.	Entrant	Mrs. E.P. Warren
49	Nash 1950	Roy Pat Connor Corsicana, Tex.	Entrant	Robert Green
50	Ford 1949	John Reber Bensenville, Ill.	Entrant	John Harper
51	Buick 1938	Fernando Duran Mejia Mexico, D.F.	Entrant	Jorge Campos Rodriguez
52	Oldsmobile 1950	Roy Sundstrom Portland, Ore.	Hershel McGriff	Ray Elliott
53	Cadillac 1950	Ricardo Lopez Mendez Mexico, D.F.	Entrant	....
54	Lincoln 1949	Jimmy Hicks Houston, Tex.	Entrant	Knobby Amos
55	Cadillac 1950	Calvin C. Connell Detroit, Mich.	George Lynch	Johnny Fedricks
56	Ford 1949	Nieders Auto Talleres Mexico, D.F.	Edward A.R. Nieders	Max Humberto Diener
57	Mercury 1950	Northern Territory of Lower California, Mexicali	Alfonso Verdugo Quirez	Francisco Armenta M.
58	De Soto 1949	Burnett E. Thatcher Pomona, Calif.	C.E. O'Brien	Joe Gumbmann
59	Cadillac 1949	Robert A. Clement, Jr. Detroit, Mich.	Entrant	Leonard Rao
60	Mercury 1950	Ruppert Motors, Inc. Pomona, Calif.	S.S. Barragan	J. Forester
61	Buick 1950	Ricardo Garcia Rendon Mexico, D.F.	Entrant	Rodolfo Garcia Rendon
62	Oldsmobile 1949	State of Chihuahua Chihuahua, Chi.	Carlos Gustavo Mass	Jose Durarte

CAR NO.	MAKE & YEAR	ENTRANT	DRIVER	ASSISTANT
63	Cadillac 1949	George Nelson Ashley, El Paso, Tex.	Entrant	Alfredo Saucedo
64	Mercury 1950	Central de Lineas, Mexico, D.F.	Marcelo Quintanilla S.	Roberto Quintanilla S.
65	Packard 1948	Harry E. Alberts, Portland, Ore.	Francisco Ibarra Somohano	Cornelio Medina O.
66	Hudson 1950	Bob Korf, Beloit, Wis.	Entrant	John Renier
67	Cadillac 1950	Rafael Norma Larranaga, Mexico, D.F.	Entrant	Guillermo Norma L.
68	Cadillac 1950	Charles Ray Royal, El Paso, Tex.	William W. Sterling	Daniel Arias, Jr.
69	....	State of Tamaulipas, Ciudad Victoria, Tamps.	(entry paid, but no car entered)	
70	Studebaker 1950	Republic of Peru, Lima, Peru	Luis Astengo Albizuri	Inocencio Ortiz G.
71	Oldsmobile 1950	Womble Olds, Lubbock, Tex.	Owen R. Gray	L. C. McMillan
72	Cadillac 1949	Omnibus Analco-Moderna, Guadalajara, Jalisco	Manuel R. Soto Lara	Enrique Verduzco R.
73	Nash 1950	Rafael Mendoza Licea, Guadalajara, Jal.	Entrant	Rafael Gonzales S.
74	Chevrolet 1950	Republic of Venezuela, Caracas, Venezuela	Ramon Lopez	Pedro Noguera
75	Buick 1942	Luciano Joublanc Zamora, Mexico,D.F.	Carlos Garcia Ruiz	Entrant
76	Hudson 1949	Calzado Canada, S.A., Guadalajara, Jalisco	Salvador Lopez Chavez	Eduardo Soto Lara
77	Lincoln 1949	State of Mexico, Toluca, Mex.	Jesus Valezzi	Adolfo Duenas Costa
78	Oldsmobile 1950	Republic of Venezuela, Caracas, Venezuela	Atilio Cagnasso	Rito Giorgio
79	Oldsmobile 1950	H. G. Littlejohn, Spartanburg, S. Car.	Lewis Hawkins	Wayland Burgess
80	Buick 1940	Andrea Gonzalez, San Francisco, Calif.	Entrant	Lucille Acevedo
81	Cadillac 1949	Lonnie H. Johnson, Jr. Shallowater, Tex.	Entrant	G. W. McGraw
82	Mercury 1950	Transportes Tresguerras, Celaya, Guanajuato	Leopoldo Almanza Vera	Arnulfo Silva Solis
83	Buick 1948	State of Durango, Durango, Dgo.	Leonel Nunez Chavez	Celestino Flores Carillo
84	Mercury 1950	Alianza de Camioneros de Mexico, Mexico, D.F.	Carlos Almazan Becerril	Leopoldo Almazan B.
85	Hudson 1949	Territory of Quintana Roo, Chetumal, Q.R.	Gustavo Ladewig Camarena	Jesus Ascencio Hernandez
86	Ford 1950	Republic of Colombia, Bogota, Colombia	Samuel Marin	Arturo Marin
87	Studebaker 1950	Hart Motors, S.A., Mexico, D.F.	Andres Wiltz	Luis Rivas Melara
88	Lincoln 1950	Harry Sents, Glen Aubry, N.Y.	Entrant	Amos Hill
89	Buick 1941	William A. Grover, Colorado Springs, Colo.	Entrant	Marcelino Garcia
90	Alfa Romeo 1950	Automobile Club of Italy, Milan, Italy	Piero Taruffi	Isidoro Ceroli
91	Oldsmobile 1950	Republic of Colombia, Bogota, Colombia	Artesio Paz P.	Juan Godina
92	Ford 1950	Conrad Barrett Anthony, N.Mex.	Rafael Almodovar	Luis Almodovar
93	Mercury 1950	Republic of Colombia, Bogota, Colombia	Gabriel Herrera R.	Carlos Gonzalez Vargas
94	Studebaker 1950	Universidad Nacional Autonoma de Mexico, Mexico, D.F.	Fernando Gallardo Amaro	Enrique Torres Caballero
95	Oldsmobile 1950	Charley L. Goldtrap, Harlingen, Tex.	Entrant	Claud W. Philips
96	Buick 1950	Joe Thompson, Carlsbad, N.Mex.	Entrant	....
97	Chevrolet 1948	Republic of Venezuela, Caracas, Venezuela	Ali Segundo Rachid Luzardo	Luis Alberto Aribe M.
98	Hudson 1947	Jack R. Gaynor, Inglewood, Calif.	Chuck Meekins	Joe Pisano
99	Packard 1949	State of Puebla, Puebla, Pue.	Mariano Garn	Erasmo Villoria
100	Buick 1949	State of Michoacan, Morelia, Michoacan	Felix Cerda Loza	Jose Aguilar
101	Chrysler 1950	Industrias Montiel, S.A. Mexico, D.F.	Jose Mateo Topete	Miguel Lecuona Ramos
102	Cadillac 1938	Fox Motor Sales, Mount Gilead, Ohio	Dwight Phillip Fox	Benjamin Shelpman
103	Alfa Romeo 1950	Automobile Club of Italy, Milan, Italy	Felice Bonetto	Bruno Bonini
104	Mercury 1950	Republic of Colombia, Bogota, Colombia	Juan Riu	Jean Mott de Riu
105	Buick 1950	Antonio Pacheco Casero, Mexico, D.F.	Entrant	Raul Carregha
106	Lincoln 1947	State of Veracruz, Jalapa, Veracruz	Arturo F. Breton	Mario Navarro Hoyo
107	Buick 1950	William M. Gillespie, Idyllwild, Calif.	Entrant	Mrs. L.H. Gillespie
108	Hotchkiss 1938	Taylor Lucas, Los Angeles, Calif.	Entrant	Johnny Von Neumann
109	Oldsmobile 1950	Julio V. Hirschfield, Mexico, D.F.	Entrant	Marcos Raya
110	Jaguar 1949	Jorgen Thayssen, Los Angeles, Calif.	Jay C. Chamberlain	Benny Long
111	Cadillac 1950	J. W. Parham, Lubbock, Tex.	Entrant	Noel Singleton
112	Lincoln 1949	Republic of Guatemala, Guatemala City	Enrique F. Hachmeister	Francisco Toscana Valle
113	Cadillac 1950	Thomas A. Deal, El Paso, Tex.	Entrant	Sam Cresap
114	Nash 1950	Edwin John Sollohub, Schenectady, N.Y.	Entrant	Nicholeo Scott
115	Lincoln 1950	Raymundo Mendoza Yniguez, Bakersfiled, Calif.	Lewis Ruwalt	Entrant
116	Nash 1949	Republic of China	Entrant	Jose O'Farrill Larranaga
117	Buick 1949	Republic of El Salvador, San Salvador, El Salvador	Manuel Luz Meneses Mexico, D.F. Capt. Alfredo Call	Romeo Lopez Mejia
118	Cadillac 1949	Tony Parravano, Manhattan Beach, Calif.	Jack McAfee	Ford Robinson
119	Ford 1949	Pentathlon Universitario, Mexico, D.F.	Emilio Portes Medina	Armando Rodriguez Morado
120	Cadillac 1939	Ray Colenbaugh, Des Plaines, Ill.	Entrant	Howard Hasse
121	Lincoln 1949	Alianza de Camioneros de Mexico, Mexico, D.F.	Abelardo Matamoros Acosta	Julio Arciniega Jimenez
122	Hudson 1950	Harry Adam Elbel, San Antonio, Tex.	Entrant	Henry A. Magers
123	Lincoln 1949	Raymond M. Ector and N.H. Fuller, Atlanta, GA.	Fontello Flock	Bob Flock
124	Buick 1950	Victor de la Lama, Mexico, D.F.	Entrant	Samuel del Villar
125	Cadillac 1943	State of Campeche, Campeche, Camp.	Manuel Lomeli Martinez	Jorge Ortiz Gomez
126	Buick 1949	Angel Gonzalez, Tacubaya, D.F.	Entrant	Ramon Macias
127	Chevrolet 1950	El Anfora, S.A., Mexico, D.F.	Porfirio Miranda Gonzalez	J. Refugio Miranda G.
128	Studebaker 1950	Republic of Venezuela, Caracas, Venezuela	Hugo Inciarte	Angel Inciarte
129	Oldsmobile 1950	C.D. Evans, El Paso, Tex.	Entrant	Ramiro Aguilar Jr.
130	Buick 1950	Arthur Daniel Boone, New York, N.Y.	Entrant	Mrs. Marie E. Boone
131	Chevrolet 1950	Cerveceria Moctezuma, Mexico, D.F.	Emilio A. Camargo	Raul Mendoza Terrazas
132	De Soto 1949	Cecil Weishuhn, Grand Blanc, Mich.	Entrant	Phillip Rhoader

Some of the Drivers and Teams

Luis Gomez Barrera #16   Alberto P. Rojas #16

Raul Arguelles Salgado #39   Enrique Paredes Herrasti #39

Tommy Francis #6   Jimmie Crum #6

Ross Barton #40   Marie Brookreson #40

Rodolfo Castaneda #9   Florencio Estrado #9

Ali Rachid #97   Luis A. Uribe #97

George H. Ashley #63   Alfredo Saucedo #63

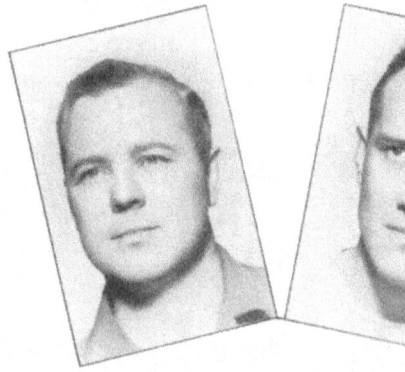
Cecil Weishunn #132   Philip Rhoades #132

Roy Connor #49 Robert Green #49 Alfonso Oviedo #27 Eulalio Rodriguez #27

Johnny Fredricks #55 George Lynch #55 G.W. McGraw #81 Lonnie Johnson Jr. #81

Gabriel Herrera #93 Samuel Marin #86 Gregorio Pirez Granier #5 Luis Leal Solares #46 Andrew Moran #36 Henry Bradley #7

Toscana Valle #112 C.D. Evans #129 Piero Taruffi #90 Luis Astengo #70 Manuel Luz Meneses #116 Nicholas Scott #114

Parade and Final Checking

A parade was held in Juarez before the start of the race.

An interested crowd watched the cars at the impound area in Juarez.

Car No. 38 before the start at Juarez. Left to Right: Johnny Mantz, Les Willand, Bob Estes, Bill Stroppe and Paul Neal.

Cars were stored overnight at Juarez on the race track. This is the morning of the start.

Lots of drivers taped the noses of their cars for protection from bugs. Driver Robert A. Clement Jr. with car No. 59.

Andre Mariotte gives the final touches to car No. 19 before start of the race.

Prominent Contestants and the Packard Pace Car

Italians Piero Taruffi (left) and his assistant, Isidoro Ceroli, stand beside their Alfa Romeo before the start. Car finished fourth.

The eventual winner before the long grind. Hershel McGriff (in winning Oldsmobile) and co-driver, Ray Elliott.

Bill France, stock car ace, and Curtis Turner with their Nash No. 37.

Right—This Packard was pace car for the race. Driver is R. O'Farrill.

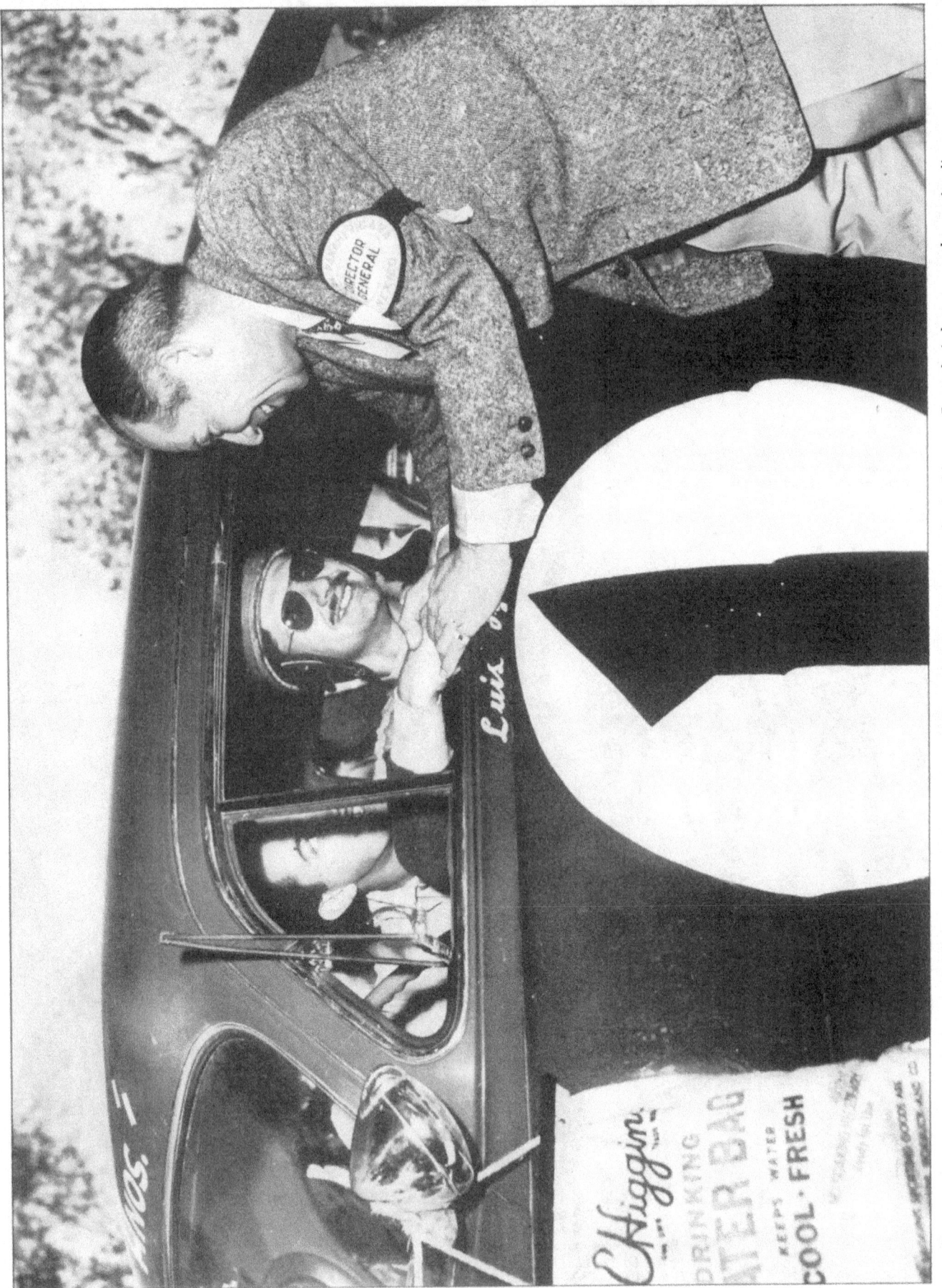

Luis Iglesias Davalos, first driver to start, gets best wishes from Sr. Antonio Cornejo C., Director General of the race, at the starting line.

CHAPTER IV

An Account of the Race... Leg-by-Leg

FIRST LEG — MAY 5, 1950
From Ciudad Juarez to Chihuahua
Official Distance . . . 375 kilometers, or 233 miles
Maximum Time permitted . . . . 6:15 hours

Summary of Standings
Cars in running for major prizes at start . . . 132
Cars disqualified during leg 19
Cars in running for major prizes at finish . . . 113

Winners of Leg

Position	Car No.	Miles Per Hour	Prizes
1	68	100.425	2,000 pesos
2	36	99.591	1,000 pesos
3	38	98.991	500 pesos

THE first leg of the Mexican Pan-American Race was a thrilling chase at high speeds under a hot sun across 233 miles of nearly level, perfectly-paved highway with no mountains and comparatively few curves.

When the calculations were completed, the winner for the leg was anonunced as lanky William W. Sterling, of El Paso. He is a salesman whose only racing experience had been on minor tracks.

Driving Car 68, a 1950 Cadillac, the former Navy flight mechanic crossed the finish line at Chihuahua in two hours, 19 minutes and 12 seconds, for a remarkable average speed of 100.425 miles an hour.

Right behind him were Andrew and John Moran, of Chicago, in another 1950 Cadillac, in 2:20:22 and an average of 99.591, and Johnny Mantz, of Long Beach, Calif., in a 1949 Lincoln with a time of 2:21:13 and an average of 98.991 m.p.h.

It was a highway that permitted speeds like that—the 50th car in the leg was only 20 minutes and 43 seconds behind Sterling—but immediately there was a chorus of protests from the South American and European entrants, who cried that there wasn't a stock car made that could reach speeds of 120 miles or more, as the leaders had to do in order to attain their averages.

The U. S. drivers remained calm, and the complaints had almost died out by the end of the race, when the Europeans had greatly improved their positions on the mountainous stretches near the end, and large numbers of the heavier early leaders had been eliminated.

The first day was one of triumph for U. S. drivers and heavy cars. The first 16 finishers were from the U. S., with a Peruvian in 17th place, a Venezuelan and a Mexican tied for 18th, and another U. S. driver in 20th. Of the European drivers, the French Delahaye entry, Car 19, was in 22nd, and the two Alfa Romeos, Cars 90 and 103, were gloomily in 36th and 39th, though less than 18 minutes off the pace. The gap between first and 20th places was only 10 minutes, 16 seconds.

Sixteen of the first 20 cars were medium to heavy—Oldsmobiles, a Buick, a Packard, Lincolns and Cadillacs. A Hudson managed to capture 10th place, and there were three Nashes among the second 10. But the big boys, pushed to the limit in the early legs, couldn't all take it. Four of the first six cars in the first leg were 1950 Cadillacs, but not one of them crossed the final finish line.

In fact, the mortality rate in the race is demonstrated by the fact that only three of the first leg's 10 leaders were present at the finish. These were Mantz's car, which ended in ninth; Car 12, a 1950 Oldsmobile piloted by professional Bud Sennett of Los Angeles with John C. Balch, Los Angeles racing veteran, as mastermind and copilot; and Car 52, the eventual winner. Car 12, fourth in the first leg, was fifth at the finish.

A CAREFULLY-PLANNED RACE

Hershel McGriff and Ray Elliott were the crew of Car 52, a 1950 Oldsmobile, and their sponsor, Roy Sundstrom, rode with them to Ciudad Juarez from Portland, Ore., their home. Their seventh place in the first leg was typical of the race Sundstrom planned for them—within shooting distance of the leaders, but never up in front until it was time to turn on the steam. On the trip south to Mexico the three men carefully calculated the maximum performance of their car, including gasoline consumption as well as speed. After the race began, Sundstrom followed by plane, and each night the next day's strategy was worked out. Most of the driving was done by 22-year-old McGriff, who had plenty of miles under his belt as a lumber-truck driver, and also had a little racing experience. The anchor man was Elliott, president of the P.S.C.R.A. and a track veteran. In the first leg their time of 2:24:59 was 5 minutes and 47 seconds behind Sterling, the leader.

For a while it seemed that the weather might frown on the beginning of the race. It was too early for rain in northern Mexico, but for two days before May 5 there had been strong windstorms that had stirred up dust clouds which cut down visibility and at times blotted out the highway.

Good luck was with the racers, however, and May 5 was a clear day. Of the 132 cars entered, 126 were on hand ready to start. One U. S. entry, Car 58, inscribed by Burnett E. Thatcher of Pomona, Calif., was among those unable to make the race, as was Car 117, the lone representative of El Salvador. The other four which did not start were Mexican entrants—the drivers of Cars 28 and 53 were flying north from Mexico City on a plane that was grounded by the dust storms, and Cars 67 and 69 simply never appeared.

The crews assembled early and paraded to the starting line, in front of a movie theater on the edge of Ciudad Juarez, where they listened from 9:30 to 10 a.m. to a program of speeches by U. S. Senator Dennis Chavez, of New Mexico; Guillermo Palmieri, of the Guatemalan Embassy in Mexico City; the Venezuelan Ambassador, Dr. Manuel Antonio Pulido; Carlos Casabianca, Colombian charge d'affaires; the Peruvian Ambassador, Dr. Vazquez Benavides, and El Salvador's Ambassador Hector Escobar Serrano.

Finally came 10 a.m., and Fernando Foglio Miramontes, governor of the state of Chihuahua, gave the signal with the black-and-white checkered flag that released Car 1. The others followed at one-minute intervals, with a five-minute break after every 20th cars, and the race was on.

The first three Cars get under way

The big race starts as cars 1, 2, and 3 are flagged out on the first leg to Chihuahua. Note the enthusiasm displayed by the ever-present crowds.

44

Excitement Runs High

Senator Denis Chavez addresses the radio audience at the start of the event.

Some of the crowd watching the start at Juarez.

There was a long line of cars at all starts.

The Flagman has a busy time

Above: Johnny Mantz, of California, leaves the starting line at Juarez.

Start of Car 32 at Juarez.

Official start of Car 34.

Right: Official start of Car No. 40 (the oldtimers).

Andre Mariotti and Jean Trevoux get the gun. The Delahaye was brought all the way from Paris.

Queen of Juarez parade waves Mexican flag at Jesus Nava Gonzalez, as he starts in '49 Lincoln.

The winner at the start — Hershel McGriff and the "City of Roses" Oldsmobile

Three Cadillacs and a Nash

Tom Deal, of El Paso, Texas, brought his sleek Cadillac to the starting line in 113th position and finished second in the race.

Below — Robert A. Clement, Jr., of Detroit has his new Cadillac ready for the long grind.

Number 37 leaves the starting line with drivers Bill France and Curtis Turner.

Al and Ralph Rogers, of Colorado Springs, Colo., get the flag in their '49 Cadillac.

48

Otto Foster and Edward Walker, of North Hollywood, Calif., take off in a '47 Lago Talbot.

A '38 Buick driven by Fernando Mejia of Mexico City, is the 51st car to get the starting flag.

Andrea Gonzalez and Lucille Acevedo, two adventurous San Francisco girls, get the checkered starting flag at Juarez.

It looks like most every make of car is represented as a 1937 Cord driven by Hugh Reilly of Chicago makes its appearance.

Ray Colenbaugh and Howard Hasse, of Des Plaines, Ill., make the entire run in a 1939 Cadillac.

A Hotchkiss was started by Taylor Lucas, of Los Angeles.

It was a hot day, and soon tires were blowing like popcorn. Planes patrolling the route reported one car after another halted for hasty tire changes. Car 65, for instance, had four flats and never got Chihuahua inside the time limit of six hours and 15 minutes.

Luck had determined the starting order, but quality quickly told, and the faster cars began passing those which had started earlier. In this race, speed determined the rating, and not order across the finish line, but it also was true, particularly in the first leg, that the car which passed the most others tended to be the fastest. First to reach Chihuahua was Car 5, which tied for 18th in the leg. A moment later Cars 12 and 14 came in, each having forged ahead of nine others. Then the Frenchmen and Car 20 flashed over the line, with a gain of 11 places each. Then there were cheers for Cars 36 and 38, respectively 24 and 25 places ahead of their starting positions. And then Sterling, with husky Mexican youth Daniel Arias, Jr., as copilot, arrived with a gain of some 32 positions.

TRAGEDY STRIKES QUICKLY

The first leg was the fastest of the race, and also the most tragic. It included the only fatality among the entrants. Enrique F. Hachmeister, driver of the only auto representing Guatemala, Car 112, took his eyes from the road for a moment as he arrived at a grade crossing 19 miles past the starting line, and lost control of his 1949 Lincoln. It was going a little more than 105 miles an hour, according to Francisco Toscana Valle, the co-pilot. The car bounced against a signal post, then careened off the road, rolling over at least six times. An ambulance took the crew to Ciudad Juarez, where Hachmeister died of a fractured skull at 6:20 p.m. Toscana, not seriously injured, was able to leave the hospital next day.

Car 56, a 1949 Ford entered by Nieders Auto Talleres, of Mexico City, turned over 28 miles from Ciudad Juarez and, with the top battered, was unable to reach Chihuahua in time after being righted, though its crew, Edward Nieders and Max H. Diener, were only scratched. Later they got it back into running order, and competed unsuccessfully for leg prizes from Mexico City to El Ocotal.

Others of the 126 starters who failed to finish the leg within the deadline were Cars 22; 30, a 1947 Lago Talbot from North Hollywood, Calif.; 43, a 1937 Cord from Chicago; 47, a 1949 Cadillac driven by Joel Thorne, of Las Vegas, Nev., a veteran of the Indianapolis Speedway; 51; 76; 85; 99; 100 and 126.

Among Mexico's stars, Jose Estrada Menocal, in Car 8, had three flats and finished 31st; Jose and Javier Solana, in Car 29, were 28th; Javier Razo Maciel, in Car 35, was 63rd; Fernando Razo Maciel, in Car 44, was 'way down in 108th, and Jesus Valezzi, in Car 77, finished 29th.

Car 9, the entry of Mexico's presidential staff, whose crew was encouraged by a phone call from President Miguel Aleman before the start, had two accidents, but got special permission to continue out of competition for prizes with a substitute for its injured co-pilot.

The first accident of the race was a minor one to one of the officials. Control Chief Enrique Martin Moreno, preceding the racers in a station wagon, turned over a few miles out of Ciudad Juarez, but neither he nor the car suffered noticeable damages, and he got to Chihuahua ahead of the competitors.

In the first day's excitement, Sterling's average speed was announced as 106.323 miles an hour, which would really have been a world record for highway races. Officials corrected this statement quickly, but long after the race some persons were still quoting the erroneous figure. As it is, Car 68 is believed to hold the open-road speed mark for stock cars.

In summary, 126 of the 132 cars entered started from Ciudad Juarez, and 113 reached Chihuahua. U. S. drivers held 17 of the first 20 places, including the first 16, and U. S.-made cars monopolized the first 20 places.

Of the first 10 in the race as a whole, Car 52 was in seventh place; Tom Deal's Car 113 was in 26th; Al Rogers' Car 21 was in 20th; Piero Taruffi's Car 90 was 36th; Car 12 was in fourth; Lewis Hawkins' Car 79 was 14th; Luis Leal Solares' Car 46 was 57th; Felice Bonetto's Car 103 was 39th; Car 38 was third, and Jack McAfee's Car 118 was 32nd. These are drivers' names, not entrants'.

SECOND LEG — MAY 6, 1950
From Chihuahua to Parral

Official Distance . . 300 kilometers, or 186.4 miles
Maximum Time permitted . . . . 4:55 hours

Summary of Standings

Cars in running for major prizes at start . . . 113
Cars disqualified during leg 3
Cars in running for major prizes at finish . . . 110
Disqualified cars which crossed finish line . . . 3
Total of cars which crossed finish line 113

Winners of Leg

Position	Car No.	Miles Per Hour	Prizes
1	55	95.885	2,000 pesos
2	38	94.614	1,000 pesos
3	68	93.888	500 pesos

The second leg of the race, between Chihuahua and Parral, saw Bill Sterling's Car 68 clinging to its leading position, though the leg was won by Car 55, a 1950 Cadillac driven by George Lynch and co-piloted by Johnny Fedricks, both of Detroit. The latter two were in a hurry because both had their names in for the Indianapolis race, too.

The first day was relatively easy, with only one leg to be run and comparatively flat country to run it over. Now the race was getting tougher. The second day included the second and third legs of the run, and in the second leg the drivers had to cross mountains for the first time. This leg was only 186 miles, and the first part of it was fairly level ground, but then the racers came to mountainous stretches on either side of the town of Camargo. The highway flattened out again near Parral.

Compared with the first day, the second leg was almost without incident. There were no crackups, and only three cars were disqualified. This time the contestants were started in the order of their finish the previous day, Sterling beginning the parade at 8 a. m.

With the going slightly more difficult, Lynch and Fedricks had an average speed of 95.885 m.p.h., making the leg in one hour, 56 minutes and 38 seconds.

Mantz took second place in the leg, driving it in 1:58:12, at a speed of 94.614 m.p.h., and thereby gained second place in the race to date. But Sterling, finishing third in the leg in 1:59:08, kept an advantage of exactly one minute over Johnny in total time. His average in the leg was 93.888 m.p.h.

Car 55 had been in fifth place after the first leg, five minutes and 35 seconds behind Car 68. The victory in the leg moved the Detroit team up to third in the total time.

Bad Luck strikes

Joel Thorne sits dejectedly on fender of his wrecked Cadillac a few miles from the start.

This Lincoln started in 112th position. Driven by Enrique Hachmeister, of Guatemala, the car crashed nineteen miles later, killing the driver.

Crowd quickly gathered after Edward Nieders rolled his Ford over early in race.

Nieders called for wrecker and continued the race.

Francisco Ibarra Somohano's Packard encountered tire trouble early on the first leg.

Colorful Chihuahua in Old Mexico

The cars were parked at Chihuahua's Sports Arena.

Looking out over a number of the cars from atop the Sports Arena we see the city of Chihuahua at dusk.

Chihuahua is revered in Mexican history as the city in which Miguel Hidalgo y Costilla, father of the nation's independence, passed his last days before dying a martyr as prisoner of the Spaniards. Tourists traveling Mexico's new Central Highway will find many historical sites in this city.

Center — Chihuahua's state capitol. This handsome building in Chihuahua serves as the Capitol of the state of the same name.

Bottom left — Drivers gather to learn their official positions at the end of the first day.

Bottom right — Chihuahua's Hotel Victoria, shown here, is typical of the up-to-date hostelries throughout Mexico which make travel pleasant for the foreign visitor. Such hotels already are open or are being hurried to completion along the 2,178 mile route between El Paso, Texas, and the Guatemalan border.

Bob Flock shows what heat and speed did to tires.

The NASCAR group gathered in Chihuahua. L to R — Curtis Turner, Bill France, Lewis Hawkins, Wayland Burgess, Bob Flock, Fonty Flock, Raymond Parks and Red Byron.

Bill France and Curtis Turner unload some groceries and prepare to cook dinner at Chihuahua.

Atlanta's Raymond Parks and Robert (Red) Byron pose after the first leg.

Dinner in the open is fine!

Johnny Mantz finished third on first day's run.

Meantime what had happened to Car 36, the 1950 Cadillac piloted by the Moran brothers from Chicago? Race officials were wondering, too. Making good speed, the car which had finished second in the first leg reached Parral in an estimated time which would have kept them up among the top two or three cars. But the Morans failed to make the obligatory stop at Parral, roaring through the town in spite of officials' frantic efforts to flag them down.

This was the only time this happened to any car in the entire race, and was the only unusual event of the second leg. The Chicago team continued on their hasty way until 12 miles short of Durango, where an accident put their car out of action without injury to them. They were the first among the early leaders to bite the dust.

Again in the second leg, the first 10 cars in the over-all standings were U. S. entrants, as were the 11th and 12th. But others were beginning to creep up. The French Delahaye, Car 19, piloted by professional Jean Trevoux with Andre Mariotti as assistant, ran a good fifth in 2:00:25 in this leg, and improved its general classification to 13th. The 14th through 18th cars were from the U. S., but Venezuelan Car 78 and Mexican Car 5, in 19th and 20th, were virtually holding their own. The over-all time difference between Car 68 and Car 5 was 17 minutes and 24 seconds.

Three cars dropped out of the first 20 in this leg. Besides No. 36, they were Car 7, the Peruvian entry which had been 17th the first day, and Car 71, a 1950 Oldsmobile driven by Owen R. Gray, of Lubbock, Tex., which had been 13th. Car 7 ranked 49th in the second leg, and slipped to 29th in the general standings. Car 71 finished 'way back in 78th place in the leg, and tumbled to 44th in the race as far as Parral.

Fighting their way upward, Mexican drivers began to show their mettle as they got their first taste of the mountains they knew so well. Car 5 had finished 27th in the leg, but four Mexicans took the 17th through 20th places in this portion of the race. They were, in order, Cars 29, 46 (which was to rank seventh at El Ocotal), 42 (which was to finish the entire race in 13th place), and 8, driven by the dauntless "Che" Estrada.

U. S. drivers had held 17 of the first 20 places in Leg One, and they captured 15 of the first 20 in Leg Two.

Here's how the 10 eventual winners did in Leg Two:

Final Position	Car No.	Position in Leg 2	Position in 1st 2 Legs
1	52	8	5
2	113	23	21
3	21	13	15
4	90	28	30
5	12	7	4
6	79	9 (tie)	10
7	46	18	36
8	103	31	31
9	38	2	2
10	118	14	26

The Sundstrom strategy was paying off; Tom Deal in Car 113 was beginning his climb, and so were the Italians in Cars 90 and 103, and Luis Leal Solares in Car 46. Johnny Mantz, in Car 38, and Bud Sennett, in Car 12, were holding their own. Farthest behind Sterling, the leader, was Leal, with 29 minutes, six seconds to make up.

Besides Car 36, those which dropped out of the running for the main prizes in this leg were Car 96, a 1950 Buick driven by Joe Thompson of Carlsbad, New Mexico, which didn't start after finishing 104th the previous day, and Car 25, which took two minutes more than the maximum time of four hours and 25 minutes. Cars 65 and 85, overtime in Leg 1, continued running in the second leg.

THIRD LEG — MAY 6, 1950
From Parral to Durango
Official Distance . . . 404 kilometers, or 251 miles
Maximum Time permitted . . . . 6:45 hours

Summary of Standings
Cars in running for major prizes at start . . . 110
Cars disqualified during leg 7
Cars in running for major prizes at finish . . . 103
Disqualified cars which crossed finish line . . . 2
Total of cars which crossed finish line 105

Winners of Leg

Position	Car No.	Miles Per Hour	Prizes
1	68	85.993	2,000 pesos
2	38	85.150	1,000 pesos
3	113	84.199	500 pesos

More accidents, more mountains, less speed and numerous changes of position were recorded as the 110 cars still in the running for the chief prizes covered the 251 miles from Parral to Durango, the third leg of the race, to wind up the second day of the speed derby.

William W. Sterling, the 31-year-old El Paso salesman, won the leg in the time of 2:55:08, averaging 85.993 miles an hour, and held on to first place with a total time for three legs of 7:13:28. John Mantz, the 1949 Pacific Coast AAA big-car champion, with Bill Stroppe, winner of the 1950 Mobilgas Economy Run, as his co-pilot, took second place in the leg in 2:56:52, for an average of 85.150 mph, and continued second in cumulative time with 7:16:17.

Mexico was beginning to wake up to the excitement of the race, after taking it fairly calmly the first day. The radio blared out a running account all day, and the newspapers covered their front pages with emotional stories. Spectators were lined up along the highway in the countryside, kept at a distance of 50 yards by soldiers, and in the villages and cities they filled the rooftops to which they had been shooed by the police.

The highway was closed to other traffic hours before the racers were to pass, so the people of Durango made a grand picnic of the day, heading out early to the finish line on the edge of town. At least 40,000 persons jammed into a couple of miles outside Durango, cheering loudly and indiscriminately as the cars dashed by.

The process of sorting out the men from the boys began this day, when the competitors were sent off in the morning from Chihuahua in the order of the times they logged on the first day. This put the fastest cars at the forefront, and the half-hour refueling stop at Parral, with each competitor being sent off 30 minutes after he reached the day's midpoint, did not change the situation.

Thus the first 15 or so cars to reach Durango were fairly well separated. After that the racers began to arrive in clusters of two or three, and the spectators were treated to neck-and-neck finishes as the drivers fought it out for the last possible second of advantage.

It was a tough leg for the best Mexican drivers. Seven more cars were eliminated from competition in this leg, only 103 remaining in the general running, with Cars 25 and 65 continuing to try for leg prizes after having been disqualified previously for the race as a whole.

And now the Race continues

Bill Sterling, an early leader from El Paso, passes the 524 kilometer mark.

Jose Menocal, the "Champion of Mexico," stirs up dust as he rounds a curve near Camargo.

Jorgen Thayssen, Hollywood, Calif., passes scenic spot in fast English Jaguar.

Left — Hershel McGriff speeds through a tight spot south of Chihuahua and crowd cheers madly.

Car No. 64 didn't make the turn and went off into the ditch. Note skid marks and the inevitable spectators.

The end of Mercury No. 64.— a Mexican entry.

"Che" Estrada Menocal flashes in to finish line in Parral in his Packard No. 8 at midpoint of the second day.

57

Many curves were sharp...

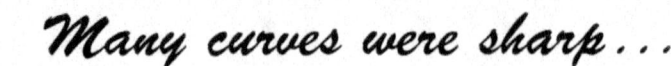

Left:
Battered Mexican Presidential Cadillac, driven by Lt. Rodolfo Castañeda, continued in race after rolling over twice in two days. He became the people's hero for his courage and performance.

Owen Gray, Lubbock, Texas, takes a sharp turn on the second day.

Two cars, one of them the French Delahaye, negotiate an S-turn.

...some, too sharp!

Salvador Santoyo lays his car into a curve on the second day.

Just one mile from the finish line at Durango two drivers find a sharp curve too much to negotiate and end up among the rocks. Jose Solana in Nash No. 29 wrecked first and then Alfonso Oviedo in Cadillac No. 27 came along and leaped over him. Neither driver was hurt!

From Durango through Leon

Left: Mexican mechanic goes over Alfa Romeo No. 90 in the rain as cars lay over for the night in Durango.

Crowd gathers around the cars in Leon at the midpoint of the third day.

Alfa Romeo No. 103 ready for the start from Durango. Felice Bonetto at wheel.

Among the seven knocked out were two of the leading Mexican teams. Car 64, a 1950 Mercury, piloted by brothers Marcelo and Roberto Quintanilla, two Mexico City bus drivers, turned over 45 miles past Parral. Roberto lay unconscious for hours with a cerebral concussion, and Marcelo suffered a broken left leg. They had reached Parral in 37th place. Car 29, a 1950 Nash driven by professional Jose Antonio Solana, smacked into a tiny hill on a curve just before the Durango finish line. The co-pilot, Jose's brother Javier, was only scratched, and Jose was unhurt, but their car was ruined. They were in a good 25th place at the time.

An hour and a half later Car 27, Alfonso Oviedo's 1941 Cadillac, hit the remains of the Solana auto, and also was wrecked. Co-pilot Eulalio Rodriguez hastily made sure that he was uninjured, then dashed around the car to help out Oviedo. But Oviedo, munching an apple, stepped out of the crumpled door also unscratched.

Engine trouble eliminated two Mexican entries, Cars 4 and 13, and two California contestants, Cars 60 and 115; none of which had been going anywhere in particular. Disqualified Car 85, which had returned to the running in Leg 2, broke down for good on this leg.

It was this leg that saw the final winners begin to move up as the route entered a region in which most of the territory was mountainous or hilly.

Tom Deal, finally beginning to get the most out of his Car 113, a 1950 Cadillac, captured third place in the leg with a time of 2:58:52, and went up from 21st to 10th in the general ranking.

McGriff and Elliott, keeping quietly to their campaign plan, took eighth in the leg with a time of 3:01:59, but that was enough to move them into fourth in the race because of the shuffling of the other leaders. Through Durango they had used up 7:28:40 hours, and they were 15 minutes and 12 seconds out of first. Deal, with 7:35:01, had 21 minutes and 33 seconds to make up.

LEADERS BEGIN CHANGING

There was a new third place car, for Lynch and Fedricks, after capturing the second leg to seize third over-all position, were able to take only 24th in the Parral-Durango run, and skidded to seventh in the rankings. Car 55 did very badly the next day, reaching Mexico City in 35th position, and the Detroit pair did not continue past there.

Elbowing out Car 55 was Car 37, piloted by Bill France, of Daytona Beach, Fla., chairman of the National Stock Car Racing Commission. France, with Curtis Turner, of Roanoke, Va., as co-pilot, shoved his 1950 Nash across the Durango finish line with a time of 3:00:17 from Parral, taking fourth place in the leg and third in the general standings with an elapsed time of 7:28:02. This was the best position France was to hold. He slipped steadily thereafter, and his car broke down halfway through the final leg.

For the first time a Mexican driver was among the first 10 in a leg. Luis Leal Solares, who was to take seventh place at El Ocotal, was ninth in this leg, moving up to 24th from 36th in total elapsed time.

The Mexicans were beginning to make themselves felt. For the first time there were three among the first 20 cars, led by Raul Arguelles Salgado, who had gotten his Car 39, a 1950 Mercury, up into 15th place. Cars 5 and 42 were in 18th and 19th.

Piero Taruffi, in Car 90, a 1950 Alfa Romeo, was continuing his steady climb with the banner of Italy. He took 19th position in the third leg, and went up from 30th to 23rd in the general standings. His partner Felice Bonetto, in Car 103, didn't do so well in this leg, slipping back from 31st to 34th. And the French team, in Car 19, really had trouble with their Delahaye. Limping into Durango in 87th position in the leg, they fell back from 13th to 44th in cumulative time.

No less than six competitors slipped out of the leading 20 in this leg—Cars 19, 45, 78, 79, 89 and 111. Their places were taken by Cars 7, 20, 39, 42, 113 and 118. Such shakeups became less violent as the race progressed and the time gaps between cars became greater. But at the end of the third leg there was a difference of only 34 minutes and 57 seconds betwen Car 20, in 20th place in elapsed time, and Car 68, in first.

Here's how the 10 eventual winners stood after Leg 3:

Final Position	Car No.	Position in Leg 3	Over-All Position
1	52	8	4
2	113	3	10
3	21	7	9
4	90	19	23
5	12	14	8
6	79	54	26
7	46	9	24
8	103	40	34
9	38	2	2
10	118	20 (tie)	17

As may be seen, two U. S. entries, Cars 12 and 79, lost ground badly on this leg. In fact, if Lewis Hawkins, of Spartanburg, South Carolina, driver of Car 79, had kept up on Leg 3 the average he maintained on other legs, he would have finished at El Ocotal in third or fourth position instead of sixth.

The hard-luck guy of the whole race, Mexico's Jose Estrada Menocal, one of the country's finest drivers, suffered one of his worst blows on Leg 3. Leaving Parral in an honorable 28th position, he ran into clutch and tire trouble on the way to Durango, and also broke a gasoline feed line, arriving at the finish mark with his last drop of fuel. His time for the leg was 6:02:58, more than twice Sterling's, leaving him in 105th and last place for the leg and 98th in the general standings. As a crowning indignity, he had to push his gasolineless 1949 Packard to a fuel pump.

●

FOURTH LEG — MAY 7, 1950
From Durango to Leon
Official Distance: 547 kilometers, or 339.85 miles
Maximum Time permitted . . . . 9:10 hours

Summary of Standings
Cars in running for major prizes at start . . . 103
Cars disqualified during leg 11
Cars in running for major prizes at finish . . . 92
Disqualified cars which crossed finish line . . . 1
Total of cars which crossed finish line 93

Winners of Leg

Position	Car No.	Miles Per Hour	Prizes
1	81	90.133	2,000 pesos
2	68	89.980	1,000 pesos
3	38	89.710	500 pesos

May 7, the third day of the race, was a festive Sunday, and the racers knew it before they had finished the two legs; the fourth, from Durango to Leon, and the fifth from Leon to Mexico City. It was the longest day's run of the entire race, and drew the biggest crowds of onlookers.

Top: Henry Bradley's Nash was demolished when it toppled from a bridge on the third day.

Bottom: A new door is made for the occupants of this house south of Durango as Harry Sents, Glen Aubry, N. Y., spectacularly wrecks his Lincoln.

At least a million persons were estimated to have watched the speeding cars as they passed through the most densely populated part of Mexico, including the cities of Durango, Fresnillo, Zacatecas, Aguascalientes, Lagos de Moreno, Leon, Irapuato, Salamanca, Celaya, Queretaro, Toluca and Mexico City.

Bill Sterling was still in the lead when the 340-mile fourth leg was over, though he didn't know till hours later that he had captured second place in the Durango-Leon run. His time for the leg was 3:46:37, his speed 89.980 miles an hour over this mountain-dotted stretch. His elapsed time from Ciudad Juarez to Leon was 11:00:05. Sterling could consider himself lucky, for he was subjected to a number of complications on this leg.

The Durango-Leon winner was youthful Lonnie H. Johnson, Jr., of Shallowater, Texas, driving a 1949 Cadillac bearing the number 81. He was assisted by G. W. McGraw. Johnson was in sixth place when the day started, and his time of 3:46:14 in this leg vaulted him into third in the over-all standings, with a total time of 11:15:53. He averaged 90.113 mph for the leg.

Johnny Mantz, plugging steadily along in Car 38, took third place in this leg and maintained his over-all position in second place behind Sterling. His leg time was 3:47:18, his average speed 89.710, and his total time 11:03:35.

It was a leg of moderate changes in the standings, and of violence on the highway. Of 103 cars in the running at the end of the third leg, only 92 reached Leon. Six of these did not start, three went out in accidents, and two broke down. Besides, U. S. Car 65, disqualified in the first leg, dropped out for good after trying for secondary prizes in two more legs. Those that did not start were U. S. entries 11, 54, 89 and 110, Mexico's Car 119, and Venezuelan Car 78. The South American entry was in 25th place when he decided that his machine wasn't in shape to continue; the others were 50th or worse. Car 110 was a Jaguar entered by Jorgen Thayssen of Hollywood, Calif. It was 53rd when a piston broke.

Car 87, a 1950 Studebaker driven by Andres Wiltz of Mexico City, hit an aqueduct at Zacatecas and was damaged, but resumed running for leg prizes after Mexico City. The other two which cracked up were cars which had been running among the first 20—Car 7, a 1950 Nash piloted by Henry Bradley, of Peru, who had been in 16th place, and Car 88, a 1950 Lincoln, driven by Harry Sents, of Glen Aubry, N. Y., who had been in fifth spot, among the leaders. Both crashed at a narrow temporary bridge over the Rio Florido, near Fresnillo, about 150 miles from Durango. Their cars were wrecked and the bridge caught fire, but the crews were hurt only slightly, contrary to a flood of rumors about death and serious injury.

The fire at the bridge caused police stationed there to hold up Sterling's Car 68 for 32 minutes. Although the officers made a notation in his route book, he wasn't sure until he reached Mexico City that the time would be allowed. It was, and he was still in the running for first place.

Sterling had been a victim of confusion earlier in the day, too, along with the other competitors. It had been announced the night before that the start would be at 6 a. m. instead of 7 a. m. In the morning, however, there was so much confusion that the first car didn't get away till 6:30, and then the officials didn't get the racers off in order. Mantz, who should have started second, was sent away first, and Sterling was the 35th to leave the mark.

SHUFFLING THE STANDINGS

This also was the leg on which a spectator was killed, the only time this happened during the race. Unexpectedly coming on a descent where the road fords a river in Lagos de Moreno, Edwin Sollohub, of Schenectady, N. Y., driving Car 114, lost control of his car for a moment and plowed into a crowd, according to Mexican newspapers. These dispatches said that a Mrs. Tomasa Lopez was killed and two other persons were hurt.

The fourth leg saw four cars drop out of the first 20. Besides Cars 7 and 88, they were Car 55, winner of the second leg, and Car 20, the entry of Charles Fraley of Columbus,, Ohio. The latter finished 86th and 88th, respectively, in the fourth leg, and dropped far down in the standings.

The four cars which thereby moved up into the first 20 included three that were among the first 10 at the finish. One was Car 79, driven by Lewis Hawkins, which was ninth in the leg and thereby returned to a position among the leaders. The others were Mexico's Car 46, which did 10th in the leg, and thereby jumped from 24th to 13th in the general standings; and Italian Piero Taruffi's Car 90, which inched up from 23rd to 20th. The fourth of this group was Car 114, which moved up to 18th place in spite of its accident.

It was looking better for the non-U. S. entrants. There were four Mexicans and one Italian among the leading 20, and one fewer car from north of the border. The standings for the fourth leg alone showed 14 U. S. cars among the first 20, plus five Mexicans and the lone French entry, which logged 15th in the leg to inch its way up to 30th place in the over-all rankings.

The time difference between the first car in the race as a whole and the 20th, Car 90, was now 58 minutes and 29 seconds, an increase of almost 24 minutes.

Notable was the performance of two drivers who were hopelessly out of the running for major prizes. Jose Estrada Menocal, in Car 8, was seventh in this leg, gaining 24 positions in the general classification, but still moving up only to 81st place after his disastrous first leg. Fernando Razo Maciel, driving Car 44, took 13th place to advance from 82nd to 77th. More was to be heard later from this pair.

Among the rest of the leaders, Car 52 kept its steady pace, again finishing eighth in the leg and fourth in the race. It was 22 minutes, 21 seconds out of first place. Tom Deal, continuing his upward rush, was fifth in the leg and advanced to sixth in the race.

This is how the 10 eventual winners ranked after Leg 4:

Final Position	Car No.	Position in Leg 4	Over-All Position
1	52	8	4
2	113	5	6
3	21	4	5
4	90	27	20
5	12	11	7
6	79	9	14
7	46	10	13
8	103	24	26
9	38	3	2
10	118	43	19

FIFTH LEG — MAY 7, 1950
From Leon to Mexico City

Official Distance . 448 kilometers, or 278.3 miles
Maximum Time permitted . . . . 7:30 hours

Summary of Standings

Cars in running for major prizes at start . . .	92
Cars disqualified during leg	4
Cars in running for major prizes at finish . . .	88
Disqualified cars which crossed finish line . . .	2
Total of cars which crossed finish line	90

Winners of Leg

Position	Car No.	Miles Per Hour	Prizes
1	113	93.169	3,000 pesos
2	38	89.078	2,000 pesos
3	118	87.278	1,000 pesos

Speeds went up in the 278-mile fifth leg, and William Sterling finally was pushed out of first place by Johnny Mantz, but the excitement of the Sunday afternoon run from Leon to Mexico City was, for the public at least, in the delirious reception the racers received at the national capital.

Easily half a million persons—some estimated the crowds at a million out of the nearly 3,000,000 inhabitants of Mexico City—were assembled that Sunday along the final miles of the leg and beside the streets between the finish line and racing headquarters.

From Leon to Toluca, 40 miles from Mexico City, the highway is through mile-high plains that are flat or gently rolling. A few miles past Toluca the highway begins to climb over a 10,000-foot-high mountain range, and there is about 18 miles of sharply rising or descending road that is an unbroken succession of curves.

The finish line was a few miles outside city limits, at the end of this mountainous stretch, and so early in the morning tens of thousands of people started out from Mexico City to park among the peaks with lunch baskets to watch the racers go by at full speed.

The drivers, after finishing the leg, had to turn in their route books at a police booth at the edge of the city, then were escorted by motorcycle policemen down the broad, tree-lined Paseo de la Reforma to their cars' overnight stopping place, the Cornejo garage on the Paseo.

The masses of people were even greater in the huge Columbus circle on which faces the Cornejo place. In a reviewing stand were Secretary of Communications Agustin Garcia Lopez and other high public officials. Fifteen hundred policemen were on duty, and there were great numbers of soldiers to help them, but it was difficult to keep the finish line clear. The crowd quickly overran the Cornejo filling station and almost managed to penetrate the large garage behind it. Pickpockets managed to snare the wallets of at least two of the U. S. drivers as they wearily forced their way out of their cars to take on gasoline.

In the confusion of the start at Durango, Sterling had gotten away late. Thus the other leaders were left to battle it out among themselves on the road, though, since the computation of course was made on the basis of elapsed time, this was more spectacular than significant.

The victor in Leg 5 was round-faced Tom Deal, the El Paso auto dealer who had entered and was driving his own 1950 Cadillac in his first race, with Sam Cresap as co-pilot. His time was 2:59:15, his average speed was 93.169 mph—the fastest for any car since Leg 2—and his total elapsed time was 14:25:56, moving him up from sixth to third. This was the fifth different car to occupy third place during the first five legs, and only two of them reached El Ocotal.

Mantz started ahead of Deal in Car 38, but Deal had passed the Californian near the end of the leg. Now they came roaring down to the finish line with Deal barely 100 yards ahead of Johnny. About a mile away Mantz' Lincoln was gaining fast, and Johnny swung out on a curve, intending to pass. He swung too far, his outer wheels caught the gravel, and for a moment he rocketed along on two wheels. The Lincoln righted itself, but Mantz had lost precious seconds, and he crossed the line 100 yards behind Deal.

For all the thrills of this duel, Car 38 was more than eight minutes behind Car 113 in the leg, with a time of 3:07:29 and a speed of 89.078 mph. Mantz' elapsed time of 14:11:04 put him into first place in the race, however, because Sterling finally had hit some bad luck in this leg.

All that Sterling and Daniel Arias, Jr., his co-pilot, reported as having happened to them in the fifth leg was two blown-out tires, but they brought their machine in 16th for the leg, with a time of 3:22:28. This made their total time 14:22:37, and dropped them into second place barely ahead of Deal.

MEXICANS, ITALIANS GAIN

Third in the leg was taken by Car 118, the 1949 Cadillac driven by Jack McAfee, of Hermosa Beach, Calif., with Ford Robinson as assistant. Their time was 3:11:21 and their speed 87.278 mph. This moved them up to 15th in the race.

As ever, the McGriff-Elliott-Sundstrom combination kept up in the running. The white Oldsmobile, Car 52, was only 14th in the leg, but this was sufficient to hold fourth position. Cars 79 and 46 took fourth and fifth in the leg. This moved No. 46, driven by Luis Leal Solares, into 10th place, and No. 79, the Lewis Hawkins car, into 11th. Leal's advance broke the U. S. monopoly on the first 10 spots— a Mexican finally was up in there as the racers reached the national capital.

The Italians were moving right along, too. Car 103 was 11th in the leg and Car 90 was 17th. The former advanced from 26th to 21st, and the latter moved up from 20th to 18th. The French team, in Car 19, was 19th in the leg and improved its standing by three positions, going to 27th.

Only one car dropped out of the first 20—No. 114, of Edwin Sollohub, of Schenectady, N. Y. It was 66th in the leg, skidded down to 29th in the race, and never got back up. Its place was taken by Car 26, a 1949 Lincoln, crewed by Raymond D. Parks and Robert N. Byron, of Atlanta, Georgia, which was 13th in the leg and advanced to 19th in the race.

Mexican Cars 8 and 44 wound up a sensational day by taking ninth and seventh positions, respectively, in the leg. Estrada Menocal, in Car 8, was 69th at the finish, a gain of 36 places during the day. Razo Maciel, in Car 44, had advanced to 47th, an advance of 35 positions for the two legs.

There was no change in the totals by nationalities of cars among the first 20 in the race—it was still 15 from the U. S., four from Mexico and one from Italy. The U. S. drivers sank to their lowest figure thus far among the first 20 in the leg alone; there were 12 from the U. S., five Mexicans, two Italians and one French car. The time gap between Mantz, in first position over-all, and Mexico's Raul Arguelles Salgado, Car 39, in 20th, was 1:14:54.

Fascinating Mexico City

Entering the Capitol of Mexico

Rodolfo Casteñada receives a cheering welcome in Mexico City.

Bud Sennett, of Los Angeles, enters Mexico City.

Leopoldo Vera, of Celaya, in his Mercury.

The Davalos brothers enter Mexico City.

McGriff and Elliott wave at the photographer as they pull on into Mexico City, having moved steadily up to the front.

Ladies of Steel

The glamor girl of the race, Jacqueline Evans de Lopez, enters Mexico City.

Marie Brookreson and Ross Barton finish at Mexico City.

Mrs. H. R. Lammons, of Jacksonville, Texas, stops to powder her nose for a photo in Mexico City. Her Buick advertises "Hi-A Brasseries, by Marja."

Columbus Circle...

Part of the thousands of spectators lining the Paseo de la Reforma at Columbus Circle, Mexico City, waiting for the race cars' arrival.

Tom Deal waves to crowd along the Paseo de la Reforma in Mexico City as he and Sam Cresap enter the Mexican capital first in No. 113.

Luis Leal Solares, popular Mexican racer, brings his Olds to a stop in front of cheering stands set up on Columbus Circle, Mexico City.

Jesus Nava Gonzalez arriving at Columbus Circle in his Lincoln No. 42.

Johnny Mantz arrives in Mexico City to a warm welcome.

The drivers were interviewed after their arrival at Columbus Circle, Mexico City. Mantz and Stroppe on the air.

68

...*welcomed tired Drivers*

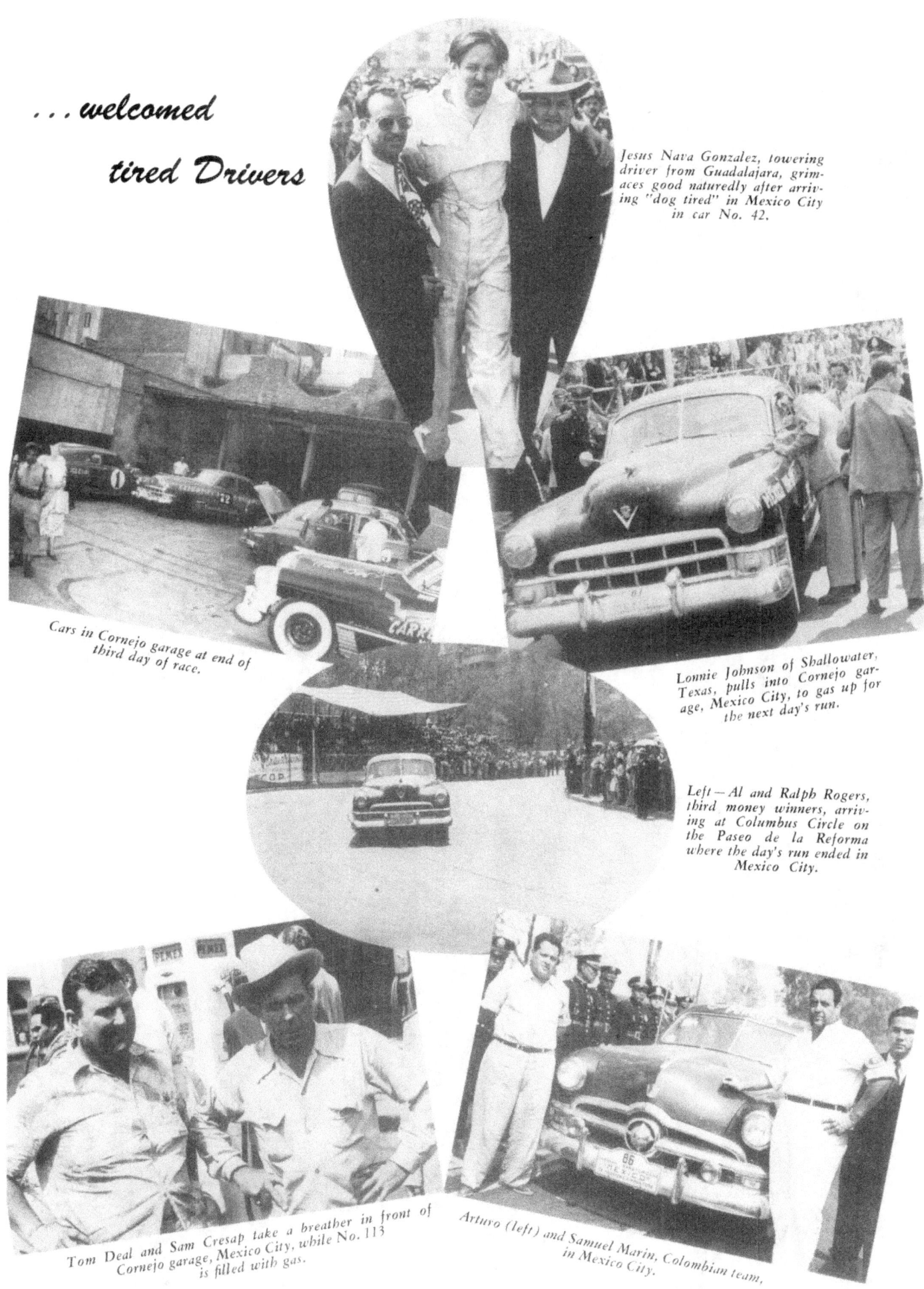

Jesus Nava Gonzalez, towering driver from Guadalajara, grimaces good naturedly after arriving "dog tired" in Mexico City in car No. 42.

Cars in Cornejo garage at end of third day of race.

Lonnie Johnson of Shallowater, Texas, pulls into Cornejo garage, Mexico City, to gas up for the next day's run.

Left — Al and Ralph Rogers, third money winners, arriving at Columbus Circle on the Paseo de la Reforma where the day's run ended in Mexico City.

Tom Deal and Sam Cresap take a breather in front of Cornejo garage, Mexico City, while No. 113 is filled with gas.

Arturo (left) and Samuel Marin, Colombian team, in Mexico City.

Even battered Cars carried on!

The battered Ford gets service in Mexico City.

A small portion of the half million people who welcomed the drivers in Mexico City.

George Lynch hit a house but was able to limp in to Mexico City.

Right—Owen Gray, of Lubbock, Texas, arrives in Mexico City.

A famous Mexican Magazine brought out a Souvenir Edition

EL AUTOMÓVIL MEXICANO

VOL. III - NUM. 29
JUNIO DE 1950
NUMERO ESPECIAL
CINCO PESOS

5a. ETAPA
3a. Jornada
LEON-MEXICO

● En la Tribuna de Honor, el Lic. García López, Secretario de Comunicaciones, en unión del Gral. Ignacio Beteta, del Lic. Alejandro Carrillo, del Dr. Antonio González Cárdenas, dieron la bienvenida a los corredores.

● Thomas A. Deal, con su enorme pericia y su magnífico Cadillac 1950, Núm. 113, fué un constante candidato al primer lugar durante todo el desenvolvimiento de la Carrera Panamericana "México". A la Ciudad de México llegó en primer lugar y aun cuando en las siguientes etapas ocupó el 7o., 31o., 3o., y 9o., siempre conservó un magnífico tiempo. El Oldsmobile triunfador sólo le ganó con ¡56 segundos!

El pueblo en masa, entusiasmado, vibrante de entusiasmo, asistió en la [capi]tal de la República a la llegada de los competidores. En la foto que pusimos da una idea remota de la verdadera algazara popular que campeó [en la]s calles de la capital el domingo 7 de mayo, día de la llegada aquí de los automóviles que compitieron en la gran justa.

● Así se vió el Paseo de la Reforma el día de la llegada de los competidores. Del lugar donde estaba situada la meta, en la carretera de Toluca, los coches fueron desfilando hasta la Glorieta de Colón.

● Los miembros del Comité de Control de la Carrera, de la Ciudad de México, estuvieron sumamente atareados el día de la llegada de los corredores. Aquí vemos a los señores Edmundo Stierle, Guillermo Prieto y Armando Fernández, miembros de dicho Comité descansando brevemente durante el desempeño de su delicada comisión.

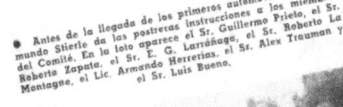

● Antes de la llegada de los primeros automóviles, Don Edmundo Stierle da las postreras instrucciones a los miembros del Comité. En la foto aparece el Sr. Guillermo Prieto, el Sr. Roberto Zapata, el Sr. E. G. Larrañaga, el Sr. Roberto La Montagne, el Lic. Armando Herrerías, el Sr. Alex Trauman y el Sr. Luis Bueno.

...s desolados a los que ...sta. La tarde del día ...volcaron en el Paseo ...espués de abrir paso ...an llegando y de so... carro "México", la ...en los alrededores ... Colón hasta altas ...da. Ante la impo-sibilidad de proveerse, en estas condiciones, de gasolina, los corredores se fueron a descansar y dejaron el cuidado de llenar los tanques para la mañana siguiente. No son las ciudades los mejores finales de etapas en una carrera de automóviles. Incluso para terminal, México es demasiado grande, bullicioso, complejo y vivo.

53

Scenic Mexico City

Statue at the Palace of Fine Arts in Mexico City.

Ben Sarkisian and Mr. and Mrs. Bob Estes on the steps to the Shrine of Guadelupe in Mexico City.

Mexico is not complete without the famous bull fights.

Mexican peon at work.

Left—a rebuilding scene in Mexico City.

View in Mexico City.

Here's the way the 10 eventual victors rated after Leg 5:

Final Position	Car No.	Position in Leg 5	Over-All Position
1	52	14	4
2	113	1	3
3	21	10	6
4	90	17	18
5	12	15	8
6	79	4	11
7	46	5	10
8	103	11	21
9	38	2	1
10	118	3	15

Only four cars dropped out of the running for major prizes in this leg, leaving 88 in competition. All were from the U. S.—Cars 50, 98, 123 and 130. Three of them were far back, but Car 98 had worked its way up to 25th position. It was piloted by Chuck Meekins and Joe Pisano, and was a 1947 Hudson owned by Jack Gaynor of Inglewood, Calif., who also entered Car 14.

●

SIXTH LEG — MAY 8, 1950
From Mexico City to Puebla
Official Distance: 135 kilometers or 83.875 miles
Maximum Time permitted . . . . 2:15 hours

Summary of Standings
Cars in running for major prizes at start	88
Cars disqualified during leg	12
Cars in running for major prizes at finish	76
Disqualified cars which crossed finish line	3
Total of cars which crossed finish line	79

Winners of Leg
Position	Car No.	Miles Per Hour	Prizes
1	44	79.777	2,000 pesos
2	8	79.336	1,000 pesos
3	118	78.715	500 pesos

Leg 6 was the shortest, but it was the best for the Mexicans. The 84-mile run from Mexico City to Puebla was the only one won by a driver from the host country, and a Mexican came in second, too.

Though the distance was brief, this leg, the first one of the fourth day of the race, was no walkover. It had fairly long straightaways at beginning and end, but the middle section climbed and descended sharply along precipices across a mountain range that included the highest point on the entire race route, Llano Grande, 10,485 feet above sea level and 33 miles out of Mexico City.

The first and second cars in the leg were driven by men who knew the road like their own homes. The winner was Fernando Razo Maciel, of Puebla, in Car 44, and second was Jose Estrada Menocal, of Mexico City, in Car 8. Both machines were 1949 Packards. As Estrada explained, "I've driven to Puebla so many times that I know every curve without having to look at it, the way you cross your living room in the dark and automatically avoid the chairs you can't see." Estrada was winning races between Mexico City and Puebla as long as 20 years ago, but the old record for the distance was held by Romulo O'Farrill, Sr., who did it in 1:05:47 in 1939.

Razo, with a time of 1:03:05 on May 8, 1950, knocked the O'Farrill record off the books, and the old mark also was beaten by Jack McAfee, Lewis Hawkins, Bill Sterling, Johnny Mantz, Tom Deal and Hershel McGriff of the U. S. and Piero Taruffi of Italy. The two Mexican leaders were far down in the over-all standings, and the time differential was so small for the leg that the foreigners' advantage was unshaken.

Razo, with his average sped of 79.777 mph, moved up from 47th to 39th as a result of his leg victory. And Estrada, making a time of 1:03:26 and a speed of 79.336 mph, advanced from 69th to 56th. Third in the leg was McAfee's second consecutive third place, and it shoved him up from 19th to 12th over-all position within two legs.

Johnny Mantz, fourth in the leg with a time of 1:04:49, not only held onto first place in the race, but increased to 12 minutes and 28 seconds his advantage over William Sterling, who remained in second. It was the first leg in which Mantz had been out of the money. Deal, seventh in the leg, remained in third for the race, and steady McGriff clung to fourth. In fact there was only one change in position among the first ten—Al Rogers, in Car 21, was 24th in the leg and thereby moved into fifth place ahead of Lonnie Johnson in Car 81, who was 42nd in the dash to Puebla.

There was some shuffling among the second 10 in the general standings, but just one change in personnel. Felice Bonetto's Alfa Romeo, Car 103, moved up one spot, from 21st to 20th, as Car 5, which had been 17th, dropped out of the race with mechanical trouble. The time gap between Mantz and Bonetto was 1:20:48.

The departure of Gregorio Pirez, five-foot-five pilot of Car 5, was a real blow to Mexican hopes, and it came on the very stretch where he had expected to do best. Pirez is an auto dealer in Puebla, and is another of those Mexicans who could almost do the sixth leg with their eyes shut. What he didn't anticipate was that just when he was making magnificent time the clutch of his 1950 Oldsmobile collapsed. It was 55 miles from the starting line, past the mountains. Pirez borrowed a motorcycle and dashed to Puebla, returning almost two hours later with the repair parts, but of course he was out of the running. He made a vigorous appeal for a "refund" of the lost time, which was forbidden by the rules and therefore refused.

There was only one serious accident in spite of the perils of the cliffs. Mexican Car 16 slipped off the road on a curve 20 miles from Mexico City and bounced off two trees. Co-pilot Luis Gomez Barrera's skull was fractured, and he was in critical condition for several days. Owner-driver Alberto P. Rojas, Jr., was unhurt.

FIELD THINNING OUT

In all only 76 cars were still in the running after this leg out of the 88 qualified at the beginning. A few, such as the Detroit team which won Leg 2, in Car 55, decided it wasn't worth while to continue past Mexico City. Others suffered mechanical troubles, such as Car 129, piloted by experienced C. D. Evans, of El Paso, which broke a steering knuckle.

Besides Cars 5, 16, 55 and 129, those which did not finish Leg 6 were Mexican entries 1, 23 and 61, none of which had been doing well, and these U. S. cars: 40, the "Abuelitos" described in the chapter on women in the race; 59, Robert Clement's 1949 Cadillac from Detroit, which had been 34th; 95, of Texan Charley Goldtrap, who had fought his way up to 25th; 102, Dwight Fox's 1938 Cadillac, third oldest car in the race, and 122, driven by Harry Adam Elbel, professional from San Antonio, Texas, which had been 38th.

In this leg, for the first time in the race, U. S. drivers failed to win a majority among the first 20 finishers in the leg itself. Ten were from the U. S., eight from Mexico and two from Italy. In the general standings, there were 15 from the U. S., three from Mexico and one from Italy among the first 20.

The start this day from Mexico City was well organized. After a ceremony in which 30 of the foreign drivers "stood guard" at the Independence Monument, the cars were lined up on the Paseo de la Reforma, then drove through the city to the starting line, on the far side of town near the airport. Deal, in Car 113, was sent away first at 10:30 a. m.

The leading drivers had been given nicknames by the Mexican press. Mantz was "Relampago," or "Lightning." Sterling, with his deep-set eyes, was "Vaquero," or "Cowboy." And huge, chunky Deal, with his round face and eternal smile, of course was "Gordito," an affectionate Mexican way of saying "Fat Boy." Mantz and Deal had driven the last part of the route on trial runs, but Sterling never had been south of Mexico City.

Mantz was in first place, but he was continuing under a handicap. He was feeling ill when he reached Mexico City, and by Monday morning he had a fever as well as dysentery.

The 10 eventual winners stood as follows after Leg 6:

Final Position	Car No.	Position in Leg 6	Over-All Position
1	52	9	4
2	113	7	3
3	21	24	5
4	90	6	17
5	12	19 (tie)	8
6	79	10	1
7	46	8	10
8	103	15	20
9	38	4	1
10	118	3	12

●

SEVENTH LEG — MAY 8, 1950
From Puebla to Oaxaca

Official Distance . . . . 412 kilometers or 256 miles
Maximum Time permitted . . . . 6:55 hours

Summary of Standings

Cars in running for major prizes at start 76
Cars disqualified during leg 4
Cars in running for major prizes at finish 72
Disqualified cars which crossed finish line . . . 3
Total of cars which crossed finish line 75

Winners of Leg

Position	Car No.	Miles Per Hour	Prizes
1	103	68.129	2,000 pesos
2	8	67.584	1,000 pesos
3	32	66.873	500 pesos

The seventh leg of the race saw the Italians come into their own at last, with Mexican drivers sharing the momentary triumph over the leading U. S. teams.

This also was the leg in which blue-helmeted Johnny Mantz, in his 1949 Lincoln, not only fell out of the lead, but was effectively knocked out of the running for the major prizes. Though no one paid any attention to it at the time, it was here, too, that Hershel McGriff and Ray Elliott, in Car 52, gained the time which eventually enabled them to carry off the 150,000-peso first money in the race.

The racers' weather luck finally changed on Leg 7, the second run of the fourth day of the competition. A torrential rainstorm, with bursts of hail, swept the last 150 miles of the 256-mile stretch. Because of the rain, and because this section of the highway is almost 90 per cent curving mountain roads, it was the next-to-slowest leg, with the leading cars only about 11 miles an hour faster than on the partly unpaved last leg.

Victor in the leg was the team of Felice Bonetto and Bruno Bonini in Car 103, a 1950 Alfa Romeo. Their speed of 68.129 mph gave them a time of 3:45:26 for the leg, and they jumped from 20th to 14th in the general standings. The other Italian team, Piero Taruffi and Isidoro Ceroli in Car 90, another 1950 Alfa Romeo, was fourth in this leg, incidentally advancing from 17th to 12th. Taruffi was the only driver among the first 10 who improved his position in every leg. McGriff had a comparable record, never slipping back at any time, though he stayed in fourth position for four consecutive legs.

"Che" Estrada Menocal was second again this leg with a time of 3:47:15 and a speed of 67.584 mph. With his second place in the sixth leg, this gave the Mexico City driver of Car 8 the best total time for the day, and advanced him to 43rd over-all, a gain of 26 places since leaving Mexico City. The winner of Leg 6, Fernando Razo Maciel in Car 44, wasn't able to keep up the pace in the afternoon run, but did finish 11th to move up to 32nd in the standings, a gain of 15 places since the night before.

Third in the leg was picked up by another Mexican driver who had been moving up steadily, Olegario Perez in Car 32, a 1950 Mercury representing the State of Morelos. His time was 3:49:40, his speed 66.873 mph, and his achievement put him among the first 20 in the race as a whole, with an advance to 18th position.

Mantz' troubles restored William Sterling's fleet 1950 Cadillac, Car 68, to first in the general standings. Sterling was 10th in the leg, but his total time to Oaxaca was 19:25:07. The leaders had gotten so far ahead of the field by this time that it was possible for Mantz to lose more than an hour to Sterling in the seventh leg, and tumble only to ninth place.

MORE HARD LUCK FOR MANTZ

Mantz' Car 38 had a total collapse of the brakes. About 65 miles short of Oaxaca they suddenly lost all their holding ability and he had to cross the last mountain range on the braking power of the engine alone. When he finally had crept across the finish line, an examination showed that the brake bands had fallen to bits. While Johnny went to bed with a fever of 102 degrees from the infection that had caught up with him in Mexico City, his co-pilot, Bill Stroppe, got permission to take the car out of the parking inclosure. Stroppe and Bobby Jones, a Oaxaca auto dealer, worked till 3 a.m. installing new brake bands with the special approval of control officials. Car 38's time of 4:58:10 was 1:01:24 more than Sterling's for the leg, and it was 69th out of the 75 cars in the leg.

Tom Deal advanced to second place in this leg, but only because Mantz had been knocked down. The carburetor of Deal's 1950 Cadillac clogged completely about 20 miles from the finish line, and he lost a precious quarter of an hour cleaning it. He was 31st in the leg.

Deal's bad luck was McGriff's opportunity. He came in fifth in the leg, and advanced to only 18 seconds behind Deal in over-all running time. With Mantz out of the lead, Car 52 was now third in the race.

South-Bound in a Hurry!

Out of Mexico City on the fourth day, the mountains began to get rugged. Note crowd on cliff overlooking road.

S-turn on the road to Puebla.

Jean Trevoux and his French Delahaye. Note how drivers used both sides of the highway.

Right—Fred J. Steinbroner Jr.'s '39 Ford at a scenic gap.

Off-Road!

Mexican soldiers help pick up pieces after Lou Figaro wrecks his Hudson on a sharp curve south of Puebla. He was hospitalized.

Off-Road!

A wet section at Oaxaca

Right—Police officials of Oaxaca before the reviewing stand where the drivers finished the leg from Puebla.

Below — Frenchman Jean Trevoux smiles cheerfully on reaching Oaxaca in his Delahaye with assistant Andre Mariotti.

Below—"Che" Estrada Menocal, driving Packard No. 8, smiles as he reaches Oaxaca.

Race officials take Bill Sterling's log book to mark time as he reaches Oaxaca.

Roy Connor and Bob Owen, driving No. 49, which was later disqualified as third place winner, reach Oaxaca in a tropical downpour.

No. 56, driven by Edward Nieders and Max Diener, of Mexico City, is still in the race at Oaxaca, although they overturned on the second day.

Luis Leal Solares arrives in Oaxaca in midst of the heavy downpour.

The only bad accident of the leg put out of the race the second car of the two entered by Jack Gaynor, of Inglewood, Calif., a Hudson dealer and president of the Stock Car Racing Association. His Car 98, a 1947 Hudson, had been eliminated before Mexico City. Now his other entry, Car 14, a 1950 Hudson, was wrecked. Dempsey Wilson, who was driving at the time, miscalculated a curve at Los Molinos, 19 miles out of Puebla, and the car went sailing off the road. Luckily it landed on a little hill that stuck up from the bottom of the canyon, and Wilson escaped with a wrenched back. His teammate, Lou Figaro, had a badly cut ear. The car was bent nearly double.

The other cars eliminated in Leg 7 were number 18, a 1939 Ford which Fred Steinbroner, Jr., of Los Angeles, Vice President of the Stock Car Racing Association, had kept rolling along in 65th place or worse; Car 114, in which Edwin Sollohub of Schenectady, N. Y., had slipped back to 27th, and Car 2, entry of the Mexican State of Guerrero, in which Oscar Lopez de Llergo had reached Puebla in 66th position. Cars 18 and 114 had minor accidents; Lopez was disqualified because he did not turn in his route book at Oaxaca. Sollohub returned to run in Leg 9, and Lopez trailed the remaining racers to the final finish line, helping with first-aid work. There were now only 72 cars in competition for the major prizes, plus three previously disqualified that were still running for leg prizes, or for the fun of it.

Car 81, driven by Lonnie Johnson, the winner of Leg 4, had trouble on the road and was tied for 41st in the leg. With car 81 skidding from 6th to 10th in the general standings, Car 38 falling from 1st to 9th, and the elimination of Car 14, which had been 7th, the classifications were shaken up considerably in this leg. Al Rogers in Car 21 climbed to 4th, Bud Sennett in Car 12 went up to 5th, Luis Leal Solares in Car 46 advanced to 6th (best position ever held by a Mexican driver), Ray Connor in Car 49 and Lewis Hawkins in Car 79 took 7th and 8th places.

Two new cars appeared among the first 20—number 32, already mentioned, and Car 6, driven by Tommy Francis, of San Gabriel, Calif., which took 20th place. Out of the select group were Car 14 and Car 26, which fell to 21st. There were now 14 U. S. drivers, four Mexicans and two Italians among the leaders. And the time difference between Car 68 and Car 6 was one hour, 24 minutes and 53 seconds.

The Mexicans finally took the most leading places in a leg—among the first 20 cars in the Puebla-Oaxaca run were 10 from the host country, eight from the U. S., and two from Italy.

The 10 eventual winners stood as follows after Leg 7:

Final Position	Car No.	Position in Leg 7	Over-All Position
1	52	5	3
2	113	31	2
3	21	15	4
4	90	4	12
5	12	16	5
6	79	20	8
7	46	9	6
8	103	1	14
9	38	69	9
10	118	22	13

EIGHTH LEG — MAY 9, 1950
From Oaxaca to Tuxtla Gutierrez
Official Distance . 540 kilometers or 335.5 miles
Maximum Time permitted . . . . 9:00 hours

Summary of Standings
Cars in running for major prizes at start 72
Cars disqualified during leg 12
Cars in running for major prizes at finish 60
Disqualified cars which crossed finish line . . . 3
Total of cars which crossed finish line 63

Winners of Leg

Position	Car No.	Miles Per Hour	Prizes
1	38	73.032	2,000 pesos
2	6	72.117	1,000 pesos
3	113	71.752	500 pesos

The seventh leg had seen the end of Johnny Mantz' hopes. Now the eighth leg of the Mexican Pan-American Race was the windup for William W. Sterling, of El Paso, the other of the early leaders. The fifth day's run, a single leg from Oaxaca to Tuxtla Gutierrez, ended with Thomas Deal precariously leading the race, and Hershel McGriff hot on his heels. All the others, including Al Rogers in third place, were too far back to have much of a chance at the top prize.

Although the weather was better for 336-mile Leg 8, second longest of the race, the racers were warned before the 9 a. m. start that the rain of the previous day had caused minor landslides in the mountains, and there were a couple of places where they would have to slow down for a total of about 10 miles. There was some rain during this leg, too.

The day's route started with about 25 miles of straight, level highway, then some 125 miles of the now-familiar mountains, followed by flat and rolling country, near sea level and hot, from Tehuantepec to Tuxtla Gutierrez.

So ill that he almost had to be carried to his Car 38, Mantz showed pure nerve in this leg. Starting in 69th spot because of his disastrous seventh leg, he passed more than 30 other cars and arrived in Tuxtla Gutierrez the winner for the day. His speed was 73.032 mph, his time 4:35:38, and he moved back up to fourth place in the race.

Meantime Sterling had the same kind of luck that overcame Mantz the day before—but worse. His brakes burned out, and he struggled into Tuxtla Gutierrez in a time of 8:22:18, last in the leg. His previous time had been so good that he was still in 29th place, but his Cadillac's condition was hopeless. He didn't even start the next and final leg.

Young Tommy Francis turned on the heat to bring his 1950 Ford in second in this leg, in a time of 4:39:08 and an average speed of 72.117 mph. This was good enough to give Tommy 15th position in the race, a gain of five places.

Third in the leg was Deal, who did it in 4:40:33, averaging 71.752 mph. With Sterling out, he was now in first, and he picked up enough time on Car 52, the white McGriff-Elliott Oldsmobile, to hold an advantage of 8 minutes and 42 seconds. The Portland team, ninth in the leg, had a total time of 24:29:49 against 24:21:07 for Deal and his assistant, Sam Cresap.

Al Rogers and his brother Ralph, piloting Car 21, a 1949 Cadillac, moved up to third in the race with an elapsed time of 24:48:55, 46 seconds ahead of Mantz. The Rogers

All-out for Tuxtla

Jack McAfee and Ford Robinson in No. 118, leaving Oaxaca on the fifth day.

Peon watches the cars leave Oaxaca.

Tom Deal (right) checks his spares for No. 113 as racers prepare to leave Oaxaca.

Drivers change tires and make last minute checks before the race starts in the early morning from Oaxaca.

Bill Sterling checks pressure in his tires before leaving Oaxaca.

Race official checks No. 113 as it leaves impound for the starting line in Oaxaca.

High in the Mountains

Bud Sennett and John C. Balch south of Oaxaca.

The Alfa Romeos proved to have an edge in the mountains and move up in the field. This is Piero Taruffi in No. 90.

Lewis Hawkins and Wayland Burgess race over top of mountains near end of race. Where are the safety rails? There aren't any!

Edward Nieders' crumpled Ford speeds along south of Oaxaca.

Mexican favorite Rodolfo Castañeda in the Cadillac No. 9 south of Oaxaca.

The Arrival at Tuxtla

Left: Olegario Perez applies his brakes to stop for official, as No. 32 reaches Tuxtla Gutierrez.

Tommy Francis and Jimmie Crum swing doors open as they brake to a stop, after crossing the finish line at Tuxtla Gutierrez.

France's Delahaye at hotel in Tuxtla Gutierrez, where drivers stayed overnight before last leg to El Ocotal. Jean Trevoux, driver (back to camera), with assistant Andre Mariotti (opposite side of car), and Olivier le Bas.

Ray Elliot holds out log book for race official as he and driver Hershel McGriff (winners of the race) reach Tuxtla Gutierrez in No. 52.

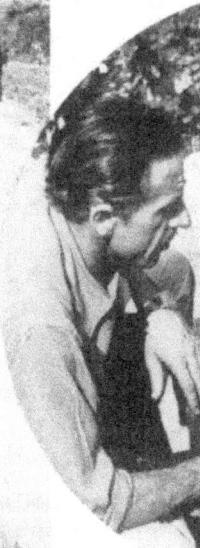

Jean Trevoux (right) checks his Delahaye with mechanic Briosi in Tuxtla Gutierrez.

Left: Crowd gathers around No. 34, representing their native State of Chiapas, after it stops on reaching Tuxtla Gutierrez.

team had been running a steady, unspectacular pace, keeping up in the first 10 since the third leg. Reaching Mexico City in sixth, they had gained three positions as Cars 81, 38 and 68 successively ran into difficulties. Al, a professional and a veteran of the Pike's Peak Hill Climb, which he has won four times, had looked over the highway before the race, and knew how to get the most out of his car, which came off the used-car lot of his sponsor, Eugene Barry. Tied for 15th in the eighth leg, Car 21 couldn't hope for much more than to hold its position and carry off third money.

Bud Sennett was still in fifth in Car 12, another 1950 Oldsmobile, more than four minutes behind Mantz. And no one was paying much attention to Car 49, a 1950 Nash driven by Roy Pat Connor and Robert Green of Corsicana, Texas. In the first 10 since Mexico City, they were eighth in Leg 8, and had inched up to sixth place. Seventh was held by Lewis Hawkins, of Spartanburg, S. C., who was fifth in the leg to pass Luis Leal Solares, Mexican driver of Car 46, who could do no better than 21st from Oaxaca to Tuxtla Gutierrez. The Mantz recovery contributed to Leal's loss of two places in the over-all standings.

EUROPEAN ENTRIES GAINING

The European entries continued to move up fast. Jean Trevoux and Andre Mariotti, the Frenchmen in a 1950 Delahaye, Car 19, had their best leg of the race, doing it fourth best right behind Deal, and advancing from 22nd to 16th, the first time they had been in the first 20 since the second leg.

The Italians were rolling right along in their 1950 Alfa Romeos. Pierro Taruffi, in Car 90, was seventh in the leg to take ninth in the general standings, and Felice Bonetto, in Car 103, was 26th and advanced into a tie for 11th with Car 39, the second-best Mexican entry. Car 39, a 1950 Mercury driven by Raul Arguelles Salgado, had been 19th at the end of the seventh leg, and never worse than 27th since Ciudad Juarez.

Leg 8 was the end for two Mexican sentimental favorites, Cars 44 and 8, which had been first and second in Leg 6. Both had engine trouble, and Jose Estrada Menocal, in Car 8, said that his gasoline feed line also collapsed. Neither he nor Fernando Razo Maciel, in Car 44 (both were 1949 Packards) was able to reach Tuxtla Gutierrez.

Altogether 12 cars were disqualified in this leg, only 60 remaining by nightfall. Two did not start—Car 48, driven by Lyle McKinley Warren, of Inglewood, Calif., with his wife as co-pilot, which had brake trouble, and Car 111, a 1950 Cadillac driven by J. W. Parham of Lubbock, Texas. The former was in 38th place, the latter in 28th. Car 81, the Lonnie Johnson entry, blew a tire 31 miles before Tuxtla Gutierrez, and somehow was stopped after tumbling 15 feet down a steep declivity more than 100 feet deep. Johnson and G. W. McGraw, his co-pilot in the big 1949 Cadillac, were unhurt. Car 93, a 1950 Mercury driven by Gabriel Herrera of Bogota, Colombia, hit a post and was damaged badly enough to be put out of the running.

Engine or tire trouble accounted for the other six eliminated: Car 35, a 1949 Packard piloted by Javier Razo Marciel, brother of Fernando, which had been in 27th place; Car 45, a 1948 Packard driven by John N. Stewart of Clovis, New Mexico; Car 63, George Nelson Ashley's 1949 Cadillac from El Paso; Car 66, the 1950 Hudson entered and driven by Bob Korf of Beloit, Wis., which had been 11th in the race and moving steadily upward; Car 73, the 1950 Nash of Mexico's Rafael Mendoza Licea, and Car 84, a 1950 Mercury driven by Carlos Almazan of Mexico City. Numbers 45, 63, 73 and 84 had held 33rd, 17th, 41st and 34th positions, respectively.

Thus four entries were eliminated from the first 20 in the over-all standings—Cars 63, 66, 68 and 81, all from the U. S. Their places were taken by machines representing four countries, Nos. 19 of France, 71 of the U. S., 82 of Mexico and 91 of Colombia. Now the select group included 11 from the U. S., five from Mexico, two from Italy, and one each from France and Colombia. And the time differential between Car 113, in first and Car 37 (Bill France) in 20th was one hour, 50 minutes and 26 seconds. The field really was spread wide.

Again half of the first 20 in the leg itself were U. S. contestants, plus six from Mexico, two from Italy, and one each from France and Venezuela.

The first 11 in the race now included the 10 ultimate winners (Car 49 was the "outsider"), which stood as follows:

Final Position	Car No.	Position in Leg 8	Over-All Position
1	52	9	2
2	113	3	1
3	21	15 (tie)	3
4	90	7	9
5	12	17	5
6	79	5	7
7	46	21	8
8	103	26	11 (tie)
9	38	1	4
10	118	10	10

Only Cars 21, 12 and 118 were in their ultimate positions. With only one leg to go, there was no such thing as a certainty in this race.

NINTH AND FINAL LEG — MAY 10, 1950
From Tuxtla Gutierrez to El Ocotal
Official Distance . 275 kilometers or 170.85 miles
Maximum Time permitted . . . . 4:35 hours

Summary of Standings
Cars in running for major prizes at start 60
Cars disqualified during leg 13
Cars in running for major prizes at finish 47
Disqualified cars which crossed finish line . . . 11
Total of cars which crossed finish line 58

LEADERS
Winners of Leg

Position	Car No.	Miles Per Hour	Prizes
1	90	57.153	2,000 pesos
2	103	56.664	1,000 pesos
3	52	55.533	500 pesos

Winners of Race

Position	Car No.	Miles Per Hour	Prizes
1	52	78.421	150,000 pesos
2	113	77.362	100,000 pesos
3	21	76.440	50,000 pesos

In the Hotel Bonampak at Tuxtla Gutierrez the night before the last leg of the race, Hershel McGriff, driver of Car 52, tried a little psychology on Thomas A. Deal, driver of Car 113. Said Hershel to Tom:

"That 100,000 pesos looks pretty good to me. I'll be plenty happy if I can hold onto second place tomorrow."

It's doubtful whether Tom Deal, a wise old hand in spite of his inexperience at auto racing, would let himself be misled by so transparent an effort to put him off his guard. But McGriff had something else up his sleeve. He'd driven lumber trucks over back-country Oregon roads, and the rough going on the last leg was his meat.

It was 171 miles from Tuxtla Gutierrez to El Ocotal, the final finish line, and 107 miles of it was unpaved. The climb to San Cristobal Las Casas, more than 5,000 feet in about 40 miles, was over an asphalt surface, but beyond there the road was 15-foot-wide gravel as far as Comitan, and then over normal-width gravel to El Ocotal on the Guatemalan border.

And on this stretch McGriff made a time of 3:04:36 against Deal's 3:14:34. The difference was nine minutes and 58 seconds, enough to give McGriff the victory in the race by 1 minute and 16 seconds. The final times were 27:34:25 and 27:35:41. Deal had driven a spectacular race, taking third in Legs 3 and 8, and first in Leg 5. Against this, he had been 26th in Leg 1, 23rd in Leg 2, and 31st in Leg 7. In contrast, 22-year-old McGriff, aided by calm veteran Ray Elliott and braintrusted by sponsor Roy Sundstrom, had been out of the first 10 in only one leg, the fifth, where he was 14th. And he hadn't won a leg prize until a ruling issued five days later gave him a third in the final stage.

The rains held off this day, May 10, the sixth of the race, but another storm was brewing. Roy Pat Connor, auto dealer from Corsicana, Texas, and owner-driver of Car 49, a 1950 Nash, felt ill that morning, he explained later, so he got Curtis Turner of Roanoke, Va., one of the best U. S. dirt-track drivers, to take his place, with Robert Green continuing as co-pilot. Turner was the co-pilot of Bill France, of Daytona Beach, Fla., driver of Car 37, another 1950 Nash. Some drivers said that Turner had studied this section of the highway in advance, and that the switch was made so that the best-placed Nash would have the advantage of his skill, but no one ever offered proof of this statement.

At any rate, Car 49, which had been in sixth place, made the best time of any entrant in the Tuxtla Gutierrez-El Ocotal run. Doing it in 2:55:57, it not only was first in the leg, but passed Cars 21, 38 and 12 to move up to third in the race. A 50,000-peso prize was at stake.

Immediately a number of drivers, including of course Al Rogers in Car 21, complained to officials about the switch in crews. The fight finally was carried to a grand commission of race authorities, which ruled on May 15 in Mexico City that Connor's admitted change in crew disqualified him for both leg and over-all prizes.

Thus the winners of the three big prizes became Car 52, first for 150,000 pesos; Car 113, second for 100,000 pesos, and Car 21, third for 50,000.

Rogers, like McGriff, had driven unspectacularly. His worst in any leg was 24th in the short sixth, and his best was fourth in Legs 4 and 9. Thus he did not capture even one of the secondary prizes.

The elimination of Car 49 gave the victory in the ninth leg to Italian Piero Taruffi in Car 90. Three and a half minutes slower than the U. S. auto, his Alfa Romeo did the dash in 2:59:22, averaging 57.153 mph, and leaping upward from ninth to fourth in the general standings. His teammate Felice Bonetto, in Car 103, was second in this leg, with a time of 3:00:55 and a speed of 56.664. McGriff's third place was gained with an average of 55.533 mph, in contrast to his speed of 78.421 for the entire race.

GRAVEL VS. RACING CARS

Bud Sennett, in Car 12, was a picture of consistency—fifth in the last leg, fifth in the race. The bad luck of Johnny Mantz permitted Lewis Hawkins in Car 79 and Luis Leal Solares in Car 46 to advance to sixth and seventh, though they were well down in the leg. Bonetto advanced to eight from 11th, and Jack McAfee, in Car 118, stayed in 10th.

Mantz' trouble was simple. He had congratulated himself on having nine special racing tires left when he reached Oaxaca. In fourth the morning of the final day, he was feeling confident—his car was in good shape and his fever was abating. But the gravel was too much for racing tires. One after another blew out, and Mantz reached El Ocotal on three tires and a smashed rear right rim. He was 36th in the leg, more than 38 minutes behind Taruffi and more than 32 behind McGriff. So his final position was ninth, 52 minutes and 45 seconds out of first place.

If there was only one Mexican among the first 10, the picture was more cheerful for the host nation when the next 10 were classified. The final score among the first 20 finishers was eight from the U. S., eight from Mexico, two from Italy, one from France, and one from Colombia. The Delahaye team was seventh in the last leg to move up to 12th over-all, a gain of four places.

Four contestants dropped out of the first 20 on this leg. Besides Car 49, there were two U. S. entrants, Cars 6 and 37, and Car 32, Mexican. Their places were taken by four Mexicans, Cars 3, 62, 77 and 121.

The exit of Car 6 was most spectacular. This was Tommy Francis' Ford. Swerving to avoid hitting a child in a village just out of Tuxtla Gutierrez, Francis sent the car against a curb. It rolled over but righted itself, so Tommy continued, but he was injured and soon was forced to pull over to one side of the road. There the driver of disqualified Car 2 found him, taking him to a hospital with serious internal injuries. Jimmie Crum, Tommy's co-pilot, took the auto on to the finish line, but arrived far after the time limit. Reports of the death of Francis and Crum were widely circulated by the United States press and radio.

Car 32, which had been in 13th place, was eliminated by an accident only 5½ miles from the finish line, and Bill France's Car 37 went out with a broken radiator in San Cristobal Las Casas. Others which never reached the final mark were Cars 10, 26, 31 and 94.

Five others passed under the El Ocotal arch after the deadline: Cars 6, 15, 105, 107 and 132. And five others, previously disqualified for major prizes, triumphantly completed the run: Cars 25, 56, 87, 114 and 130.

In all, 47 entrants made the entire race without disqualification, and another 11, including Car 49, also got there. By countries, the totals were: U. S., 20 out of 59 entered; Mexico, 27 out of 57 entered; Venezuela and Colombia, each 3 out of 4; Italy, 2 out of 2; Peru, 1 out of 2; France and China, each 1 out of 1; Guatemala and El Salvador, each 0 out of 1.

What happened to Car 94 is a separate story. This was the Mexican university students' car, a 1950 Studebaker bought for them by President Aleman. There had been many rumors about the condition of the last stretch of road because of the recent heavy rains, so Guillermo Ostos, the representative of Secretary Garcia Lopez, and Gov. Francisco Grajales of the State of Chiapas took over No. 94 to inspect the route before the race. They found it transitable, and the last leg was ordered run. There had been rumors that it would be called off, or stopped at San Cristobal Las Casas.

Antonio Cornejo, general manager of the race, decided to send the racers off at four-minute intervals from Tuxtla Gutierrez, beginning at 9:30 a. m., so that there would be a minimum of passing on the narrower sections, and he stuck by his guns in spite of the urging of some other race officials who discounted the safety factor.

After six days of racing, the cars were far apart in total elapsed time. Number 52 was 2 hours, 30 minutes and 28 seconds ahead of Car 3, in 20th place, and no less than 13 hours, 7 minutes and 1 second ahead of Car 80, the last to qualify.

And so the Mexican Pan-American Race was over. McGriff told the story of his victory in a brief interview:

"I had a good trip. Everything went well for me. I didn't have a single mishap."

That summarized it—nearly all his rivals did have accidents or mechanical trouble.

All that remained was the protests, the banquets and the presentation of the prizes.

A Mexican woman takes chickens to market at Tuxtla.

Car 38 leaving the impound area at Tuxtla for the last leg.

Car 33 leaves impound for the last leg from Tuxtla to El Ocotal.

The two Alfa Romeos at the impound at Tuxtla.

Mist on the Mountain

Lewis Hawkins stops to let out steam as rain falls in the mountains near the finish.

Felice Bonetto's Alfa Romeo corners on a curve south of Tuxtla.

McGriff overtakes Hawkins on the rocky road to El Ocotal. Look at that winding highway!

A precarious place to fix a flat—but Lewis Hawkins and Wayland Burgess had to risk it on the last day.

Top: Tom Deal heads toward El Ocotal and the finish line.

Center: Jacqueline Evans passes through a village on last leg of race.

Left: Spectators gather on high cut overlooking the road at finish line in El Ocotal to see the drivers come in.

Journey's End... a dusty Finish of 2135 grueling miles

Left — Olegario Perez crosses El Ocotal finish line in No. 32.

Badly battered rear wheel of Johnny Mantz' Lincoln. After blowing three of his special racing tires he traveled the last few miles over heavy gravel on the rim.

Weary drivers relax with food and drink in a hut in El Ocotal after finish of race. Johnny Mantz sits with arms folded in foreground. Standing, left, is Tom Deal, who won second place in No. 113.

The Lincoln No. 38 gets a new wheel in El Ocotal after coming in on a rim.

No. 77 driven by Jesus Valezzi and Adolfo Costa in El Ocotal after finish of race.

El Ocotal, Chiapas, where the race ended. It was thatched huts, lush jungle on rugged mountains and 300,000 pesos in prize money.

Congratulations and Investigations

Congratulations for a hard job well done.

Left: The winning Olds was inspected thoroughly for strictly stock specifications and was pronounced O.K.

Left: Curtis Turner's Nash was the subject of heated debate at the finish line and was ultimately disqualified because of a change in drivers.

Right: This is the heart of El Ocotal, where the Pan-American Highway ends.

CHAPTER V
Protests and Decisions

THREE formal written protests were submitted to the Race Committee after the end of the competition, and Secretary Agustin Garcia Lopez, president of the Central Executive Committee, considered them so important that he convoked a "Grand Commission" of race officials to rule on them.

The commission met in Mexico City on May 15, five days after the finish date, and handed down its rulings that evening, just two days before the delivery of trophies and prize checks to the racers.

The three protests concerned the change in crews of Car 49, the Roy Pat Connor entry, which finished first in the ninth leg and third in the race; the claim of Tom Deal, whose Car 113 took second place, for a three-minute time allowance which would have given him first; and the request of Bruno Pagliai, representing the Italian entries, Cars 90 and 103, that the first 20 finishers be inspected, rather than the first 11, as had been done.

Car 49 was disqualified, and the other two protests were rejected. Because of its interest to general readers as well as to actual participants, here is a translation of the text of the commission's ruling, with the omission of some unimportant passages:

"First there was presented the claim formulated by Messrs. Tom A. Deal and Sam Cresap, driver and co-pilot, respectively, of Car 113, consisting in the request that the Grand Commission recognize the three minutes which said gentlemen say they lost in helping Car 112 when it met with an accident 30 kilometers from the Ciudad Juarez starting line.

"The Grand Commission considers: First, that the detention of the petitioners was not obligated by obstacles in the road; second, that the claim was not presented in the manner prescribed nor within the time fixed by Article 46 of the rules of the race; third, that the rules do not authorize obligatory detentions of the racers as a result of accidents; fourth, that no matter how meritorious may have been the action of the petitioners in aiding a racing comrade, it is not possible to take into account either the reason for the detention or the time lost by them; and fifth, that the race functionaries cannot take this detention into account, in regard to either the deed itself or the time involved.

"In view of the foregoing, the Commission unanimously issues the following decision: 'The claim presented by Messrs. Tom A. Deal and Sam Cresap is rejected.'

"Second, the Commission studied the claim presented by Messrs. Al and Ralph Rogers, the crew of Car 21, and by Messrs. John C. Balch and Bud Sennett, the crew of Car 12. Examining said claim and analyzing the respective rules, the Commission agrees: First, in view of the fact that driver Roy Pat Connor, in his letter of this same date, admits in the first point the substitution of his co-pilot Robert Owen, at that time driver of the car, by Curtis Turner, co-pilot of another competitor, it is clear that there was a violation of Article 19 of the race rules, which says: 'Either the driver or his assistant may drive the automobile at will, but under no circumstances may a substitute take the place of either driver or assistant once the race has begun'; second, in view of this, it is not necessary to consider whether the protest against said action was opportunely presented, since this Commission must apply the terms of the race rules, and penalize violations of them; third, the foregoing does not subtract in any way from the merits of the competing Nash No. 49, nor its crew, Roy Connor and Robert Owen, for the total time employed in the competition and in the final leg from Tuxtla Gutierrez to El Ocotal.

"In view of the foregoing, it is decided: First, the Nash marked with the number 49 must be and is disqualified for an admitted violation of Article 19 of the race rules, and that as a consequence it ceases to occupy third place in the general classification and first place in the classification in the final leg from Tuxtla Gutierrez to El Ocotal; second, consequently the Cadillac marked with the number 21 and driven by Al and Ralph Rogers is granted third place in the general classication, and the Alfa Romeo marked with the number 90 and driven by Piero Taruffi and Isidoro Ceroli is granted the first prize in the Tuxtla Gutierrez-El Ocotal leg; the second place in the leg goes to the Alfa Romeo marked with the number 103 and driven by Felice Bonetto and Bruno Bonini; and third place in the leg to the Oldsmobile marked with the number 52 and driven by Hershel McGriff and Ray Elliott.

"Third, there is submitted to the consideration of the Grand Commission the claim formulated by Mr. Bruno Pagliai, entrants' representative, regarding the technical inspection of the cars. Studying said claim, the Commission unanimously agrees on the following: First, the Race Organizing Committee reports that the inspection of the winning cars was carried out by a technical commission composed of experts from the automobile assembly plants of Mexico, as thoroughly and minutely as was necessary to be able to make a responsible decision; second, in anticipation of the possibility that alterations might be found in one or all of the autos which won the first three places, it was ordered that the first 10 cars in the classification remain in El Ocotal to be examined, and said technical commission proceeded to inspect them, delivering its unanimous decision that the three winning cars, as well as the eight following ones, which were examined, agreed with the specifications for 'standard' type automobiles according to series and catalog; third, that there would be no object in examining 20 automobiles, as is requested by Mr. Bruno Pagliai; fourth, that the Commission understands that the articles which the claimant cites are part of the International Sporting Code, although this is not mentioned in his petition, but that on reviewing said code there is not found in the cited articles the least reference to support the request submitted by the claimant.

"Therefore it is decided: 'The claim presented by Mr. Pagliai is not pertinent and is unfounded, and therefore is rejected'."

The Commission then worked out the list of trophies to be presented, and agreed on a public statement which:

1. Gave "enthusiastic homage to the great interest, cooperation and sporting spirit" of Secretary Garcia Lopez, "faithful interpreter of the wishes of the President of the Republic, Attorney Miguel Aleman."

2. Congratulated the Army for its safety work.

3. Thanked the Mexican Red Cross and the Military Medical Service for their assistance.

4. Thanked all members of race subcommittees.

5. Hailed the "magnificent work" of Antonio Cornejo, general manager of the race, and Enrique Martin Moreno, control chief.

The Grand Commission was made up of Ramon Llano, president, and Edmundo Stierle, Jose Rivera, Pablo Macedo, Armando Herrerias, Alfonso Villaseñor, Pedro Viyao, Ricardo Estrada Berg and Manuel E. Razo.

Gallant Work by Red Cross and Safety Patrol

Top: Mexican radio operator signals for ambulance and wrecker at site of accident. Center: A Red Cross unit waits at a dangerous spot along the highway.

Bottom: Tommy Francis, driver of Ford No. 6, is brought injured to El Ocotal after overturning his car to avoid hitting a child who darted across the road in his path.

CHAPTER VI
The Race Summary

QUONSET huts, food and cots waited at El Ocotal for the racers, officials and press. For some, especially McGriff and Elliott, it was a gay arrival. As soon as it was certain that they were the winners, they were besieged by reporters and photographers, who suddenly realized that they hadn't bothered to take many pictures of this quiet pair, nor to find out much about them. Smiling McGriff told about his wife and two children back in Portland, Ore., and of his plans to use his share of the prize money to expand his little trucking business.

Tom Deal, finding himself nudged out of first place, and with 50,000 pesos less than he had been counting on, took it well, though later he was heard to complain that the unpaved section of the road was strictly for burros. A fighter to the end, Deal renewed his claim for a three-minute allowance for the time he said he had lost on the first leg as a result of the Guatemalan entry's fatal accident.

And of course, as stated previously, Al and Ralph Rogers, supported by a number of other drivers, asked for the disqualification of Car 49.

First, though, the winning cars had to be examined. The first eleven—the 10 eventual winners plus Car 49—were sequestered, and experts from the Mexican auto-assembly plants went to work on them. It might be explained that only in special cases is the import of assembled cars permitted by Mexico; all major U. S. manufacturers ship parts into the country for assembly there. Thus factory experts were available for this inspection.

There was nothing private about the going-over the cars got. Drivers were permitted to hover over competitors' autos, and they took full advantage of this, kibitzing every move and offering voluminous suggestions. But the only thing found that was the least surprising was the fact that winning Car 52 had unusually high compression, though it was within factory specifications.

Thus the early complaints against some of the U. S. entries fell by the wayside. If the winning cars had been tuned up and put into perfect condition, this certainly was part of the job of preparing for a race. There was no evidence of trickery. Bruna Pagliai, operator of the Mexico City horse-racing track and one of the backers of the Italian team, still was dissatisfied and formally requested that the inspection be extended to include all of the first 20 finishers.

First to hurry out of El Ocotal were the reporters and photographers. There was communication trouble at the end of the highway, and by light plane and auto the press had to hurry back to Tuxtla Gutierrez to get their stories out to the world.

Most of the competitors and officials caught a night's sleep in the Quonset huts before starting back north. In a day or so El Ocotal—now officially Ciudad Cuauhtemoc by action of the legislature of the state of Chiapas—was again a quiet mountain village.

As the participants hopped planes or took their cars back over the highway at a more leisurely pace, the scene of activities shifted to Mexico City.

There were to be plenty of festivities for winners and losers. Meantime the evaluations began. Since all entries were standard models, the test of success or failure was not in what was done to the cars before the race, apart from the obvious need to put them in perfect condition, and the equally obvious matter of taking full advantage of such permitted changes as the installation of heavy shock absorbers.

Everyone agreed that the various types of automatic transmissions were a handicap in a race, not permitting the quick shifting which could make many minutes' difference over more than 2,000 miles.

COMPARING THE RESULTS

On makes of cars there was less agreement. The score is indisputable: Among the first 10 there were four Oldsmobiles, three Cadillacs, two Alfa Romeos and one Lincoln; among the first 20 there were seven Oldsmobiles, four Cadillacs, four Lincolns, two Alfa Romeos and one Delahaye. It was a sweep for General Motors, Ford Motor Co. and European cars.

Continuing this analysis, the Oldsmobiles come out even better: Of the 13 which started, more than half were among the first 20. The percentages are lower for the Cadillacs, of which 20 started; the Lincolns, with 16 starting, and the Mercurys, with 11 starting. The Alfa Romeos and the Delahaye had perfect records, of course.

On the other hand, some other makes had even better marks for durability: Every DeSoto, Chrysler and Chevrolet which set out from Ciudad Juarez was able to cross the finish line, and the same would have been true of the Studebakers if the officials hadn't taken over the students' car, No. 94. Fords did well, too—five out of eight got there. It would seem that these had the lasting power, if not the speed.

Now let's look at the makes which had the worst records by percentage.

Out of seven Packards, none finished. All Packards entered were 1948 and 1949 models, which is one extenuating circumstance. Mechanical trouble put three of them out of the race, two went out with tire trouble, one because of a rules violation, and the seventh because of unknown reasons.

Out of nine Hudsons, one finished. Car 14 had an accident, two (including Car 4, a 1937 model) had mechanical trouble, and there is no record of why the five others dropped out.

Out of eight Nashes, four finished, including Car 49, which would have been third except for a rules violation. Two had mechanical trouble and two had accidents.

Out of 16 Buicks that started, six finished. One had an accident, three had mechanical trouble, and six dropped out for unknown reasons.

Out of 20 Cadillacs which started, eight finished. Three had accidents, three had mechanical trouble, five quit for unknown reasons, and one went out for a rules violation.

Out of 11 Mercurys, five finished. Three were eliminated by accidents, two by mechanical reasons and one by an unknown cause.

Out of 16 Lincoln, seven finished. Two had accidents, one had tire trouble, two had mechanical troubles, and four dropped out for reasons not recorded.

Seven of the Buicks were pre-1949 models; so were six Cadillacs, three Hudsons, two Packards, and one each of the following: Chevrolet, Ford, Lincoln, Chrysler, Cord Lago Talbot and Hotchkiss. Of these 25 only eight finished: Two Buicks, two Cadillacs, a Chevrolet, a Hudson, a Lincoln and a Chrysler.

In contrast, of the 61 1950 autos which began the race there were 33 among the 58 finishers. So age counted.

It can be seen that the statistics do not give an absolutely clear claim to superiority to any manufacturer, since tires, drivers and age were factors as well as the quality of the cars.

The two chief problems for the drivers were brakes and tires, both of which took a beating they wouldn't have experienced under normal driving conditions. Tire trouble was a time-consumer, but knocked only a few cars out of the race. When brakes went, the auto also was likely to be eliminated, sometimes for the lack of repair parts. It was brakes which forced out Bill Sterling. Johnny Mantz suffered his first blow from brakes and got the finishing wallop from tires.

Curves, of course, were what took it out of the brakes and tires, with heat alone causing plenty of blowouts the first day. Racing writers have pointed out that it is curves which make most of the difference between track and road racing. Though the Mexican route had well-banked curves, they were constructed for a maximum speed of 50 miles an hour, and not the 70 or more which most of the racers averaged over the entire run. To keep up their speed, the racers had to enter the curves from the inside and slide across, and back this up with last-second brake action. Bud Sennett, driver of Car 12, who didn't know the road, remarked that he judged the curves in part by the amount of rubber that the cars ahead of him laid down in black marks which he read as a ship pilot reads the ocean waves.

Another factor of importance was quickness of pickup; the driver who could resume full speed quickest after coming out of a curve had the advantage. Here is where the Alfa Romeos and Delahayes shone. They are constructed for that type of driving.

Gasoline was not a comparative factor, since all cars had to use Pemex' Super-Mexolina. Pemex pointed out after the race that this 80-octane gasoline was sufficient to maintain speeds that were well above the usual marks in over-the-road runs.

Whether it was luck or superiority of cars or drivers, in the end it was the entries with the least tire and mechanical trouble that finished best. McGriff's car ran well the whole distance, and he had few tire changes. The same was true for Al Rogers. Tom Deal could trace a loss of 50,000 pesos to a clogged carburetor. The Italians had almost no tire trouble, changing rubber completely a couple of times during overnight stops as a precaution. Just to show that there are no rules, Jesus Nava Gonzalez finished a good 13th with 16 tire changes on the road, however.

The rehashing of might-have-beens went on endlessly during the drivers' trip north and the post-race parties in Mexico City. But the ample Mexican hospitality was sufficient to heal most wounds.

THE VICTORY PARTY

Biggest event for the racers was a dinner at the luxurious Hotel Del Prado with Secretary Garcia Lopez as host. Public officials, race committeemen, auto industry leaders and the press attended, too, and there were lots of pretty society girls. Boyish McGriff just isn't the man-about-town type, so his wife probably merely smiled at the picture of her happy husband surrounded by three lovelies at the banquet.

Tony Cornejo also threw a party at his handsome home, and got back at the racers by unlimbering his camera to make his own collection of photographs of drivers at ease.

There were innumerable smaller gatherings, of course, and the Liga Nacional de Transporte (National Transportation League) paid special honors to Luis Leal Solares, one of their own, the bus driver who was the only Mexican among the first 10 in the race. And an oil company gave checks of 3,000 pesos to Leal and 1,000 each to Raul Arguelles Salgado (Car 39, 11th place) and Nava Gonzalez (Car 42) for using its lubricants.

Meanwhile businessmen gave banquets for the two most active officials of the race, Antonio Cornejo and Enrique Martin Moreno. Successively the Rotary Club, the Lions, the Puebla auto dealers and the Mexican auto industry honored these two men.

The prizes and trophies were to be handed out on May 17. But first the three major protests had to be settled. As told in a separate chapter, this was done by a "Grand Commission" which ruled on May 15 that Car 49 was disqualified, but turned down Deal's bid for a three-minute refund and Pagliai's request for the examination of more cars.

Finally came the culminating event. Drivers and officials assembled at Los Pinos, Mexico's White House, to receive their money and cups from the hands of President Miguel Aleman. Present were Secretary Garcia Lopez and Antonio Cornejo, on either side of the President, as well as Martin Moreno and the diplomatic representatives of Guatemala, Venezuela, Peru and Colombia.

The ceremony was simple. Opening at noon with the Mexican national anthem and a speech by Guatemalan Ambassador Francisco Conzenza, it consisted chiefly of the delivery of the awards to the accompaniment of innumerable flash bulbs.

First trophies were given to Guatemalan Car 112, and to the crews representing Colombia, Venezuela, China, Peru, Italy and France. There was a special cup for Francisco Toscana Valle, co-pilot who survived the fatally injured Guatemalan driver, Enrique Hachmeister.

Then there were trophies for leading Mexican finishers who didn't get into the first 10: Arguelles of Car 39, Nava Gonzalez of Car 42, Leopoldo Almanza Vera of Car 82, Carlos Gustavo Mass of Car 62, Jesus Valezzi of Car 77, and Abelardo Matamoros Acosta of Car 121. Sentimental awards went to Jacqueline Evans, Ismael Alvarez, who tried so hard in Car 4, the 1937 Hudson, and Oscar Lopez de Llergo, of Car 2. Next came the trophies for the broadly smiling drivers of the first 10 cars, plus checks for those who had them coming. Leal Solares was given an ovation when he stepped up for his award for seventh place. For each driver the Mexican Navy Band played the first bars of his country's national anthem, so that "The Star Spangled Banner" was heard often.

Special premiums went, after this high point, to Rodolfo Castañeda, the driver of "Coche Mexico," and his two co-pilots, Florencio Estrada G. of Mexico City and Guillermo Palmieri of Guatemala. There was special recognition for some hard-luck Mexicans who tried hard. Jose Estrada Menocal of Car 8, Gregorio Pirez of Car 5, Javier Razo Maciel of Car 35, and Fernando Gallardo Amaro and Enrique Torres Caballero, who drove Car 94, the national university entry.

Finally there were awards for four U. S. entrants who had caught the public eye: Bill Sterling of Car 68, the early leader; "Grandma" Lammons of Car 10; Tommy Francis, who turned over Car 6 rather than hit a child, and Andrea Gonzalez of San Francisco, who captured last place.

And then gold medals, to top off the ceremony, for Antonio Cornejo and Enrique Martin Moreno.

It was seven days after the checkered flag had been waved for the last time at El Ocotal. The Carrera Panamericana Mexico was now history.

President Aleman officiates at Victory Celebration

President Miguel Aleman of Mexico (at right of microphone) and other dignitaries prepare to start the ceremonies at trophy meeting.

Some of the 80 trophies which were awarded participants.

Happy Winners...

Winner McGriff gives with a big smile, check in one hand and trophy in the other.

Tom Deal, second place winner, receives check and trophy.

Below—Piero Taruffi, driver of Alfa Romeo No. 90, receives his award. He captured fourth place.

Al Rogers, third place winner, gets his prizes.

94

...share Prizes and Trophies

Jacqueline Evans de Lopez received two awards from the President.

Johnny Mantz receives large trophy from the President. He finished ninth.

Lt. Rodolfo Castañeda G., the "people's choice" receives trophy and congratulations from President Aleman.

Luis Leal Solares, driver of No. 16, before being presented his trophy by President Miguel Aleman (center, group of three facing camera). At left of President Aleman is Sr. Garcia Lopez, Secretary of Communications, and at right is Sr. Antonio Cornejo C., Director General of the race.

During a break in the presentation ceremonies a trio of "Mariachis" sang the story of the race in a special prepared song.

Jacqueline Evans and Owen Gray with trophies.

Johnny Mantz received a large trophy from the President of Mexico.

Receptions and banquets followed the race in Mexico City. Here we have, Left to Right, front: Ray Elliott, Miss Doree Clark, Hershel McGriff; back row: Mr. Clark, G. M. Engineer, Roy Sundstrom and Bud Sennett.

A toast to victory. Left to Right: Sr. Antonio Cornejo C., Miss Lolita Meek, Secretary of Sr. Cornejo, Hershel McGriff, and Miss Doree Clark.

It must have been a good one as Wayland Burgess, Red Byron, Lewis Hawkins and Owen Gray have a laugh with Señor Cornejo.

Felicitaciones a
EL AUTOMOVIL MEXICANO

Autographs of famous Personalities at Reception held in Hotel del Prado in Mexico City.

HOW THE PRIZE MONEY WAS DISTRIBUTED
(All sums in pesos -- owners' names given)

Car 52 -- Roy Sundstrom,
Portland, Ore., U.S.A.

1st place in race 150,000
3rd in 9th leg 500

Total 150,500

*

Car 113 -- Thomas A. Deal,
El Paso, Tex., U.S.A.

2nd place in race..... 100,000
3rd in 3rd leg.......... 500
1st in 5th leg.......... 3,000
3rd in 8th leg.......... 500

Total 104,000

*

Car 21 -- Eugene Barry,
Colorado Springs, Colo., U.S.A.

3rd place in race   50,000

*

Car 38 -- Bob Estes,
Inglewood, Calif., U.S.A.

3rd place in 1st leg 500
2nd place in 2nd leg 1,000
2nd place in 3rd leg 1,000
3rd place in 4th leg 500
2nd place in 5th leg 2,000
1st place in 8th leg 2,000

Total............. 7,000

*

Car 68 -- Charles Ray Royal,
El Paso, Tex., U.S.A.

1st place in 1st leg 2,000
3rd place in 2nd leg 500
1st place in 3rd leg 2,000
2nd place in 4th leg 1,000

Total............ 5,500

*

Car 103 -- Automobile Club of
Italy, Milan, Italy

1st place in 7th leg 2,000
2nd place in 9th leg 1,000

Total 3,000

*

Car 55 -- Calvin C. Connell,
Detroit, Mich., U.S.A.

1st place in 2nd leg 2,000

*

Car 81 -- Lonnie H. Johnson,
Shallowater, Tex., U.S.A.

1st place in 4th leg 2,000

*

Car 44 -- Techo Eterno Eureka,
S.A., Mexico, D.F., Mexico

1st place in 6th leg 2,000

*

Car 8 -- Industrias 1-2-3, S.A.,
Mexico, D.F., Mexico

2nd place in 6th leg 1,000
2nd place in 7th leg 1,000

Total............... 2,000

*

Car 90 -- Automobile Club of
Italy, Milan, Italy

1st place in 9th leg 2,000

*

Car 118 -- Tony Parravano,
Manhattan Beach, Calif. U.S.A.

3rd place in 5th leg 1,000

3rd place in 6th leg 500

Total 1,500

*

Car 6 -- Frank Carroll,
Los Angeles, Calif., U.S.A.

2nd place in 8th leg 1,000

*

Car 36 -- John and Andrew Moran,
Chicago, Ill., U.S.A.

2nd place in 1st leg 1,000

*

Car 32 -- State of Morelas,
Cuernavaca, Morelos, Mexico

3rd place in 7th leg 500

DISTRIBUTION BY COUNTRIES

	Main Prizes	Leg Prizes
U.S. Cars....	300,000 (3)	24,500 (20)
Italian Cars...	...	5,000 (3)
Mexican Cars..	...	4,500 (4)
Totals	300,000 (3)	34,000 (27)

Rodolfo Castaneda, driver of Cadillac No. 9, official car of Mexico, is given trophy won by Bill Sterling, No. 68, for speed record established by Sterling first day of the race. Sterling asked the trophy to be given Castaneda and that another to be presented family of Enrique Hachmeister, who was fatally injured the first day.

The Ladies of the Race

Andrea Gonzalez and Lucille Avecedo always managed to finish last, but not least.

Five of the six women competitors: Left to right: Jean Mott de Riu, Andrea Gonzalez, Lucille Avecedo, Mrs. Marie Boone, and Marie H. Brookreson.

Left: Crash helmets were customary for the race. The shock-resisting chapeau is obligingly modeled by one of the female contestants. Nearly all the drivers used crash helmets, and some had their cars equipped with safety belts.

CHAPTER VII
Panamericana...a la Femme

AMONG the women who entered the Mexican-Pan-American Race was one movie actress, but several of the others were pretty enough to rate appearance on the screen. On the other hand, at least a couple were in the grandmother class.

Probably this was the only major race ever held in which one of the contestants was sponsored by a brassiere manufacturer. But that's the kind of contest it was.

No less than nine of the 132 cars entered had women in their crews. All showed up at the start, and five crossed the finish line at El Ocotal, a much better record than the all-male crews, of which only 53 out of 123 went the whole distance. The percentage, if you're interested, is 55 against 43.

The movie actress is a lovely athletic blonde named Jacqueline Evans, who came to Mexico a few years ago on a vacation, met and married a bullfighter, Fernando Lopez, and of course stayed. In Mexico she has acted in movies and sung in nightclubs.

She was interested in the race from the time she first heard of it, but someone told her women were barred, and she gave up the idea of entering. Then she went to the Secretariat of Communications on some other business, and happened to ask why women weren't allowed. She was told that this was wrong, that two women already had entered from the U. S.

It was only a couple of days before the entry deadline, but Jacqueline hastily got 3,500 pesos backing from a cosmetics firm. With this money and 320 pesos from friends (including 20 from a poor woman who insisted on helping) entered her 1947 Chrysler in the race.

All this was a surprise to Fernando, who found himself waiting anxiously by the fireside while his intrepid wife dashed down the highway with Arturo Medina, a friend who is an expert with cars, as co-pilot. Jackie did the driving though, and dropped off her assistant early, making nearly all the race alone. Her biggest adventure was when her plane was grounded on the way to Ciudad Juarez—Medina took the car north—and she barely got there in time for the start.

Near the end in each leg's classification, Jacqueline stayed within the maximum time throughout, and finished in 45th place. Her Car 17 was cheered by crowds the whole distance.

Another British girl, equally as pretty as Jacqueline, was in the car that finished 33rd. She is Jean Mott, married to Juan Riu, a native of Catalonia, Spain, who now owns a garage in Bogota, Colombia. She went along as co-pilot in his 1950 Mercury, Car 104, and they kept up a steady position throughout, well up among the second half of the cars in the race.

The only all-woman team was made up of two San Francisco girls of Spanish descent, Andrea Gonzalez and Lucille Acevedo. In Car 80, Andrea's 1940 Buick, they stayed near the end of the general classification until the final leg, when they managed to get in under the wire in 47th place. This was, among those who finished within the official limit, last, and for that they carried off a 2,000-peso prize offered in a spirit of sportsmanship by the ANA (the National Automobile Association of Mexico) for the final car in the race.

Andrea and Lucille shared with Miss Evans a recuperative ability which amazed their male rivals. The British-Mexican girl, for instance, arrived at Tuxtla Gutierrez dusty from the run from Oaxaca, but emerged for a party in the evening fresh and sparklingly clean in a white evening gown.

One of the grandmothers stuck in the race until the final leg, when her 1948 Buick was unable to complete the run to El Ocotal. She was Mrs. H. R. Lammons, of Jacksonville, Texas. Her driver was a young fellow named Merryl Bedford, but she was equal to him in enthusiasm.

Mrs. Lammons' photos submitted along with her application blank showed her in a dress-up afternoon gown and wearing a string of pearls. No posing in dungarees and goggles for her. And her sponsor was a brassiere manufacturer in Jacksonville. To prove it, a pair of brassieres was tastefully painted on each side of the Buick.

In Car 10, Mrs. Lammons and Bedford stayed just ahead of the Gonzalez-Acevedo entry as far as Tuxtla Gutierrez.

Two autos with woman assistants which reached the finish line, but later than the time limit, were Cars 107 and 130. No. 107 was a 1950 Buick entered and driven by William Gillespie of Idyllwild, Calif., with his wife, Mrs. L. H. Gillespie, as co-pilot. They were within five to ten places of final position throughout the race.

No. 130 was the entry of Arthur Daniel Boone, of New York City, the only car in the race from the metropolis. With him was his wife, Marie. A chipper couple well into middle age, they made dozens of friends among the other teams, and everyone was sorry when their 1950 Buick broke down at Queretaro on the fifth leg, and had to be towed into Mexico City.

The Boones weren't daunted, however, though they had lost the respectable 54th place they had gained among the 93 cars still in the running at the end of the fourth leg. They wanted to go on to the end, so they continued to El Ocotal, having their route book signed at the finish line of each leg, but not bothering to have their times recorded.

Two other woman co-pilots were Mrs. Lyle McKinley Warren, of Inglewood, Calif., whose husband entered and drove Car 48, a 1950 Buick, and Margie Allen of San Antonio, Texas, who aided Byster Anthony Hemesby, also of San Antonio, in a 1949 Mercury, Car 11, entered by Earl Allen.

The Warren car's brakes went bad on the seventh leg, between Puebla and Oaxaca, and they were unable to start the eighth leg. They were in 38th place at the time, about halfway up the list. The Allen car never reached Mexico City. After getting to Durango at the end of the second day in 50th place, it failed to start in the fourth leg on the third day.

The romance of the race centered around Car 40, a 1949 Lincoln entered by Marie R. Brookreson of Willcox, Ariz., in which she rode as assistant to Ross Barton, of Long Beach, Calif.

As they told it, Barton, 72, a veteran of the Spanish-American War, with the Silver Star and Purple Heart decorations, is an amateur pilot. A couple of months before the race he was forced to set down his light plane on Miss Brookreson's ranch in Arizona. In the two days he stayed there, he fell in love with Miss Brookreson, whose hair is white, though she isn't telling her age.

Miss Brookreson said, "There's going to be a big highway race in Mexico in May. If you'll drive my car in it, I'll marry you after the race." Naturally, Barton agreed.

Although a war injury left him with a bad right arm, Barton kept the Lincoln in the running as far as Mexico City. But a breakdown 20 miles out of Mexico City on the sixth leg to Puebla, forced the couple out of the race.

Unhappy at being unable to reach El Ocotal, the couple returned to Mexico City to get married. The Mexican press christened them "Los Abuelitos," or "The Little Grandparents," and followed their romance sympathetically.

As a footnote, market research experts may be interested in which cars women select for an auto race. The score, in Mexico at least, is as follows: Five Buicks (1940, 1948 and three 1950s); two Mercurys (1949 and 1950); a 1949 Lincoln, and a 1947 Chrysler.

Jacqueline Evans de Lopez, driver of No. 17, waits in her car before the drivers leave Oaxaca on the next to the last leg.

"Grandma" Lammons heads for starting line in Oaxaca after overnight rest.

Oldest pair in the race—Marie H. Brookreson and Ross Barton.

Jean Riu, wife and assistant driver of Juan Riu, of Colombia's car No. 104, talks with newsmen at Cornejo garage in Mexico City.

A short pause for the wives of some of the drivers, who were following the race.

CHAPTER VIII
Prospects for the Future

WILL MEXICO stage another major road race in 1951? It is quite possible that it will. At least the machinery has been set up.

At a meeting in the home of Gen. Ignacio Beteta, president of the ANA, a new Mexican Automobile Sport Commission (**Comision Deportiva Automovilistica Mexicana**) was set up on June 15, 1950, to take over the supervision of all auto races held in Mexico under International Automobile Federation (F.I.A.) regulations. The ANA, until then the holder of F.I.A. representation in Mexico, voluntarily relinquished its rights to the new organization.

With Gen. Beteta as prime mover, the new commission named Enrique Martin Moreno of the ANA and Ricardo Estrada Berg of the AMA and Mexican Tourist Association to draft a code.

Included are representatives of the ANA, AMA, National Association of Auto Distributors, Mexican Highway Association, Mexican Tourist Association, Pemex, six auto assemblers and five tire manufacturers.

If there is another race—and many persons in Mexico want to make it an annual affair—it will probably be different from the first one.

For one thing, there is talk of dividing the field into as many as three categories: Standard cars, sports cars and special racing cars.

Then there is a variety of possible routes. Some have suggested repeating the 1950 race from south to north, so that it would end in a more-developed part of the country. There is a new highway under construction from Nogales, on the Arizona border, to Guadalajara, where it will connect with cross-country highways that lead to Mexico City. This might be completed in 1951, but 1952 is a safer guess.

Some have spoken of an east-west race across Mexico. This could now be held from Tampico or Veracruz, on the Gulf of Mexico, to Acapulco, on the Pacific. By 1951 it also will be possible to start from Coatzacoalcos on the Gulf and end at Manzanillo or Mazatlan on the Pacific. All these routes could pass through Mexico City, and any sort of combination could be worked out. Too, all include plenty of mountains for those who like them.

Of course there are questions of financing and organization which haven't begun to be considered at this writing. But there's at least a 50-50 chance that those U. S. drivers who said, "Be seeing you next year," will have another race to run.

Aftermath

Mr. and Mrs. Arthur Boone of New York prepare to leave Mexico City for home. They took the race in a more or less leisurely way and made an adventurous vacation out of it.

Bill Sterling, back home in El Paso, gets a congratulatory handshake from C. R. Royal, car owner.

Bill France, Red Byron and Ray Parks try to figure out what to do with damaged Lincoln after the race. Many had to sell badly damaged cars in Mexico.

CHAPTER IX
The Race in Retrospect

PRESIDENT MIGUEL ALEMAN, as the busiest man in Mexico, could have rested content with his designation as honorary president of the Organizing Committee for the Mexican Pan-American Race, but instead he took an active interest in the preparations, and eagerly followed the progress of the race itself by radio.

Two entries in the race were due directly to action by President Aleman. One was the famous "Coche Mexico," which represented the Presidencia, a term difficult to translate, referring to the presidential offices and staff. This was a 1950 Cadillac, supplied by auto dealer Thomas A. Deal, of El Paso, who incidentally drove his own Car 113 to second place in the race, and also backed Car 68, the early leader. "Coche Mexico," which bore number 9, was driven by Lieut. Rodolfo Castañeda, of the presidential staff, with Florencio Estrada as assistant.

Car 9 had two accidents on the first leg, rolling over completely each time, but Castañeda refused to abandon the race, arriving at Chihuahua in 3 hours, 8 minutes, 28 seconds, in 91st place for the leg. At Chihuahua it was discovered that Estrada had a broken shoulder. Castañeda had numerous cuts and bruises, and the body of the car was crumpled, the windshield smashed.

The car was inspected and the engine was discovered to be in running condition. Estrada was taken to the hospital, but Guillermo Palmieri, of the staff of the Guatemalan Embassy in Mexico, a member of the race's public relations committee, volunteered to accompany Castañeda. The lone Guatemalan entry, Car 112, had cracked up 19 miles after the start, fatally injuring its driver, Enrique Hachmeister, and sending his assistant, Francisco Toscana Valle, to a hospital. Palmieri made his offer so that Guatemala might still be represented.

Race officials conferred. A change of crews was forbidden by Article 19 of the rules. So a special ruling was made—Car 9 could continue with Palmieri as co-pilot, and would be classified in each leg, but would be considered legally disqualified as far as prizes were concerned. This was satisfactory to everyone, and Castañeda and Palmieri were cheered as heroes as they took Car 9 across Mexico to the finish line, ending in 25th place and capturing ninth position in the last leg. The pair drove with goggles and helmets because of the lack of a windshield.

The other car in which President Aleman took a direct interest was a 1950 Studebaker which he bought for the students of the Universidad Nacional Autonoma de Mexico, the national university from which the President was graduated with a law degree in 1928. President Aleman naturally has maintained an interest in the university, and when a group of students called on him on April 3 at his official residence, Los Pinos, to ask his help so that they could take part in the race, he agreed to buy them a new Studebaker.

With the car went some advice. The President said:

"I wish you much success, and recommend that you take good care in all the aspects of the race. Don't have so much eagerness to win that you don't reach the finish line. Use the necessary technique, but with perspicacity. Study carefully all the maps and routes so that you'll know in what places there is danger. Remember that you don't win with boldness alone, unless you also use your heads."

These words were quoted widely, and mentioned more than once by other Mexican drivers besides the students.

The Studebaker was driven in the race under the number 94 by law students Fernando Gallardo Amaro and Enrique Torres Caballero and reached Tuxtla Gutierrez in 54th place, more than six hours behind the leader. Since they had no chance at a prize, the pair there turned their car over to race officials to make a test run over the last leg, to check on the condition of the unpaved final portion.

Another team of students, from the Pentathlon Universitario, an advanced military school in Mexico City, also competed in the race. In Car 119, a 1949 Ford, Emilio Portes Medina and Armando Rodriguez Morado finished the third leg in 99th place in the race, but were unable to continue.

-----o-----

Spanish-language personal names often cause confusion for English-speaking people. This arises out of the custom, followed by most Mexicans, of attaching the mother's name after the father's name. Thus the Secretary of Communications and Public Works, the president of the Central Executive Committee for the Mexican Pan-American Race, is the son of a Mr. Garcia and a former Miss Lopez, who gave him the name of Agustin. He writes his full name "Agustin Garcia Lopez," and would be called "Secretary Garcia" for short. A person is free to write his name as he pleases, of course, and ex-President Manual Avila Camacho often was spoken of as "President Camacho," using the mother's name. Thus there is no unbreakable rule for names, but this explanation may help the reader understand some of the usages followed in this book.

-----o-----

A "flying saucer," a huge structure of tin-covered wood, made its appearance early in April in one of the main downtown squares of Mexico City as an advertisement for the race. A miniature car was driven about its elevated platform by a man in a fanciful costume that was supposed to be Martian. This was during a time when "flying saucers" were being reported seen all over Mexico, and the imaginative structure drew a lot of attention. Press officials of the Secretariat of Communications, whose idea it was to erect the "saucer," said that it would be used as an information booth during the race, but somehow this never happened.

-----o-----

The most exalted "messenger boy" who called at race headquarters was the charge d'affaires of the Ecuador Embassy. Alberto Cucalon, an airplane pilot from Guayaquil, wanted information about the race, but lacked the committee's address, so he wrote in care of his embassy. The head of the embassy delivered the letter in person. That was the last that was heard of Cucalon; however, a rules book was sent him, but he never wrote again.

-----o-----

Valuable help in promoting the race was given by Capt. Eddie Rickenbacker, president of Eastern Air Lines, who was one of the great U. S. racing drivers in the years before World War I. Rickenbacker donated an impressive trophy, and also wrote letters about the race to a number of his old friends in the fraternity, including Wilbur Shaw, who took over direction of the Indianapolis Speedway after World War II.

-----o-----

An amusing mixup occurred in connection with the trophy donated for the race by Gov. Earl Warren, of California. He delivered it to Adolfo Dominguez and Salvador Duhart, two of Mexico's consuls-general in California, at a ceremony, April 25 in Sacramento.

Everyone was mystified to note that the plaque on the trophy finished with the words "Una Compra," followed by a blank space. This means "one buy" in Spanish. A phone call to the San Francisco jewelers who made the trophy resulted in an explanation. Warren had ordered the inscription to read "Won By," which, when translated to Spanish, comes out "Ganada Por." The oral instructions caused the confusion.

When the trophy reached Mexico City the inscription had been corrected.

----o----

The race entry fee included public liability insurance for all cars, covering injuries and damage to persons or property not connected with the race. Arrangements also were made for insurance on the racers and their cars, but this was optional and at the entrant's expense. Ironically, the only driver killed, Enrique Hachmeister, was among those who did not buy added insurance, so his widow received nothing more than the wreck of his 1949 Lincoln.

----o----

A special plane was chartered to carry race officials, diplomats and the press along the route during the race. It took off from the starting point for each day's run after the cars had begun running, and landed at the afternoon's finish point before the first car arrived. In charge of the plane was Guillermo Ostos, right-hand man of Secretary Garcia Lopez. Control Chief Martin Moreno and General Manager Cornejo preceded the racers each day by auto so they could be present at the intermediate finish lines when there were two legs in one day. Communications problems became really tough on the final leg of the race, however. It proved to be impossible to send news out of El Ocotal, except a few brief radioed bulletins, and only a light plane could land there with some of the reporters, while the rest had to make the dash by auto.

----o----

Hershel McGriff, winner of first prize, had never been over the race route before. On his return trip north he got a look at the precipices which border much of the road, and suddenly was "scared to death." Going south at full speed, he hadn't lifted his eyes from the asphalt. Coming back, he got his first good view of the dangers he'd skirted at more than a mile a minute.

----o----

After blowing three tires in the first leg, Mexico's Jose Estrada Menocal, in Car 8, went on to establish what he wryly claimed was a record. He used up 13 more tires on his 1949 Packard before being forced out on the eighth leg, for a total of four complete sets.

----o----

The first race-connected death came on May 3, north of the city of Durango, when Jesus Valezzi, driver of Car 77, was hurrying north to Ciudad Juarez. Major Aurelio Altamirano Campa was strolling beside the road with his four-year-old son, when the child suddenly darted in front of Valezzi's car and was killed. Authorities exonerated Valezzi, who continued on his way and took part in the race.

----o----

With freedom to use any type of tires and tubes they preferred, most of the drivers strung along with more or less standard equipment. They figured that heavier tires and puncture-proof tubes would heat up too much at racing speeds on an asphalt highway. Some used carbon dioxide to inflate their tires, on the theory that it would heat up slower.

----o----

The European entrants in the race were also goodwill ambassadors, with an eye to the Mexican auto market. Jean Trevoux and Andre Mariotti, the Frenchmen, made numerous friends in Mexico City, although they avoided night life until after the race. Mariotti stayed in Mexico City some weeks following the competition, and there was talk of beginning the importation of Delahayes, the make he and Trevoux drove in the race, a luxury automobile costing $10,000. Piero Taruffi and Felice Bonetto, drivers of the two Italian Alfa Romeos, a more popular-priced and lighter car than the French entry, also were feted much in Mexico City, and it was reported that Alfa Romeos soon would be sold in Mexico.

----o----

At the starting line, Lucille Acevedo, San Francisco social worker who was co-pilot of Car 80, told reporters that she and Andrea Gonzalez, owner-driver, were going to drive slowly "because we're in a hurry to reach El Ocotal." The girls said that they knew they had no chance to win, but wanted to see the highway, and show the men that this was a woman's world, too. Their Buick sported a pair of painted butterflies for the feminine touch. The girls kept their word—they chugged along near the end of the classification, but completed each leg within the maximum time and finished in last place.

----o----

Dr. Mario del Rio, publicity-conscious Mexico City plastic surgeon, not only donated a trophy for the winner of the Mexico City-Puebla leg, but offered to treat without charge any injured competitor.

----o----

Control Chief Enrique Martin Moreno, entering Durango in his station wagon ahead of the first competing cars, was promptly arrested by an over-zealous policeman who knew that the highway had to be kept clear. He was released as promptly by the cop's superiors.

----o----

The enormous crowd which greeted the racers in Mexico City on Sunday, May 7, was soon beyond control at most important points, in spite of the assignment of 1,500 policemen, 25 radio cars, 65 motorcycle officers, a fire brigade and numerous soldiers to duty along the route.

One race driver remarked:

"The toughest leg of all was between the city limits and Automotriz Cornejo."

Five hundred first-aid workers were on duty, and 90 persons were treated for sunstroke and minor injuries.

At least 20 times spectators dashed across the road in front of drivers at the finish line, but all managed to avoid crackups.

----o----

Bill Sterling and his Mexican co-pilot, husky Daniel Arias, Jr., won applause when they were presented with trophies at a banquet in Durango after the third leg of the race, when they were still in the lead. And then they won Mexico's affection by immediately presenting the trophies to Lieut. Rodolfo Castañeda, driver of the smashed-up Mexican presidential car, and the widow of Enrique Hachmeister, the Guatemalan who was killed in the first leg.

Hachmeister, 30 years old, was married to a Mexico City girl, and they were living in Mexico City at the time of the race. A son was born to them only 15 days before the fatal crash, and they also had a boy, 4.

----o----

The Mexican press reported two "mystery cars" on the Leon-Mexico City leg: One was a Leon shoe merchant who, according to the dispatches, filled his car with gasoline and himself with something out of a bottle, and set off after the racers in his own car. He was said to have cracked up at Silao, being killed instantly.

The other mystery was a black 1950 Mercury with a "press" sticker that followed the racers from Leon to Mexico City, creating "an unpleasant impression" according to Mexican reporters. The truth can now be told—it was two U. S. correspondents who had been taking pictures of the race, and decided to follow the contestants in order to get back to Mexico City promptly.

---o---

Considering their lack of experience in covering auto races, plus the handicap of having to work from the finish lines without the ability to check immediately on what had happened up along the highway, Mexican radio announcers did a good job of telling the public what was going on.

They did tend to pass along rumors, however, and as a result "killed" a number of drivers who later turned up in reasonably good shape. One of these was Tommy Francis, of Los Angeles, whose Car 6 had an accident on the last leg which sent Tommy to a hospital with some broken ribs.

The worst day for false reports, however, was Sunday, May 7. Cars 7 and 88 had cracked up at a bridge between Durango and Leon, but their drivers and crews were only shaken up and scratched. Somehow, perhaps in reports from planes hovering over the highway, perhaps in stories from other drivers in the race, the numbers were confused in the first news reaching Mexico City. Both Car 78—the Venezuelan car driven by Atilio Cagnasso—and Car 97—the Venezuelan entry piloted by Ali Rachid—were said to have had accidents, and the rumors said that in each case the crews had been killed. The press office of the Secretariat of Communications later added to the mixup by announcing "officially" that it was Car 97 that had had the accident, and repeating that Rachid was dead.

It turned out that Cagnasso hadn't even started that day, since he had reached Durango with his car in such bad condition that he couldn't continue. Rachid not only reached Mexico City without any mishap, but went on later all the way to El Ocotal. It was necessary to cable denials to Venezuela, because the rumors had traveled there quickly.

Cagnasso, a native of Italy, was said to have had a fatal accident in his first race in Venezuela in 1949. His wife was riding with him as his assistant, and lost her life, the Mexican press said.

---o---

The Mexican Pan-American Race wasn't the only highway speed contest in Mexico City on Sunday, May 7. A mountain climb for bicycles from Mexico City to Tres Cumbres, on the road to Acapulco, took place the same day. There were 109 entrants, no accidents, and few spectators.

---o---

Car 9, the Mexican sentimental favorite which represented the presidential offices, had another accident between Leon and Mexico City, but without doing further damage to its battered body. Lieut. Rodolfo Castañeda, the driver, reported that the Cadillac smacked into an adobe house near Ixtlahuaca, north of Toluca, ruining the dwelling. Then a tire blew out. He had used his last spare, but was rescued by a man living along the road who astonished Castañeda by producing a tire that fitted the Cadillac.

As everywhere, Castañeda was greeted as a hero when he reached Mexico City. At headquarters the public enthusiasm rose to its highest point. The Mexican driver, his forehead and left hand bandaged, was lifted onto the shoulders of the spectators, as was Guillermo Palmieri, his Guatemalan co-pilot. The crowd sang the national anthem.

Car 9 was showered with flowers and confetti as it drove into the capital.

---o---

Asked near the beginning of the race why they were lagging, the Italian teams replied laconically, "We'll be seeing you in El Ocotal." At Mexico City some of the European and Mexican drivers said, "For us the race begins tomorrow." A study of the statistics reveals that this was true for the Europeans at least.

---o---

The surprising fact is that if a new race had been started from Mexico City among the cars which continued beyond that point, there wouldn't have been a Mexican driver among the first 10. Piero Taruffi, in his 1950 Alfa Romeo, would have won by more than 10 minutes, and Hershel McGriff would have been second, with Taruffi's teammate Felice Bonetto in third place, Jean Trevoux's 1950 Delahaye in fourth, and Tom Deal in fifth. McGriff had an Oldsmobile, Deal a Cadillac.

Nine of the second 10 would have been Mexicans, and Johnny Mantz, who had all kinds of trouble on the 7th and 9th legs, would have been 27th. Here is the chart:

Position	Car No.	Mexico City - Ocotal Time	Country
1	90	12:39:50	Italy
2	52	12:50:15	U. S.
3	103	12:55:35	Italy
4	19	13:07:38	France
5	113	13:09:45	U. S.
6	21	13:09:55	U. S.
7	12	13:11:52	U. S.
8	79	13:14:30	U. S.
9	91	13:15:52	Colombia
10	118	13:15:55	U. S.
11	9	13:17:00	Mexico
12	34	13:18:25	Mexico
13	77	13:18:49	Mexico
14	39	13:19:49	Mexico
15	46	13:22:16	Mexico
16	71	13:22:56	U. S.
17	82	13:35:21	Mexico
18	42	13:40:21	Mexico
19	3	13:42:08	Mexico
20	121	13:43:07	Mexico

And so on. Venezuelan Cars 128, 74 and 97 rated 21st, 22nd and 26th, respectively, on this stretch, and Mantz had a time of 14:16:06.

Several surprising things are noticeable. Colombia's Artesio Paz, who got virtually no attention at any time, made a splendid run from Mexico City to the end. But, because he left the capital in 44th place, he was able to advance only to 16th in his 1950 Oldsmobile.

The five best U. S. drivers did the latter part of the run in the same relation to each other as they did in the race as a whole. Jack McAfee, in Car 118, would have finished in 10th place in any case.

Among the Mexicans, the smashed-up Car 9 was the best in the mountainous south, and it turned out that the Mexican cars who did best in the race as a whole—Cars 46, 39, 42 and 82—would have wound up further back if time had been counted only for the kind of roads they were supposed to prefer.

Jacqueline Evans, who started out from Ciudad Juarez with a male co-pilot in Car 17, reached Mexico City alone and finished the race unaided. Just wanted to show that she didn't need any help.

———o———

The "heart" of El Ocotal consists of four thatch-roofed houses, with the rest of the 250 to 300 inhabitants living in buildings scattered over the surrounding hills. The race committee met this problem by erecting Quonset huts with running water and enough cots to accommodate racers, officials and newsmen. There also was a dining pavilion where soft drinks and beer were sold as well as food. One thing that proved impractical was to set up a gasoline depot there. All cars had to take on enough gasoline for a round trip when they left Tuxtla Gutierrez for the final leg of the race.

———o———

Tom Deal learned to drive on Mexican roads as the result of numerous business and pleasure trips south from the border city of El Paso. His co-pilot, Sam Cresap, was equally familiar with Mexico's highways, with emphasis on the sierras. So Deal drove Car 113 on the level stretches, and Cresap took over in the mountains. Deal, in introducing the team, would say: "Sam's Mr. Curve and I'm Mr. Straightaway."

———o———

Wanna thumb a ride? Bill France's and Curtis Turner's car was damaged in an accident. The tree is an organ cactus.

CHAPTER X
To the Victor belongs the Spoils...$17,391.00

By HERSHEL McGRIFF
Winner of the Pan-American Road Race

Mr. Clymer asked me to tell some of my experiences in winning the Mexican Pan American road race—the troubles I encountered, the close shaves I had, and that sort of thing—but the truth is I didn't have any troubles and my experiences were not what you would call melodramatic. No doubt that's why I won. My 1950 Oldsmobile ran like a clock all the way. Except for the last 1,000 yards of the race (I'll get to that later) it was just a case of cruising along.

Even before the race started I never had any doubts that I was going to win. Sometimes during the race I didn't quite know how it was going to be accomplished, but, sure enough, everything came out all right. To begin with, I didn't enter the long haul as what you would call a novice driver. For five years—ever since I was seventeen—I had competed in more stock car races than I can remember, most of them around my home in Portland, Oregon. In 1949 I won the northwest drivers' championship in the Pacific Stock Car Racing Association. At Oakland, Calif., I set the world's record for a five-eighths track with a time of :25.17, or slightly better than 89 miles per hour.

Although I have never driven big cars or midgets, I guess I know as much about getting the stock cars over a prescribed course as the next fellow, so when Roy Sundstrom, my sponsor, came back from the factory with a new Oldsmobile which I was to drive in stock events, I hastened to persuade him to enter the Mexican marathon. It looked like a good deal to me all along.

We arrived in El Paso four days before the start of the race. The only part of the Pan American highway I saw before the race was the first five miles out of Juarez, which we drove one day just to see if there was really a road down there.

Now, in a long race such as this, with nine separate legs, it isn't necessary to break your neck trying to finish first every day, or even at all. Consider the position of the winning car on each of the legs. I finished like this: Seventh, eighth, eighth, eighth, fourteenth, ninth, fifth, ninth and fourth. So I was consistently among the leaders, assuring myself of an early start each morning, but not particularly pointing for the small daily lap prizes.

My co-driver, Ray Elliott, a Portland, Ore., policeman, and I had one serious difficulty, perhaps more psychological than anything else. Neither he nor I liked Mexican food and we were afraid to eat anything out of the ground or drink any water that wasn't bottled. In the mornings we always were among the early starters and didn't have time to find the right restaurant. They gave us a couple of sandwiches each day before the start but we couldn't eat them except at Oaxaca, where we ran into some fresh chicken.

The result was that we went four days without anything to eat! Lewis Hawkins, driver of Car 79, gave me a can of tomato juice one morning, but outside of that there was nothing. My digestion was so disorganized that even at the inevitable evening banquets I couldn't eat a thing except a small piece of cooked meat. When we finished at El Ocotal, Elliott rashly ate some pork and had to pay a hurried visit to the hospital. He was all right next morning, though.

In the six days of the race I lost fifteen pounds and Elliott dropped twenty-eight. But when we got back to Mexico City we were able to resume our normal diet and suffered no ill effects.

Our accommodations at night were always the best in town, because we were always among the first finishers and had our choice of places to stay, and we were glad to get that rest. Driving three or four hundred miles a day, most of them with the speedometer stuck on the last peg, 110 miles per hour, over strange, winding roads is not the most relaxing thing in the world, believe me. We wore Clymer crash helmets and if we hadn't had safety belts we would have gone through the roof of the car a dozen times.

We didn't do anything to the car all through the race except at one stop where we changed oil and cleaned the plugs. We had three flat tires and changed three sets in all. On the extremely rough last leg of the course going into El Ocotal I used Mexican tires, General Popos, and they performed nicely. A tire dealer gave them to me in Tuxtla, remarking that if I won the race I wouldn't have to pay for them.

We had a close call near Mexico City. A horse was standing on the highway—they love to do that down there—and a soldier patrolling the course threw a rock at it as we approached, attempting to frighten him away. Instead of running off, the horse fell down smack in the middle of the road. I slowed down to 90 and just brushed the beast as I went by. That was the only thing even approaching an accident that we experienced. I drove all legs except one. Elliott took the wheel between Parral and Durango.

All the competing drivers displayed fine courtesy of the road and gave me plenty of room when I wanted to pass. At the sharp U turn where Lou Figaro cracked up, I thought for a minute I had lost it. I couldn't see the turn and we came close to going over the bank after taking the turn broadside all the way around.

The morning we left Tuxtla on the last leg, it seemed pretty sure that either Tom Deal or I would win the race. He was leading me by 8 minutes, 42 seconds, but I figured I could make that up over the rough, rocky road to El Ocotal. After all, I had had much experience with difficult highways, driving trucks over mountainous country in Oregon.

When we crossed the finish line at El Ocotal and drove to the impound area, Deal was there and immediately congratulated me as the winner. I didn't know whether I had won or not, but as Elliott and I walked back to the finish line, the crowd came running and cheering. That was when we knew we were in.

It was only when the officials tore the car apart in the impound that we found out how close we came to making it. About a thousand yards from the finish I had hit a nasty bunch of rocks and the car bounced in the air and bounced hard when it came down. Now, we discovered, we had no oil or gas! There was a big hole in the oil pan and the gas tank was damaged so badly we couldn't have lasted another mile. So that's how close I came to NOT winning the Carrera Panamericana.

El C. Presidente de los Estados Unidos Mexicanos

LIC. MIGUEL ALEMAN

y el C. Secretario de Comunicaciones y Obras Públicas

LIC. AGUSTIN GARCIA LOPEZ

confieren el presente

DIPLOMA DE HONOR

a *Hershel McGriff*

por su relevante participación en la CARRERA PANAMERICANA "MEXICO", celebrada con motivo de la inauguración de la carretera Ciudad Juárez - Ciudad Cuauhtémoc, de 3,440 kilómetros de frontera a frontera, como *Piloto* cuyo mérito aquí se acredita.

México, D. F., 17 de mayo de 1950

Lic. Miguel Alemán

El Secretario de Comunicaciones y Obras Públicas
Lic. Agustín García López

THIS IS A REPRODUCTION OF THE DIPLOMA DE HONOR SIGNED BY PRESIDENT ALEMAN OF MEXICO AWARDED TO HERSHEL McGRIFF AS FIRST PLACE WINNER IN THE 1950 CARRERA PANAMERICANA (MEXICO ROAD RACE) OF 2,135 MILES FROM THE U.S. BORDER ACROSS MEXICO TO GUATEMALAN BORDER.

The next morning we welded the gas tank and fixed it so we could use our reserve supply. But on that stretch to El Ocotal we must have hit the bottom fifty times. I didn't realize the bottom of the car was so low, or I never could have driven over that rough gravel road at 100 miles per hour. On the last stretch I was thankful that the Oldsmobile had a standard gear shift. I drove a lot in second gear using compression to help in braking.

During the race we carried four spare tires, seven gallons of water, a small set of tools, our extra clothes and a 35 gallon reserve gas tank. The next time all I'm going to take is food!

On the way back to Mexico City we were given hysterical welcomes at every town. The Mexicans really went for this race and it's a pity that their great hero, Lt. Rodolfo Castañeda G., who drove "the president's car," didn't win. They really would have gone crazy. As it was, at the award banquet in Mexico City I got one trophy and he took away six! But then, of course, I got $17,391.

Returning through San Cristobal, the welcoming crowd practically carried me out of the car and into the hotel for a big banquet. It was that way every place, and of course I had to make several speeches through an interpreter. So many pictures had been published in the Mexico City newspapers that I couldn't walk the streets without the fear of being mobbed. That's the reason I flew back home from Mexico City. I don't know what they would have done to me in Juarez.

In the Mexican capital my gifts included a watch from a Mexico City dealer to whom I had loaned a couple of tires and wheels so he could return from El Ocotal. He gave Elliott a watch, too. From the Mexico City Oldsmobile dealer, Morris Brothers, I received a solid silver model of a 1902 Olds, valued at $1,000.

I'll always remember Mexico City because of the start we made from there on the sixth leg of the race. The crowds watching the start were so dense there really wasn't room for the cars to get through. They would see us coming at top speed and form a narrow lane for us to pass, closing up behind us immediately as we brushed through. I still don't know why several people weren't killed in that screaming mob.

Since everything turned out all right I have no complaints, but we actually were at a disadvantage through a slight misunderstanding. As we interpreted the rules each car had to carry all its supplies throughout the race, so that's what we did. However, several of the boys turned up with pick-up trucks and trailers and they were allowed to use them all the way. This made a considerable difference, especially in weight. Next year I'll have a truck for everything.

And, incidentally, I'm pretty sure they will have a race in 1951, and I'm listening to all offers to drive.

Returning to Portland I was greeted by my wife, Delores, and children; Douglas, four, and Marilyn, two. There was little time to rest, because I was slated to tour several eastern cities for Oldsmobile. Consequently I missed out on a lot of my regular racing dates, although I did manage to enter the Darlington 500-mile stock car care, in which I finished ninth.

Most of my prize money went straight into my towing business in Portland. I am associated with a firm which operates a fleet of ten tow trucks, but they're not as much fun as the Pan American road race—especially if you win!

McGriff and his famous Oldsmobile "City of Roses."

Mexico is Careful about Disease

Johnny Mantz and Bill Stroppe of No. 38 take the foot bath for hoof and mouth disease. Oaxaca, Mexico.

Members of the hoof and mouth disease commission spray cars as they leave the impound in Oaxaca for the starting line. No. 66 is driven by Bob Korf and John Renier.

CHAPTER XI
My Experience in the Race

By BUD SENNETT
Los Angeles Driver of Car No. 12, Winner of Fifth Place

I got into the Mexican Pan-American Road Race by the back door, so to speak. J. C. Balch, of Los Angeles, asked me to drive the James Motor Car Co.'s 1950 Oldsmobile which had originally been scheduled for Troy Ruttman. Ruttman, however, had a stomach ailment and besides was anxious to get to Indianapolis for the 500-mile race. It was a most enjoyable break for me, and although I didn't make any money by finishing fifth in the long race, it was a most interesting experience. Incidentally, the Mexican newspapers and magazines still think Ruttman drove No. 12; at least he's listed among the leading finishers!

When we arrived in Ciudad Juarez for the start of the race, we were just in time for a terrific dust storm. And I mean terrific! It threatened to blow us all away the night before the start, but fortunately it had spent itself by the next morning. I was fortunate to draw a low starting number, 12, and after that I was seldom out of the first ten in elapsed time on any of the nine legs.

The large entry list of 132 cars—and it cost $258 to enter a car—surprised the race authorities, who had only provided for three top prizes besides small prizes for the three leaders of each leg. Although I didn't get a peso for finishing fifth, I'm sure that will be remedied if the race is renewed. It was good training for a bulging waist line, though. During the six days of the race I lost ten pounds and Johnny Balch, who rode with me, lost eighteen. Johnny is the worrying type, you see.

The start of the race at Juarez was really something. The cars were sent away at one-minute intervals, with five minutes allowed after every twenty cars. We had to be ready to go at 6 a. m.; the authorities were very insistent. Actually no wheel turned until about 9:30. I had never seen any part of the course, but that had its advantages, as I later found. The Mexican drivers thought they would have a pronounced advantage over the Americans because of their familiarity with the highway, but actually that didn't seem to make a bit of difference.

We were cautioned to take bottled water with us, and it was a good thing we did. The natives have drunk the Mexican water all their lives and are immune to it, but it's poison for a foreigner. Several American drivers, including myself, suffered from dysentery somewhere along the road; at Oaxaca, I really had the screamers. Our car carried two gallon water bags, one for drinking and the other for the radiator if needed. In one day—it was hot!—Johnny and I drank both water bags dry, plus a couple of warm cokes.

You had to be in good condition to finish this one. After it was over Johnny Mantz told me he would rather drive three Indianapolis races than one Mexican road race, and I knew how he felt.

Before the start at Juarez all cars had to be taken to an impound area for an engine seal. This consisted of a wire wrapped all around the engine, and the seal was checked at the start of every leg. An official had to be present if it was ever necessary to break the seal at any time during the race. Our seal was still on when we got back in Los Angeles. "I guess we can take that off now," Johnny said.

The first leg from Juarez to Chihuahua was about 236 miles, mostly straight with a gradual upgrade. I passed eight cars to finish fourth. If you wanted to pass, you were supposed to toot your horn once, politely. If nothing happened, you were supposed to toot again. If you still couldn't get around, the officials said you could file a protest! We thought that was pretty funny.

We soon found out from the actions of the crowds along the way that there was really a "people's choice" in this race—and how! He was the driver of "the President's car," No. 9, a handsome Mexican army officer, Lieut. Rodolfo Castañeda. He turned out to be a national hero. He piled up his Cadillac once but was able to continue, uninjured. The newspapers said that Castañeda. was "continuing the race with a broken left arm."

I can't say enough in praise of the way the Mexican army patrolled the highway during the race. There are no fences; it's all open range and nothing but cattle. Horses, burros, steers, goats, sheep, pigs and dogs are everywhere, but the soldiers kept them clear of the road at all times. A couple of times we saw cattle a mile or so ahead, but by the time we got there they had been herded out of danger. Coming back after the race it was different! Several times we had to stop completely because of cattle and even peons sitting in the middle of the road! Everything that walks was in our way, it seemed. In the leg between Durango and Chihuahua coming back we hit a coyote at about 90 miles an hour and knocked him half a mile. On the return trip a peon on a burro started across the road directly in our path. We blew the horn as loud as we could, but he just kept coming. I swear he was fast asleep. We missed him by six inches.

We were really loaded for the race. In the back seat we had four spare wheels, a large box of tools, a small hydraulic jack, a case of oil, a spare fuel pump, a spare carburetor, spare ignition, two suitcases and an extra thirty-gallon gas tank. Altogether we were hauling 700 extra pounds.

One thing everyone found out for sure—a car with an automatic shift is at a big disadvantage in a long road race through twisting, mountainous country. But our Olds didn't have the slightest bit of trouble in the 2,100 miles. All we did was change tires and oil and check the fuel pump. All cars used the same kind of gasoline, furnished free by the race committee. We didn't need a full tank at any time, but the attendants would fill us up with forty or fifty gallons regardless. Mobiloil furnished oil to all who desired it.

Most of the race officials spoke only Mexican, but I knew enough Spanish to make my wants known, and at all stops there were usually some English-speaking people around to help out if needed.

The course was mostly mountainous, but our pace was "full bore" where we could do it. On the second leg the road was so straight for such a long stretch I had to shift my right foot off the accelerator and use my left. I didn't take my foot off the accelerator for ninety minutes. It was more than 100 miles of sheer straightaway.

Our accommodations all along the way were the best. Usually there was a banquet in the evening, thrown by whatever local dignitaries who felt some speeches coming on. The nicest place we stayed was at Durango, in the motel-like American Courts. It was really hot there, and I lost no time in jumping in the swimming pool with an ice-cold beer.

At Mexico City most of the drivers stayed at either the Rejis or the El Prado, both fine hotels. All our hotel bills were paid, but we usually bought our own meals except for the ever-recurring banquets. At the start of each leg we would receive four bottles of Coca-Cola and several sandwiches to eat on the road. We had the banquets every stop except at Oaxaca. The one at El Ocotal was excellent. But when we got down to the finish at El Ocotal, we really found out what "jumping-off place" means. There we ate barbecued burro, I'll swear to this day. The meat was prepared in huge steaming jugs buried in the ground.

El Ocotal consists of a couple of grass huts and that's about all. While I was trying to discover where the town was, someone came up and said, "There's a night club up on the hill." I thought he was joking but I went up to a thatched hut and, sure enough, there was a night club. Eight Mexicans were playing the same marimba. It was almost worth the trip to see it.

The last leg, we were warned, was partly over "gravel." The gravel turned out to be rocks, and the farther we went the bigger the rocks got. We all made it except Tommy Francis, who was brought into El Ocotal suffering from shock after his car had crashed.

The start and finish of each leg drew large crowds. Sometimes the specators would form a V and the cars could hardly get through. We got a terrific welcome at Mexico City. The finish was about five miles from the center of town, but thousands of people were there. They threw flowers in our path, yelling and screaming. Then we were escorted by the fabulous Mexico motorcycle policemen to the receiving stand to be greeted by numerous high officials.

We could always tell where the finish lines were because of the crowds waiting for us; it was either the finish or a bad curve. At Oaxaca I got sideways just at the finish on a sharp curve. It was raining hard. I thought I was out of business right there and was going to take twelve or fifteen peons with me in the process. I was going about 85 and dived the car into gravel purposely to regain partial control. However, I still crossed the finish line sideways. Other than that it was a smooth ride. I only stopped during one leg—the eighth—to change three tires. It cost me seven minutes and third money in the race. We used eight tires in the whole race and four more getting to and from Los Angeles.

We did have a little front end trouble after Oaxaca. The right front tire was half flat and we were running on the safety tube. The tube was showing; one more curve would have blown the tire. We put on the best tires we had left on the front, and they were rags, too. After that we blew the right rear and it went flat again just at the finish.

The highway had very few guard rails, and there are places on it where, if you fell off, you'd be falling yet. Small rock markers served the purpose of guard rails, and you had only to blow a tire to fall 4,000 feet. Otherwise the safety precautions were pretty efficient. There was supposed to be an ambulance station every twenty miles. Planes often patrolled the course and there were many soldiers on horseback along the way. However, one car completely disappeared in the middle of a leg and no one ever learned what happened to it.

Since the highway was closed to all other traffic, it wasn't necessary to drive on the right-hand side of the road. It was a little awkward to break ourselves of the habit at first, but we grew accustomed to using the left side or going straight down the middle.

Everyone was most helpful along the way. I want particularly to thank officials of the Mexican division of General Motors Corp., including Mr. Moore, the general manager; Ralph Clark, service manager, and Bob LaMontaign, publicity director. The Mobiloil people also deserve thanks for their courtesy. Also worthy of mention was the sportsmanship of all drivers. They gave us all the breaks in the world, and when we went around them they would wave us on with a good luck sign.

I guess about the closest call I had during the race was at a 90-degree turn which Hershel McGriff and I entered side by side. Just as we entered the sharp downhill curve we saw a Mexican car and driver in the ditch, ten feet below. And he had gone into the turn alone! Well, if McGriff had been a little less skillful and I had lost my head, he could easily have shoved me off the road end over end. However, we just barely made it. It was a close call.

If they decide to make the race an annual affair that's all right with me. It was a great experience and if there is a "Carrera Panamericana" in 1951 you can count me in now. And I wouldn't drive anything but an Oldsmobile!

Seeing Mexico at 100 M.P.H.

By JACK McAFEE
Driver of Car No. 118, Winner of Tenth Place

Most of the drivers in the 1950 Pan-American road race would like to do it all over again tomorrow, I suppose. I know I would. Although my assistant, Ford Robinson, and I had our share of troubles before the finish line, we managed to finish tenth in elapsed time. I was satisfied to do that well, after losing so much time on the road with various troubles.

Our 1950 Cadillac was entered by Tony Parravano, of Manhattan Beach, Calif. I managed to get a leave of absence from my job as refrigeration engineer for a frozen food concern in El Segundo and really snapped up the chance to drive the car.

At the start of the race in Juarez we drew 118th starting position, down near the tail end. During the leg to Chihuahua we passed about twenty cars and wound up with the thirty-second fastest time of the day, just mediocre. Along the way, since we had started so late, we saw all the wrecks that occurred that day. In fact we were held up somewhat nineteen miles out of Juarez as the fatal wreck of the Guatemalan entrant still was being cleared way. A few miles farther on, Joel Thorne was in the ditch.

We soon discovered that we would have to be careful with our fuel supply. On the first leg we had to stop and switch over from our main gas tank to a reserve. On the second night we revised the fuel system once and for all so we wouldn't have to switch fuel lines again. It quickly came to our attention that every second was going to count.

On the next leg the car "vapor locked" and we had to stop and free the fuel line. The stop cost us about five minutes, but we still managed to finish fourteenth for the day. Our troubles weren't over; on the third day, from Durango to Leon, we vapor locked twice. That settled it. We pulled out the fuel system entirely from the reserve tank. The gas line was getting so hot it was vaporizing the fuel and it was necessary to stop and pull the line free from underneath the car. We stuck the free end into the regular Cadillac gas tank so when the regular fuel supply ran low we could simply pump fuel from the reserve tank. We should have done that in the first place. Anyway, our time for that morning leg was only forty-third fastest.

We were determined to make up lost time on the leg from Leon to Mexico City, and we did so. We had the third fastest time for the leg, passing the French Delahaye and the Italian Bonetto on the way. We reached Mexico City on the same set of tires with which we had left Los Angeles. The tire men there were amazed we were able to do it. The boys up front, like Tommy Deal, were using a set of tires a day. Altogether, during the race we used eight tires, blowing four when we got into the really tough terrain.

On the fourth leg from Mexico City to Puebla we again had the third fastest time. That morning we started third behind Johnny Mantz and Deal, and passed both of them before reaching Puebla.

Next day, on the stretch from Puebla to Oaxaca, we blew two tires and ran out of gas! We used more than fifty gallons in the 339 miles from Mexico City to Oaxaca—pretty poor mileage, but the 10,000-foot altitude and driving in second gear probably explained it. We found ourselves fortunate in having a standard gear shift instead of a hydramatic when we got in the mountainous country. A lot of the boys really moaned about their automatic transmissions.

Twenty-seven miles out of Oaxaca our fuel gauge read "Empty" and we actually coasted the rest of the way with the motor off. Gravity pulled us to a service station.

Having used up all our Firestones, we put on Mexican tires at Oaxaca and promptly blew them on the last leg to El Ocotal. In addition we had lost all the fluid in our shock absorbers and drove over the rocks to the finish without any shocks whatever! You can understand why we took it easy on the last leg, having no shocks, no wheel balance and no tires to speak of. Still, we had the fourteenth fastest time for that stretch and wound up tenth in the race. By El Ocotal, I had lost twelve pounds.

I'll drive the same Cadillac again in the next race. We had no mishaps whatever and used no oil or water on the entire journey. I changed the oil and lubricated the car every night and the oil was always up to the "Full" mark. Fuel trouble was our only woe.

Ours was one of the few cars in the race which used a pick-up truck to carry supplies ahead on each leg. Later we found we didn't need it because at any good-sized town there was always a Cadillac agency available for parts or servicing. Ralph Cramer drove our truck, leaving Juarez the midnight before the start. Having no special race credentials, he had plenty of trouble getting through to Leon. Those Mexican soldiers really guarded that highway, believe me. We dispensed with the truck at Mexico City.

I believe everyone was impressed by the excellent way in which the race was handled from start to finish. Of course in a first-time venture there are bound to be some "bugs," but there were remarkably few in this one. All the American drivers remarked at the courteous way in which we were treated by everyone concerned.

I'll be back for the next one, all right.

Jack McAfee and Ford Robinson cross fingers by their Cadillac in Mexico City, while race was still on.

Personalities and Festivities

Some drivers and friends gathered at Sr. Cornejo's home for dinner. Left to right: Ray Crawford, Bob and Mrs. Estes, Ben Sarkisian, and Amos Hill. Standing in rear are Thomas Deal and Vincent Lopez.

Bill Sterling (seated second from right) talks with guests at the reception given the drivers at the Hotel Del Prado, Mexico City.

Sam Cresap (left) and Tom Deal, second prize winners, at the reception at Hotel Del Prado, Mexico City.

Above—Jose Antonio Solana (left) and brother Javier look at helmet Jose was wearing when they cracked up at Durango on second day. Photo taken at post-race reception at Cornejo home.

Left—Group of South American drivers at Cornejo home after race. Left to Right: Artesio Paz, Samuel Marin, and Gabriel Herrera, of Colombia; Atilio Cagnasso of Venezuela, and Arturo Marin, of Colombia.

CHAPTER XII
The Race from behind a Movie Camera

By T. E. (Ted) MacDONALD
Crown Film Productions

On the afternoon of April 25 I answered my telephone and a voice excitedly asked, "Mac, how soon can you leave for El Paso?"

"What's going on down in El Paso?" I asked, and he replied: "The Mexican Road Race starts from Juarez, May 5 and we want you to cover it."

The voice was that of N. F. Lawler, director of national advertising for Nash Motors, and he was calling Los Angeles from Detroit.

"Well," I replied, "it will take some doing, but you can depend on me."

Having been in the motion picture business more than twenty years, I know only too well that these "quickie" assignments can be awful headaches if a cameraman isn't plenty careful in his preparations.

The only information I could get over the phone was that there were eight Nash cars entered in the race and that a factory representative, Ross Grower, was already in El Paso. I called Grower, made arrangements to meet him, and started getting the necessary equipment together. Believe me, no one will ever know just how much equipment a cameraman has to carry unless he is in the picture business. Air travel was out of the question, so I took the S.P.'s Golden State to El Paso.

Before leaving Los Angeles I had contacted Miguel (Mike) Gallagher at the Mexican government's National Tourists Commission offices and he gave me letters to officials at El Paso and Juarez, and they were a big help. At El Paso I met Joe Gondora, who was in charge of the Pemex Travel Bureau. He went out of his way to assist me in getting lined up with the proper authorities to get clearance for my equipment.

I finally ended up at the Mexican consulate where all my papers were issued to film the race, plus a very official-looking letter authorizing all persons who were in charge of the event to recognize me as an official cameraman. Another letter was given me by Sr. Antonio Cornejo C., general manager of the race. All my credentials were in Spanish.

All the Mexican officials were most helpful throughout the entire proceeding. No one I came in contact with was under any obligation to help me, but each one seemed eager to do all he could so that my task (which was a rough go) would be made easier.

Three or four days before the start of the race the U. S. Health Department office in El Paso informed me we would have to be vaccinated for small pox, which is quite prevalent in some of the jungle country through which we would pass. Grower and I took the treatment from an El Paso doctor. On me it didn't take because I had been shot in the arm too many times already, but Ross really had one sore arm for the next week.

The day before the race we started on a shopping tour. We knew we would have to take such things as drinking water, canned food, a Coleman stove, coffee pot, pans, paper cups, lantern, flash light, mattresses, blankets, knives, forks, spoons and many other things. After we had finished our all-day tour, we really had a lot of stuff to pack into out Nash Ambassador. When we got through packing our equipment the car was loaded from the floor to the top and packed solid.

We checked out of our El Paso hotel at 5 a. m., May 5 and were off to Juarez. Anyone who ever has crossed the International bridge at Juarez knows there is usually a constant round of inspections, but as we approached the Mexican customs and the officers on duty saw the lettering on the Nash, which read "Carrera-Panamericana, Nash Motion Picture Unit," they motioned us on. We were relieved to find that through our connection with the race we could take anything we wished into Mexico. We had had visions of the customs officials taking away our cigarettes, and that was one item we didn't want to lose.

The starting line was quite a distance south of town, and there was much activity at this early hour. The closer we got to the starting line the greater the crowd became, until it was almost impossible to get the car through. We were thankful to have made such an early start; otherwise we might never have reached our destination. Driving partly on the edge of the roadway but mostly in the ditch, we finally found a parking place about a quarter of a mile from the starting line. Taking my Bell & Howell 70 D. A. camera which I was using newsreel-style with a hand-pod (a tripod would only have been in the way), and tucking several hundred feet of 16mm. Kodachrome in my gadget bag, I was off to the starting line, stopping on the way to talk to Bud Sennett, Johnny Balch, Johnny Mantz and many other drivers who have fallen victim to my lens for many years.

A milling mass of humanity was pushing and shoving, trying to get closer to the contesting cars and their occupants. The Mexican army was in charge of all civilian activities. It was the soldiers' job to keep the people away from the starting line and out on the course the army had a squad of soldiers stationed every four or five miles during the race. Each day, the army would block off that section of the highway which the race cars were to travel. The daily distances averaged from 226 miles to more than 600 miles, and this was quite a task for the army to perform.

The cars were started at intervals much the same as in our Grand Canyon Economy Run, except that in this race the officials allowed twenty cars to start at short intervals, and then held up the field for five minutes, so there would not be too many cars traveling the highway at one time and they would not get bunched in the bad spots.

At a time designated by the official starter the first car was rolled to the starting line and the starter counted in Spanish, "Ten seconds, nine seconds, eight seconds," and so on until the flag was dropped and a great roar rose up from the mass of humanity. It sounded like "yah." The first car was on its way to Chihuahua on the first leg of the Pan-American road race.

Car after car was brought to the starting line and each time I had the same problem of getting my picture. The throngs of screaming Mexicans would rush in front of my camera at just the wrong time, and the soldiers would push everyone back, including the cameraman, and that was bad. After discussing the matter with several "still" men who were having the same trouble, we found an officer and asked him to explain to the soldiers that when they shoved the crowd back they should not do the same to those of us with arm bands and cameras. After several minutes of explanation the officer went along the line pointing out their mistakes to the soldiers, and from then on we managed to do pretty well.

After what seemed like days, the last car was started and we fought our way back to our camera car with the intention of getting way right behind the last starter. But there was that mass of people and when we did reach our car it took us a good half hour to get in the highway. Blowing our horn constantly and creeping along an inch at a time we managed to get clear, but it was plain to see we were not going to make very good time because for the next ten miles people, cars and dogs were a solid mass right down the middle of the road. I have seen some after-race crowds in my time, but this was the pay-off as far as I was concerned.

About twelve miles out of Juarez things started looking up and we were able to make a little faster time. As we approached a curve and railroad crossing some nineteen miles south of Juarez we saw a huge crowd of people. It was not long before we saw the first and only fatal wreck of the race. The Guatemalan entry No. 112, a Lincoln, had flipped over and landed right side up but was a complete washout and its driver had been killed. After getting several shots of the wreck (a job I don't relish when a man has been killed) we proceeded on down the road only to come upon Joel Thorne's Cadillac which had gone over a bank. Joel was walking around the badly smashed-up vehicle shaking his head and saying something about "everything happens to me."

Without further incidents we arrived at Chihuahua late in the afternoon and went directly to the huge sports center which was the impound area. We found all the cars lined up and most of the drivers were gathered in groups in the main hall. Not having any food since 5 a.m., in El Paso, we proceeded to break out our stove and prepare something to eat. I was elected to do the cooking. Frying half a dozen eggs and making toast and coffee was not so bad, but when those guys started walking away and leaving their dirty dishes, I screamed. "Hey, you birds! Get husky in the pots and pans department or you'll cook your own breakfast in the morning," I said. When I got back after shaving I found everything cleaned up and put in its proper place.

In the sports center the race committee had 200 cots with sheets and blankets for the drivers and members of their crews to sleep on. But that didn't include us, so we had to figure out a way to use the twin beds with which the Nash was equipped. With soldiers walking their posts all night we figured we could unload our equipment from the car and get some shut-eye without the danger of getting anything stolen, because we were in an enclosed area anyway. We did just that, and after asking one of the building attendants if he would wake us at 4 a.m., we removed our heavy boots and collapsed with our clothes on into those soft mattresses.

It hardly seemed to me that I had been asleep five minutes when there was pounding on the window and I heard a voice say, "Eet eze four o'clock, señors." Looking at my wrist watch, I found that the guy was telling the truth. We rolled out and started packing our equipment back in the car, deciding that we would wait until later in the morning for breakfast. During the night it had turned very cold at that elevation, so we washed our faces in ice-cold water. The night before, we had picked a spot on our map about 100 miles south of Chihuahua at a town called Camargo where, we were told, there should be some pretty good picture material owing to the crooked highway at that point. In the early morning darkness we sped along the highway south, keeping an eye open for army patrols which had been ordered to keep the highway closed from midnight on. We ran into several of these patrols and were stopped on each occasion. Sometimes we were lucky enough to be stopped by a patrol which was headed by an officer, but if there was no officer present and none of the soldiers could understand English, we really had our troubles getting through. Each patrol consisted of from four to eight men and each was well heeled with a tommy gun, carbine or pistol. Although most of the solders were good natured, there were some who took their orders seriously and would poke those guns in our faces and order us off the road.

If you have ever been in a strange country and it's pitch black outside and you're at the wrong end of a gun that looks like a 16-inch cannon, you just don't argue with the guy. In most cases, however, we would show our credentials and after some deliberation we would be told, "Pass-a" and again we were on our way. That morning it took us four hours to travel 100 miles over a beautifully-paved highway because of the patrol stops, but that was good because those army boys were sure seeing to it that the road was going to be clear when the cars started coming through, and that was the important thing.

It was long after daylight when we approached Camargo and the sun was getting hotter. Suddenly we came on a sign which read "Slow, Bad Curve" in Spanish and, believe me, the sign wasn't put there just for an ornament. Down the road it looked as if the highway had disappeared into thin air and directly at its end was a bank about ten feet high. We could understand why we had been told this place would be a good one for filming motion pictures. The long, smooth stretch of highway came abruptly to an end, making a right-angle turn, proceeding another 100 feet and making another left turn just as sharp. It was necessary to drive between two very high, thick cement walls. Then we crossed a series of narrow cement bridges over two brooks, then made another sharp turn, then another at right angles, and finally we hit Camargo.

We figured we would have time to eat before the first car came through, and we did so, with a crowd of people coming out of nowhere to watch us. By the time we had put away all our utensils a crowd of about 200 had gathered, plus an ambulance, internes and all.

Previously we had become acquainted with two small boys, about ten and twelve respectively, and to my surprise I found the younger one spoke perfect English. I decided to make a deal with the kid to stand on the old railroad abutment and watch for the race cars. When he saw one he was to signal me, and shout in English. A U. S. dime closed the deal and he and his friend started off. I was checking my camera equipment when it happened. All along the ridge of a hill which overlooked the highway to the north there came a murmur of voices and then my lookout started waving his arms and shouting frantically in Spanish. The first contestant was coming, hell bent for Durango, and the boy became so excited he forgot he could speak English and was yelling his head off in his native tongue.

Needless to say I was off and running. I shot plenty of footage at that point throughout the morning and into the afternoon, and I still get a bang out of that kid forgetting to shout in English, "Here they come!"

After the last car had passed and the army jeep control car with its green flags had gone by, we fell in behind for the trip to Durango. Along the road I stopped and made shots of many wrecked cars, but fortunately there had been no serious injuries. The impound area at Durango that night was a hive of activity. All contestants were busy changing tires and checking motors, with Coleman lanterns and flashlights blinking all over the place.

Looking for a bath and a bed was our next concern. Unfortunately the American Motel, which had been recommended to us, was full and we had to look elsewhere. As we were leaving the motel a fellow stopped us and asked if we would like to use his cabin in which to wash. Right then, I knew there was a Santa Claus.

Unfortunately we couldn't shave because there was no outlet for electric razors, but we could clean up somewhat. It was now nearly midnight and we felt the smart thing for us to do would be to leave for Mexico City immediately so we could get pictures of the finish there the next day. It is a distance of about 600 miles from Durango to the capital.

It's difficult to explain, but in Mexico it seems as though every mule, burro and dog likes to use the highway to roam or sleep on, and cattle seem to think the nice warm pavement is a good place to lie down for the night. When you're rolling along pretty fast and a group of animals suddenly looms up in your headlight beam, it just takes a few years off your remaining days, that's all.

We travelled all night through unknown territory and when the sun came out it seemed we were as far from Mexico City as ever. About noon we arrived at the outskirts and proceeded across the city. The closer we came to the course which would lead the race cars into the impound area the greater became the throngs of people. Some three miles from the finish line we had to abandon the car and take off on foot. After having been stopped a dozen times by soldiers and having had my camera taken away twice only to be returned by an officer, I arrived at a point where I could take some pretty fair pictures. As the cars came roaring in I ground out foot after foot, long shots, close-ups, running here and there trying to catch lots of the human interest stuff. Meanwhile Grower had been working on the proposition of getting our car closer to the finish line, and when I returned to the point where all competing cars were being stopped by the race committee I found the car, so things again were looking up.

The racers were escorted to Sr. Cornejo's garage, which was that night's impound area, by motorcycle policemen. Grower had managed to get an officer to ride in the camera car with us so I could make some shots through the windshield as we drove to the center of the city. Headed by a squadron of army motorcycle officers with their sirens wide open and red lights flashing, we were really traveling. Thousands of people lined the beautiful parkway as we went speeding along behind our escort, but we were traveling so fast at times that the throng looked just a blur through my camera.

When we stopped at the impound area, I thought every human being in Mexico was trying to get in our car. A sea of yelling, screaming faces were everywhere atop a wave of surging bodies, which seemed that it would capsize all the cars. Soldiers with fixed bayonets tried hopelessly to maintain order. At last we cleared the gates into the impound area and heaved sighs of relief.

Next we made our way, having parked the car, across the square to the Hotel Reforma, where we had reservations and when we reached the lobby we were a sad-looking sight if ever there was one. Never in my life did a bed and a bath with tub and shower look so good to me. For three days and two nights we had been going almost constantly, with only four hours' sleep the night at Chihuahua. Chihuahua! How long ago and far away that name sounded! After bathing we went down to the dining room and really put away a meal. We were asked if we were going to attend the Governor's banquet that night at his mansion for the contestants, to which we replied, "Are you kidding?"

That night we went to sleep to the noise of the vast celebration going on in the streets below. Early next morning we got the car and headed for the town of Rio Frio, 10,000 feet up in the mountains on the road between Mexico City and Puebla. The road up was good but chuck full of sharp switchback turns. I finally selected a spot there for filming and history repeated itself with still more spectators and soldiers. Where they all came from in such a sparsely-settled country I couldn't figure out, but they had been waiting long hours before the cars even left the starting line at Mexico City, 50 miles away.

At last the cars swished by and my camera ground on. At the foot of a hill was a sharp curve leading straight on to a bridge. Perhaps you have heard of the great skill of the foreign road-race drivers, and some of them were in this race. But I'm here to state that some of our American race drivers are pretty good at this road-racing business too. Although the foreign cars were equipped with shifts which certainly were a distinct advantage on hills and curves, that seemed to make very little difference to drivers such as Johnny Mantz, Bud Sennett, Lou Figaro, Dempsey Wilson and many others. When they wanted to pass any of these foreign "hot shots" they just did it, and that's all. You can always depend on a real American race driver giving a good account of himself while his car lasts.

After the control car had passed we started off again for Puebla, where we turned south again toward the next night's stop, Oaxaca. Just after leaving Puebla we saw a crowd of people looking down a bank and we realized a car was off the road. There it was about 30 feet down and really smashed up—No. 14, driven by Figaro and Wilson. We learned that neither boy was hurt badly, but their car sure was a mess.

As we continued the countryside was taking on a jungle atmosphere. Trees were taking on that flat-top appearance and candlestick cactus rose long and tall on all sides. The atmosphere had become humid, leaving us with that hard-to-breathe feeling. But it was only the beginning.

We reached Oaxaca that night late and drove to the city square. It had been raining and a clammy jungle fog was beginning to rise from the streets with an eerie effect. At the hotel there were no rooms, of course, but we were too tired and hungry to worry about a little thing like that. We merely sat in the front seat of our loaded car (we couldn't use our beds again because there was no room to put the equipment) and slept sitting up until the church bells started ringing at 6 a. m.

Tired and with our joints stiff from sitting up all night, we left the car and went to the hotel in search of a dining room. Luckily, the restaurant was open. After some scrambled eggs and three cups of the blackest coffee I ever drank, we were back in the car and headed for a point 40 miles below Oaxaca where I was going to stake out and wait for the coming racers. Here it was different; only a handful of people were waiting, although there was the ever-present ambulance, as there always was where there was a bad turn or where there might be a crack-up. These ambulances were equipped with short wave radios and if they were needed at another point within their area a call could reach them. Most ambulances I saw were of the U. S. Army type.

When the cars had passed we hurried back to Oaxaca in an unsuccessful effort by Grower to put through a long distance call to Detroit. In that part of Mexico there are only radio-type telephones. After many hours we gave up and started south toward Tuxtla Guitierrez, the next night's stop.

The territory south of Oaxaca is very mountainous and we reached the worst part of these mountains after dark. Tropical thunderstorms made it difficult to see more than a few feet in front of the car, but they would last only a few minutes. Near the town of Tehuantepec, which is just about at sea level, we encountered our first hoof-and-mouth disease inspection station. We had been told about them, but this was the first along the road. We were disconcerted to see a lantern swinging back and forth across the road indicating a stop. The guard motioned us off the road to the right, and then we saw the buildings. The odor of disinfectant was very strong. The attendant ordered us to walk through a covered trough, on the floor of which was heavy dirt mixed with disinfectant. While this was being done the attendant was spraying the chassis of the car with disinfectant shot from a long pipe. When this was done we were allowed to proceed. Both the Mexican and U. S. governments are fighting this dreaded animal disease which is such a scourge to Mexican beef. There were three such stations and all cars had to be disinfected each time they passed in either direction. The racers did not have to stop during the race, however.

About two in the morning our gas supply was getting low and we saw the lights of Tuxtla. We headed for the first station we could find open and we pulled in, only to be told we couldn't have any gasoline. The man said he was only the watchman and that the owner had all the keys for the pumps. Brother, were we in trouble! We had planned to gas up and head straight for El Ocotal, which would be the finish of the long race, and of course I had to get pictures there.

So there we sat at two in the morning figuring out the distance our gasoline would take us and trying to get the watchman to tell us which of the towns on the map would have a gas station, if any. He said we might get gas at Comitan in the morning, but that was 165 miles away and we were going over a rock ballast road and through mountains before we would reach there. After another half hour of deliberation we decided that with good luck and Nash economy we might make it.

After we had passed through the town of San Cristobal we came to the end of the pavement. Then it was a narrow dirt road winding through the mountains. After daylight we made a little better time, but both of us had our eyes glued on the gas gauge, which had been on the empty peg for some time. We prayed for some downhill going, and we did start downgrade! We rolled into Comitan with the motor off, and at the service station we were told that it would not be open for another hour because the owner had not arrived.

It was now about seven o'clock and we knew the race cars would be starting on their last leg from Tuxtla in another hour! We were desperate, but the attendant told us that down the road a few miles was a place where a gasoline distributor kept his drums and if we could make it there we could get some fuel. It was beginning to look bad for me and the picture business. However we figured the chance was worth it so we rolled out of the station, going as far as we could without turning on the motor. Soon we saw a truck and gasoline drums and a gentleman who spoke very good English said he would be happy to fill our gas tank. The words were right out of heaven to our ears, and our thanks must still be echoing across the very desolate jungle.

The last 25 miles to El Ocotal was an unfinished section of highway of solid rock ballast. We were forced to drive carefully, hoping we would not be stopped by any patrols and also hoping the race cars didn't overtake us. At last we reached El Ocotal, which was easily identified by a framework about fifteen feet high displaying a picture of President Miguel Aleman and covered with flowers and green leaves. This was the finish line. The impound area was about a mile beyond and to the right were several thatched huts which comprise the village. Far to the south, the towering mountains of Guatemala rose above the peaceful countryside.

When we had parked our car near the finish we both sat there and fell asleep. The trip from Mexico City of more than 850 miles had been a tough one without sleep, a shave or a bath, and with only what canned food would keep us sustained.

We didn't have long to sleep before the first racers were upon us. There were very few people to greet the racers because that section of Mexico is primitive and sparsely settled. The region in which the natives plant corn and raise beans is decidedly tropical in appearance.

An army radio was receiving a mile-by-mile account of the cars' progress over short wave, with an army plane spotting the cars as they headed south, then relaying the information to those at the finish line. Punchy from lack of sleep, I got out on one side of the highway and waited. A Paramount newsreel man who had flown down from Mexico City was the only other cameraman present and there were only a couple of still photographers there.

Then, with great clouds of dust and the thumping of tires over the rock ballast, came the first contestant across the line. From then until late afternoon I kept grinding away, not knowing one car from another, but getting each on film. About five o'clock it appeared that all the finishers had arrived, so Grower and I decided to find if there would be a place for us to sleep. We were told that only the drivers and crews would be accomodated in specially-built dormitories in the impound field. By this time I had begun worrying about all the exposed color film I was carrying. Tropical climate is dynamite on exposed film unless you have a special container, which I didn't. Lacking a place to sleep, we decided in the interests of the film as well as ourselves we should head back to Mexico City. Starting at El Ocotal at 6 p. m., we refueled at Comitan and took off again.

By driving in short reliefs to give both of us a chance to nap, we made good time, arriving in Mexico City late the next afternoon. Then to the Reforma. Since we had left the hotel, which was the last place we had had a bath or shave, we had traveled some 1900 miles through tropical storms and hot jungle country with a total of about five hours' sleep, all of it sitting up. But now we slept fourteen hours.

At four the following afternoon we loaded once more and started for Juarez and El Paso. Driving two hours on and two hours off, we reached the international boundary in slightly over 24 hours. The next day I said good-bye to Grower and boarded the Golden State for Los Angeles.

At last I arrived home with 1600 feet of Kodachrome in the bag. The next day the film was processed at the laboratory. It came out a lot better than I had expected, everything plainly visible to stand as a record of one of the most grueling assignments I have ever undertaken.

As we sat in the studio watching the film, I lived over

and over again every mile of the race from Juarez to El Ocotal, just as I have lived it over and over in the comfort of my own living room, and I somehow feel that the race has been run many times in scores of living rooms all over the nation by those drivers who pioneered the Pan American Highway.

An emergency service station in the mountains.

The snow-capped peak of towering Mt. Popocatepetl (17,822 ft. high) appears above the clouds.

Picturesque Old Mexico

View of the church of Taxaco.

Church at San Cristobal.

Typical American tourists at Taxaco.

Scenic Xochimilco Gardens, Mexico.

Mexican Magazines and Newspapers gave much Pre-Publicity to the Race

This Article from Pemex Travel Club Bulletin

From Aguascalientes, through the picturesque little village of Encarnación, the magnificent highway goes on southward, toward Mexico's southern border.

PAN-AMERICAN auto race Ciudad Juarez-EL Ocotal

by LUIS VILLAFRANCA.

A spectacular cross country border-to-border automobile race, marking completion of a through route from Alaska to Guatemala, is being staged in Mexico next month.

The race begins on May fifth —national holiday celebrating the victory of Mexican troops over French armies in 1862—. Competitors start out from Ciudad Juárez, border city in the State of Chihuahua, across from El Paso, Texas.

With this race, revival of cross country auto competition, Mexico officially inaugurates her latest portion of the Pan American Highway System.

The Central Highway —from Ciudad Juárez to Mexico City and the Cristóbal Colón Highway —from the capital to El Ocotal in the State of Chiapas—, a 3,505 kilometer stretch from north to south, winds and pushes through mountains, canyons, jungles and desert lands; through old colonial towns and modern industrial centers. It crosses two great mountain ranges between the cities of Toluca and Puebla highest point reaching an altitude of 10,000 feet.

The race, organized in accord with the International and the Inter-American Sporting Codes, is under management of an Organizing Committee, with government backing.

President of Mexico, Lic. Miguel Alemán, is honorary president of the Organizing Committee. Secretary of Communications and Public Works, Agustín García López, is acting president, and Antonio Cornejo C., prominent in the Mexican automobile business general manager.

The six-day cross country competition is an open test of speed over the highways from Mexico's northern border to its southern frontier. The route is paved all the way, with the exception of the last 107 miles in the State of Chiapas, but these have a good gravel surface. The highways —magnificent engineering feat— measure up to the highest standards for grades curves and other construction factors. Cost was five hundred million pesos. Another three hundred million are being spent by Mexico this year on her paved road program

Competing vehicles in race are five-seat closed body passenger cars, using 80-Octane Super Mexoline, supplied as part of entry fee —demonstrating progress of Mexico's petroleum industry. Entry fee also covers insurance for damage to property and persons not connected with the race.

Rules governing competition permit entry of any automobile, if it is standard type, five-seat, closed body, with factory equipment and without change or special added equipment. Any person, organization or company in the world is allowed to enter any number of cars. Each competing one carries a driver and an assistant. Competitors must maintain a minimum speed of 80 kilometers an hour on each lap to be eligible for major prizes but may compete for minor awards if they fall below 80 kilometers; not however, if they go below an average speed of 50 per hour, in which case they are disqualified.

On May 5, President Alemán, presiding highway inaugural ceremonies, will cut the ribbon across the Río Grande, and competitors start off on their six day speed test. The first lap ends in Chihuahua for over night stop. The second day stretch, from Chihuahua to Durango, has a half hour stop at Parral; third stretch, from Durango to Mexico City, also allows a half hour stop at León; the fourth, from Mexico City to Oaxaca; the fifth from Oaxaca to Tuxtla Gutiérrez; and the sixth from Tuxtla Gutiérrez ands at El Ocotal, on the southern border. Total coverage is 3,505 kilometers.

President Alemán will preside at delivery of prizes in Mexico City. Major awards for winners are 150,000, 100,00 and 50,000 pesos. There are minor prizes for each leg of the race and, in addition to cash rewards, winners will receive trophies, including one presented by Captain Eddie Rickenbacker.

The entire Mexican highway network provides a variety of routes across the nation. Besides the Central Highway, three other entrances to Mexico from Texas are an invitation to U.S. tourists. From Matamoros, opposite Laredo; from Reynosa, opposite McAllen, from Piedras Negras, opposite Eagle Pass, excellent paved roads lead southward. The new route, providing a direct approach from the far west, is of great importance to tourists as well as to commerce.

Chihuahua, the first stop in

race schedule, is a modern city, capital of the State of Chihuahua, in the Tarahumara region. The Tarahumara Indians are probably of the same racial stock as the Pueblos of New Mexico. The State is a wealthy cattle raising section. The people are extraordinarily hospitable and cordial. Second stop is Parral a small, pleasant town in the same State.

Durango, ending the second day's jaunt, is the capital of the State of Durango. From the quiet, charming city with shaded parks and an Old World air about it, a branch road leads to Mazatlán, the port city on the Pacific.

Set on a narrow peninsula with beautiful curved beaches that slant down into the ocean, Mazatlán is an ideal winter resort, pleasant the year around. In the vicinity are excellent hunting grounds —pheasant, deer and wild bear— and fishing —bass, mackerel, trout, dolphin, giant manta ray—.

Speeding southward from Durango, the racers pass through Zacatecas and Aguascalientes before reaching León, a progressive little city agricultural center and railroad junction noted for its carved leather and shoe manufacturing. Zacatecas is charming old city built on a hill. Interesting, colonial monuments remind one of its mining wealth of yesterday. The hot mineral springs of Aguascalientes gave the city its name which means "hot waters". It is gay with parks and orchards. From here a branch road leads to Guadalajara, a beautiful city built on a gently sloping plain.

Guadalajara's climate is warm and dry The city is filled with parks and plazas, always thronged with gay crods. Most of the houses are built around tiled patios of Andalusian type, beautifully cared for and filled with flowering trees, potted plants, luxuriant ferns and caged birds. Among the city's important colonial buildings are: the State Capitol, a fine example of Churriguera; the Church of Santa Mónica, plateresque in style and with an elaborately carved facade; the Museum, built at the beginning of the XVIII Century and, for more than a hundred years a monastary; San Francisco Church, massive and imposing, constructed in the XVI Century. In the State Capitol, the University and the Museum, there are magnificent José Clemente Orozco frescoes The Museum houses a very interesting collection of early Mexican paintings and a number of Murillo oils

A short paved distance from the city —almost a suburb of it— is Tlaquepaque, pottery manufacturing center colorful and noisily gay with unending mariachi music.

Guanajuato and San Miguel Allende are in the vicinity of León, which marked the first lap of the third day, and are easily reached over paved roads.

Guanajuato, stretching down a mountain side to three ravines, is one of the most beautiful cities in Mexico. Once a small Tarascan village it flourished into Colonial prominence in the XVI Century. Cobble and flag-stoned streets wind up and down, lined by handsome colonial buildings. Because of its uneven terrain, the roof of one house is often on a level with the ground floor of another; houses that have entrances on two streets sometimes have the living room, opening out on one street, one floor above the garage or the bedroom, which gives out on the back street.

The Guanajuato churches of La Compañia, San Cayetano and San Diego, and the magnificent house that was once the home of Count Rul de Valenciana, are extraordinarily lovely. An interesting historical site is the Alhóndiga de Granaditas. Once a grain market, the Royalist troops —during struggle for Mexican independence— were entrecched within its massive walls when the city was beseiged by the insurgents under the command of the fighting priest Miguel Hidalgo. When Hidalgo called for volunteers to brave the Spanish gunfire and set fire to the huge wooden door of the Alhóndiga, a miner called "Pípila"; answered the summons. Protecting his shoulders with a huge slab of stone and carrying a flaming torch in his hand he crawled to the fortress and set fire to the door. A tremendous struggle followed, ending in the defeat of the Royalists.

In the same State of Guanajuato, San Miguel Allende was founded in 1542 by Franciscan friars, on the old site of a Chichimec outpost A center of conspiracy for Independence, San Miguel Allende clings, nevertheless, to its Spanish past: It is a lovely colonial town which during the past few years has become one of the most important art centers in the Americas.

Querétaro, only a few hours drive from Mexico City, is another colonial city rivaling Guanajuato. Morelia and Puebla in beauty of architecture. Its perfect climate —never cold, never warm— and the fertile surrounding country are added attractions.

At some remote period, Otomi Indians settled a spot which was called Querétaro, meaning "where ball games are played", and it was until the beginning of the XVI Century, when Emperor Moctezuma of Mexico was successfully continuing the imperial policy of the warlike Aztecs, that the Otomi city fell under Mexico-Tenocthtitlan's sphere of influence. Later, it fell under Spanish rule, and nothing was left of the primitive Otomi village.

The seventy four graceful arches of a colonial aqueduct frame the entrance into Querétaro, and everything about it is Spanish colonial.

Querétaro is the church bells breaking the silence, the trickle of water in stone fountains, the sun slanting on the beautifully carved stone of ancient churches, tzentzontle birds singing in shaded patios, the memory of Spanish rule, of struggle for independence, and the more recent memory —less than a hundred years ago— of a short lived empire.

Querétaro was imperial in the eighteen-sixties. Its people swore allegiance to Maximilian of Hapsburg, and were loyal. Outside the city, on the little Hill of the Bells, the Empire ended as Archduke Maximilian and his brave and loyal Mexican generals, Miramón, and Mejia, fell before a firing squad.

Two extraordinary architects, Eduardo Tres Guerras and Mariano de las Casas, gave to Querétaro some of its most cherished relics of colonial art: the Churches of Santa Rosa and Santa Clara, the House of the Gargoyles and the Convent of San Agustín, now State Museum.

Still nearer to Mexico City and close to the highest point on the route, is Toluca Its Friday market offers the visitor all kinds of Indian arts and crafts, especially the colorful as well as useful Toluca baskets, and an immense variety of foods, fruits and herbs. The small modern arts and crafts museum at the entrance of the city is interesting.

To the northwest of the city, the Nevado de Toluca volcano rears its imposing height, hiding within its crater a pair of clear twin lakes which according to legend, were formed by the tears of an Indian monarch. In remote times —goes the story— the inhabitants of Toluca were conquered by a warring tribe. The vanquised ruler fled to the summit of the volcano, determined to perish in its crater. As he looked down on his lost land and his fleeing subjects, the monarch wept bitterly. His tears formed the twin lakes in the heart of the Nevado de Toluca.

At the end of the third day, the racers reach Mexico City. The Mexican capital, with a population of approximately two and a half million, is ultra modern and cosmopolitan in spots, with swank hotels, bars, nightclubs and cinemas; bullfighting, jai alai games, excellent polo and and golf fields and a magnificent race track. Modern architecture in the city is really spectacular. However, there is a strong colonial seal on the old Aztec capital, clear in its magnificent churches and palatial homes built during the Spanish domination. There are also vestiges of Indian architecture in the very heart of the city, and markedly Indian suburbs in close proximity. The solid grandeur of French-influenced architecture of the Porfirio Díaz regime, marks another period and adds to Mexico City's contrasts

Southward from the capital is the Spanish City of Puebla. The four volcanoes —Popocatépetl, Iztaccíhuatl, Malintzin and Orizaba are in full view. The city was founded in 1531, and legends has it that the Angels chose the site, hence its name Puebla de los Angeles —city of the angels.

The Puebla Cathedral, with its fine paintings, exquisite carvings and Flemish tapestries, is second in importance only to that of Mexico City. The Capilla del Rosario, ornamented with tiles, polychrome sculptures and gold leaf Churriguera alters of Indian craftmanship, is unique. The Casa del Alfeñique, the churches of San Francisco and Nuestra Señora de la Luz the Convent of Santa Rosa and the Jesuit Convent which is now State College are notable examples of colonial architecture.

Farther south is Oaxaca, capital of the State of Oaxaca, called the green city because of the green hued stones of its buildings. It is set in a valley and the surrounding hills seem to shoot up abruptly into the sky. Folklore, Indian crafts and magnificent architecture are part of the Oaxaca scene. The main plaza is shaded by enormous trees; scores of squirrels dart about and race across the flower beds. Near the plaza is the Cathedral, built in mid-XVI Century, with massive walls and a beautiful plateresque facade. A fine collection of paintings is found in the old church. The XVIII Century Santo Domingo church is a wealth of gold, color and carvings And, the Museum guards a splendid collection of preCortés treasures.

Near the city are two fascinating archaeological zones: Mitla and Monte Albán. Long before the Spaniards reached the New World, Mitla, under the Mixtec government, had reached great splendor. The Toltec-influenced Mixteca monuments of Mitla are spectacular proof of that splendor. Zapotec Monte Albán, with Mayan and Teotihuacan influence, reached its Golden

Age about the year 500, lasting until 1,000 A.S. Its ruins are tremendously interesting.

Near Oaxaca, in a gorgeus tropical setting, lies Tehuantepec, home of Zapotecan Indians, with unmistakable mixture of Spanish, French and Irish. The Tehuantepec zone is one of the most colorful of Mexico. The town itself is divided into 15 barrios, or neighborhoods, and as each one celebrates its patron saint with a several-days-long fiesta, there are few fiesta-less days for the Tehuanos. Because men work at down in the fields and take a long siesta during the hot noon hours, while the women are seen going to and fro and attending to household tasks, tourists, who are not up at daybreak, believe that all the work is done by the women.

Folklore, colorful costumes and charming folksongs are as much a part of Tehuantepec as the tall statuesque Tehuanas who walk gracefully balancing baskets and gourds on their heads.

Tuxtla Gutiérrez capital of the State of Chiapas, a lush tropical zone crossed by wide rivers over which aigrettes and parrots form fying clouds of color, also has some delightfully cool spots

There are many Indian tribes in Chiapas, all speaking their own tongues and governed by their own Indian governors, under State - Government control. The capital city itself is small and pleasant.

From Tuxtla Gutiérrez, the road southward leads to El Ocotal, in the same State and on the Mexico-Guatemala border, a tropical town which marks the limits of Mexico and the end of the cross country race.

The two highways which cross the country from north to south, passing through important centers such as Chihuahua, Durango, Aguascalientes, León, Querétaro, Puebla and Oaxaca, and within easy access —by branch roads, to Mazatlán, Guadalajara, Guanajuato, San Miguel Allende, and a number of charming towns and villages, are of tremendous importance. Not only do these roads benefit Mexico's tourist trade, as well as her agriculture and commerce by making transport of products possible, they are also in benefit of that friendship and understanding between the peoples of the two countries, which the governments of Mexico and of the United States have warmly sponsored, and which can only be reached by the people of one nation knowing the people of the other.

Durango is an aristocratic little city, peaceful and charming. View of one of the streets; the theatre in foreground to the left.

Scenery and Tradition Abound

The rebozo, Mexican women's finely-woven scarf, is fashionable now in the U. S. Here it is seen at its best, embellishing and embellished by two senoritas from Leon, ancient city along the new Pan-American Highway through Mexico, which links the U. S. and Guatemala.

Guanajuato is one of Mexico's most amazing cities. Many of its streets are really stairways. The city is just off the highway which spans Mexico from El Paso to El Ocotal.

Above and right: Mexico walks on shoes made in Leon, city of nearly 100,000 in the west-central part of the country on the new border-to-border highway. Though the products are turned out in modern factories, the Machine Age can't displace the faithful burros, which still find work transporting hides for the city's many tanneries.

Mexico has large deposits of real gold under its soil, as well as petroleum. Just as precious is the water impounded in its dams. These views show the canals and the General Lazaro Gardenas Dam at El Palmito, in the mountains a few miles west of La Zarca in the north-central State of Durango. La Zarca is along the new Pan-American Highway which sweeps across Mexico from north to south.

Distinctively Mexican scenery along the country's thousands of miles of paved highways.

Left: The new north-south highway route between El Paso and Guatemala has made this little known yet interesting archeological site, Chicomoztoc (the Seven Caves) easily accessible to tourists of north-central Mexico. The Aztecs are said to have built it while on their long journey towards the present site of Mexico City, in 1170.

Center: Ancient aqueduct at Queretaro, Mexico, just a short distance from the Pan-American Race route.

Right: Another view of Chicomoztoc, located some 35 miles southeast of Zacatecas. The high, dry climate has preserved these steep pyramids and round columns, which are held together with a cement made of red clay and corn husks. These structures were part of an extensive city at one time.

Right: The old and the new in Mexico—A modern statue stands near the classic Sanctuary of Guadalupe Church in Chihuahua. Tourists will be impressed with this typical contrast all along the new Mexican border-to-border highway.

Center: A Monument of Chihuahua, capital of the northern Mexican state of the same name, is its 16th Century cathedral, a baroque masterpiece designed by Juan Antonio Travina y Reyes. The new highway passes through this historic town, which is today a progressive industrial and commercial city.

Left: This picturesque Mexican taxi runs on 80-octane hay, still typical transportation in many cities of Mexico. This particular cabby operates in Aguascalientes, a north-central town along the Pan-American route.

131

The World's Toughest Road Race!

THE WORLD'S TOUGHEST ROAD RACE

by JACK CANSLER

> Speed Age's ace cameraman and correspondent Jack Cansler faced many unexpected troubles and hardships during the 2178 mile Pan-American road race. He reports:
>
> "I had to make some hasty arrangements in El Paso for processing and mailing, and the arrangements didn't work out satisfactorily. Well, anyhow, I have thorough arrangements made in Mexico City, to handle all my work next year, if the race is repeated, as it is expected to be.
>
> "I took over 400 shots on 4 x 5 film pack, which kept me jumping day and night—the event was so big. Everybody wanted pictures, although there were plenty of Mexican photographers, their coverage was pretty skimpy, consisting mostly of start and finish. I found the event almost too big for one man to cover completely, but it was a great experience and adventure even with the sunburn, thirst, inconvenience, lack of food and sleep.
>
> "The combination of all these knocked me out on the last day of the race, and as they say in good old England, 'I thought I had it,' but luckily recovered in a few hours."

SIX DAYS and 2178 miles comprised the biggest, toughest and most adventurous race ever held—the 1950 Pan American border to border stock car road race, won by American Hershel McGriff and co-driver Ray Elliott in the City of Roses, Portland, Oregon 1950 Oldsmobile.

Returning to Mexico City from the Guatemalan border, the drivers—successful and otherwise—were feted and honored with receptions and banquets by the populace, for this event has been the most outstanding single happening to the Republic of Mexico since the war. It was programmed by the government as an international attraction to celebrate the opening of the inter-continental highway which stretches the length of the Republic.

The event attracted 132 starters, giving their home destinations as Italy, France, England, China, South America, United States and the host country of Mexico. Almost every make of standard automobile was entered and scheduled to start from Juarez at 10 a.m., Friday, May 5.

All cars were impounded and sealed 24 hours before the race, and a drawing was held for starting positions. Mexican drivers secured the first five positions, with the sixth going to Tommy Francis of Los Angeles, driving a 1950 Ford.

Francis, incidentally, is the young man who gathered himself considerable publicity in the desperate, but futile effort to save little Kathy Fiscus from the deep pipe well into which she had fallen a year ago. Francis was lowered into the pipe head first, after being greased all over, and was lowered to the point where he could hear her, before being ordered up by the little girl's father—not wishing another life to be lost in the rescue attempt.

Two entries caused considerable discussion. They were the Alfa Romeos from Italy. Their appearance was that of a racing car, but officials, after checking with the parent company, announced sufficient numbers of this model had been produced and sold to put them in the stock classification.

Americans seemed to show little concern over the formidable looking Italian cars, feeling their own product had little to fear from foreign importations. The confidence was well based.

Following an impressive ceremony headed by the Governor of Chihuahua, the first car, a 1950 Hudson driven by Luis Iglesias Davalos of Mexico was flagged on its way, between the thousands of spectators that lined the roads. The finish was 229 miles away, towards Chihuahua— the first leg.

Cars were started at one minute intervals, each driver carrying a log book on which the officials stamped the starting time and finish time at the end of each leg. The mathematical undertaking, in this scoring, was a big one and many felt concern over the complexity of the huge event and the possible margin of errors. As the race progressed, drivers realized the entire fairness of the officials and were complete in their agreement that an accurate record had been compiled.

All cars rolled away from the starting line smoothly. At 12:12 the 132nd entry started. One unfortunate driver, Enrique Hachmeister, driving a 1949 Lincoln and starting 112th, lost control of his car just 17 miles from the starting line and was killed. His co-driver was uninjured and continued in the race, taking as a driver Rodolfo Castaneda, a favorite of the Mexican populace, who had rolled his 1950 Cadillac near the same spot where Hachmeister lost his life. Later Castaneda rolled this car, but being an entry of the Mexican Government, continued with his battered car, finishing the race. He was hailed as a hero the entire way. In private life Castaneda is a lieutenant in the Mexican army.

The first leg, from Juarez to Chihuahua, was a monotonous stretch of almost straight road through flat, desert like, hot country. The stretch took a heavy toll of tires, causing many cars to fall out and some to turn back. A Cord, driven by Hugh J. Reilly of Chicago, suffered mechanical trouble and turned back. Joel Thorne, of Indianapolis fame, and driving a 1949 Cadillac, was forced off the road and rolled at a point 38 miles from the start. He was unable to continue. At a point 26 miles from the start, a Ford, driven by Edward Neiders of Mexico City, rolled off the road and was badly battered, neither he nor his co-driver being hurt. Pulled back to the road by a wrecker, they continued.

A Buick, driven by Angel Gonzales of Mexico City, went out at 45 miles with engine trouble, while a Packard driver, Mariano Gomez of the same city, suffered the same fate with but 64 miles on his speedometer.

The heat increased and in the boiling sun it was a common sight to see drivers out of their cars, changing tires. Francisco Somohano of Portland, Oregon, in a Packard, blew four tires within the first 165 miles. Rubber came off in chunks, some as big as a man's hand, while other tires became so hot streams of white smoke spurted from them in dozens of places.

At 194 miles, Edward Walker of North Hollywood had to see his Talbot towed from the race, while at the same mark Felix Loza missed a turn, clipping fence posts and requiring a tow back onto the road and into the race.

Cars began to arrive at Chihuahua and surprisingly soon after the time limitation was up, the first day's official results were posted. Bill Sterling, driving a 1950 Cadillac from El Paso, Texas, was in the number one spot with an average speed of 98.4 MPH for the entire 229 miles—a record unsurpassed on any of the following legs. Sterling, an amateur driver, had never previously participated in a race of any kind.

Another 1950 Cadillac, driven by Anthony Muste of Chicago, was second while Johnny Mantz, 1949 Lincoln driver of speedway fame and one of the hot favorites to win the contest, was third. Mantz had previously driven the entire course, taking notes on curves, grades and road surfaces.

Fourth was Troy Ruttman in a 1950 Oldsmobile and George Lynch of Detroit was fifth in a 1950 Cadillac. Both, like Mantz, famed speedway drivers. Hershell McGriff, the eventual winner, was seventh at this point. All American cars and drivers held the first ten positions. Out of the 132 starters, 113 finished this first leg.

Starting positions for the second leg, the next day, from Chihuahua to Parral, a distance of 183 miles, were determined by the finish position on the first leg. This was the procedure to the end of the race. The third leg was to be run the same day, after a 30 minute stop in Parral. This was to Durango, 301 miles, making a total of 484 miles for the day.

Positions did not change too much on this second leg. Sterling was still first, Mantz second and Lynch third, but on the third leg, after the stop at Parral, changes were rapid. It began to look as if the contest would center between Sterling and Mantz, as they were again one-two at the finish. Tom Deal of El Paso, driving a 1950 Cadillac and 113th the first day, had charged up into third spot, while fourth was the NASCAR pace car, driven by Bill France and Curtis Turner. Although 37th the first day and fourth on this leg, their elapsed time placed them

133

in third position for the three legs. The car was a 1950 Nash Ambassador. McGriff had dropped into eighth place, but still the first ten cars and drivers were American, with only the Nash upsetting the Lincoln and Cadillac dynasty.

Finishing this period were 194 cars. Of those that dropped out, a 1950 Mercury, driven by Marcello Quintanilla of Mexico, was badly wrecked when he lost control on a sharp curve. Both drivers were injured severely. One mile from the finish, a Nash entry of Jose Solana of Mexico spun into the rough rocks alongside the road. Minutes later, a 1941 Cadillac, driven by Alfonso Oviedo of Mexico, rounding the same turn, crashed into the wrecked Nash, did a complete somersault over the car and landed upside down among the rocks. None of the four drivers were injured.

At this point it was notable that those who had safety belts and crash helmets were uninjured, while those riding without this equipment were the ones being hurt. The Guatemalan who had been killed the first day had no protective equipment.

The third day schedule was one of 620 miles, also in two legs. The first from Durango to Leon, with a check stop scheduled, and thence to Mexico City.

Tires were now becoming a concern. Drivers who hadn't previously experienced trouble, now suffered blowouts over the rough macadam road surface. Other tires were wearing thin, while some drivers had expended their supply of spares—the rules reading that all spare tires had to be carried from the start of the race.

Before the start, it was predicted that overheating would be the big problem, but strange to say, very little overheating had been experienced. Burning rubber off on curves, when cars were taking them at every ounce of speed possible, had turned out to be the big bugaboo, and the contest was just nearing the half-way mark.

Tire trouble hit Bill France and Curtis Turner on this leg, two successive blowouts causing them to lose considerable time and to fall well back in the standings. At a little village south of Leon, a Nash driven by Henry Bradley of Lima, Peru hit a bridge railing and toppled into the dry bed of a river. Both co-drivers were injured.

Thirty minutes later, near the same spot, a 1950 Lincoln driven by Harry Sents of Glen Aubry, N. Y. rounded a turn entering the village and rolled into a house, knocking a large hole in the house and damaging the car. Again no serious injuries. At Leon, the first three were Lonne Johnson, Sterling and Mantz.

From here into Mexico City a half million people lined the roads. Police and the military fought the populace to keep order, but it was nearly hopeless. Drivers told of approaching a solid mass of people at 100 MPH, seeing a lane open at the last minute and then close solidly again behind them as they passed. It was most harrowing.

The first car into the capital city was that driven by Deal. But 50 feet behind was Mantz. Three Mexican drivers, for the first time, crashed the first 10, but still the cars were all American. Cadillac, Lincoln, Olds, Nash, Hudson and Packard were listed. The finishing field numbered 89 cars.

Pulling out of Mexico City on Monday morning, the fourth day of the race, the drivers faced 86 miles of narrow, sharply curving road through high mountains to the city of Puebla. Ten cars dropped out on this short but dangerous stretch of road. The next leg was 253 miles to Oaxaca, during which Lou Figaro lost control of his Hudson at a steep curve and crashed. He was hospitalized and the car demolished.

Drivers were encountering mountain range after mountain range and the race was getting to be more of a rugged adventure with each mile. At the high altitudes it was chilly, with rain and hail being encountered. In a matter of minutes the cars would surge down into almost sea level country in flat, humid tropical country. All kept the windows closed tightly to cut down wind resistance, causing great discomforture in the hot areas, adding to the natural hazards of a hot, heavy helmet and only warm bottled water to drink. It was far from the picnic some imagined, at the start.

At the end of each day's running, discouragement could be seen plainly written on the faces of the contestants. Many wondered out loud what had prompted them to get into such a hellish thing as this. Many felt it was futile to go on, as their chances of winning were slim and towns getting more primitive, with accommodations scarce, and poor at best. Food was at a minimum, canned goods, mostly brought along, had dwindled and the bottled water brought from El Paso had almost disappeared. Still, many determined to see the contest to a finish, come what may. Here was the greatest test of drivers and endurance yet experienced, taking a huge toll of both.

The loss of sleep and lack of food, coupled with tropical heat, made many ill, including your reporter, who was grounded some three hours by the side of the road near Guatemala. We could see ourselves spending several weeks in some remote hospital with some form of tropical fever, but luckily nightfall brought a quick recovery—and so, on to the border.

In Oaxaca, at the end of the fourth day, the American flag was not raised until that of Italy, then Mexico twice, and again Italy was raised. At the start, the Alfa drivers had expressed the thought they would make their best showing when the mountains were reached, losing to American cars on the straight and flat roads. This proved to be true. Taruffi and his Alfa was first while Monetto was fourth. Between them came the Mexicans Menocal and Olegario Perez in a Packard and Mercury. McGriff, the Olds driver, was sixth and Owen Grey of Lubbock, Texas, in another Olds, seventh, before Mexicans took over to complete the ten.

Johnny Mantz suffered his worst lap during this running—mechanical and tires taking him into 64th finishing position out of the 75 cars that remained.

The fifth and next to last day, brought a stretch of 345 miles that took the drivers down to sea level and very close to the Pacific coast line on their way to Tuxtla. The tropical foliage began to show up profusely, with cocoanut palms and cactus dense.

On this run, we found a likely spot for pictures and stopped to wait for the cars to come along. Hardly stopped and esconsed when a big Mexican, bearing a wicked three foot knife, approached. Visions of Pancho Villa, movie villians and unmarked graves filled our mind as we remained, fear-frozen, to the spot.

Nearing us, the unsmiling peon whipped the lethal looking instrument into a high arc .... and lopped off the end of a large cocoanut, offering us the cool, refreshing milk that is contained inside.

Many such interesting and humorous experiences were told by the drivers. Bill France and Curtis Turner tell of an incident that was humorous and puzzling as well. They were in the middle of a hot, dry desert, working like mad changing a tire and not believing a human being was within a hundred miles, when a native materialized out of nowhere and offered them a "cerveza fria" (cold beer). The pair refused, although barely able to speak from thirst-parched lips, hopped into their car and charged back into the race. They then realized what they had done. What puzzled them was, where the native had come from, in an area that seemed void of habitation, and how he could have had cold beer in such a tepid atmosphere.

Quite some adventure, this race.

At Tuxtla, Mantz had regained the lead, Francis was second and Deal third. Andre Mariotti of Paris brought a French Delahaye into fifth while the first Alfa had dropped to seventh. McGriff was ninth.

Only 62 cars completed this run, Red Byron and Raymond Parks being listed among those out. They had skidded on a rocky embankment. Bob and Fonty Flock were out with a cracked block on their 1950 Lincoln. Elapsed time leader Sterling was the victim of tire trouble and he dropped out of sight in the standings.

The sixth and last day came May 10, with 160 miles of unpaved and treacherous narrow road that wound up and over a mountain, ending abruptly at the little village of El Octotal—the Guatemalian border—the objective for which all drivers had been punishing themselves and their machines for six days. The stakes were pretty high for the first three winners, and all seemed determined to throw all caution into the winds on this last leg.

At the start from Tuxtla, Roy Connor held eighth position in a Nash. He stood a good chance to come among the winners, except that the tropical sickness had visited him. Bill France, co-driver of Nash No. 37, offered his driver Curtis Turner to Connor, and the switch was made. Turner was ordered to push the Nash and push he did.

Due to the dangerous condition of the road, the cars were started four minutes apart, rather than the customary one.

In a feat that almost overcame the eventual winner, Turner made up the four minutes between each car, passing all seven who started previous to his Connor entry, placing him well out in front —when he blew a tire but 10 miles from the finish. Making a fast change, he still finished first, placing the Nash third in total elapsed time for the race.

The two Alfas followed Turner, then McGriff, the French Delahaye and two Mexicans.

Total time was then computed, with the personable young man Hershel McGriff of Portland, Oregon, driving the 1950 Oldsmobile, the winner of the six day marathon. He had but one blowout in the entire race. One minute and 16 seconds later came Tom Deal, the Cadillac driver from Texas, while Connor was disqualified for changing drivers, although the entry was third. Al Rogers of Colorado Springs, Colo. came fourth, moving into third.

Fifty-two cars finished the race, out of the 132 that started. France came to grief when he hit a large culvert but 50 miles from the finish, damaging his radiator until he was unable to continue.

Over 80 trophies were presented at the huge banquet which was presided over by Presidente Miguel Aleman in Mexico City. McGriff's check was for $17,400, Deal $11,600 and Rogers $5,800.

The two Alfa Romeos were the only cars able to break into the American dominated — Oldsmobile, Nash, Cadillac and Lincoln—first ten in elapsed time. The Delahaye was thirteenth. First driver other than American and Italian to finish was R. Salgado, Mercury driver in twelfth.

The drivers were unanimous in saying the race was well managed and fairly conducted. There is a general belief it will be repeated next year. All found our neighbors to the south of us very friendly and cordial.

Thus closed the first Pan American road race. The first of such scope since the Paris-Madrid event at the turn of the century. Adios!

NOTE: THIS ARTICLE, ALONG WITH MANY NEWSPAPERS, LISTED TROY RUTTMAN AS DRIVER OF CAR No. 12. THIS WAS AN ERROR AND WAS NOT CORRECTED UNTIL RACE ENDED. BUD SENNETT, NOT TROY RUTTMAN, DROVE No. 12.—CLYMER.

Jack Causler

Photos OF THE Mexican Race

— GET A SELECTED SET NOW —

or you may obtain copies of any of mine appearing in this book.

— WRITE —

Jack Causler

614 S. ELM STREET   GREENSBORO, N. C.

1.—VOS OS LLEVAIS LA LANA...

(FOR YOU, THE REWARD...)

2.—...PERO NOSOTROS, LA GLORIA!...

(... FOR US, THE GLORY.)

The Race thru Italian Eyes

By PIERO TARUFFI
of Rome, Italy

(Italian Driver of Car No. 90, Winner of Fourth Place.)

Bruno Pagliai, an Italian-Mexican sportsman, made it possible for Bonetto and myself to compete in the Carrera Panamericana. He issued invitations for us to bring over two Alfa-Romeos because he wanted Italy represented by a team in this fine classic.

Also assisting us in the big expense entailed were the Italian Olivetti typewriter factory and the "Ippodromo Las Americas."

Before leaving Italy Bonetto and I discussed the regulation of the race that strictly stock tourist cars were the only ones eligible. Accordingly we entered two 2500 cc. Alfa Romeo "Freccia d'oro," which had only 90 h.p. and a maximum speed of 90 m.p.h.

When we started the long race at Juarez we soon discovered we were at a disadvantage. For the first two-thirds of the entire race we were far back in the pack. At Mexico City, my car was about one hour behind a fast Cadillac which had an engine with a cubic-inch capacity of more than twice that of our Alfas!

After leaving Mexico City the course lent itself to expert driving, with much cornering to be done. Since our cars had splendid maneuverability, Bonetto and I regained much of the time we had lost on the long straights in the first part of the race.

This greatly revived our hopes, but unhappily we began to have tire trouble. The new rough road surface and the necessity for taking the turns in skids obliged us to proceed at slower speed than would have been necessary under better conditions.

I had already had bad luck in the first leg, running out of gas. I lost more than ten minutes before I found some in a spectator's car near where I had stopped. But I was happy that my teammate, Bonetto, showed well on this leg for Alfa Romeo.

Another satisfaction I received was winning the ninth and last leg of the race to El Ocotal. Here the road was very winding and I could use my cornering experience to good advantage. This incompleted stretch of road was the most difficult of the long and interesting highway over which the Carrera Panamericana was run.

Our positions at the finish—myself in fourth place and Bonetto in eighth, was highly satisfactory for our team, since we had started with two really stock cars and arrived at the finish line in perfect condition.

The organization of the race, especially from the point of view of highway maintenance and policing, was perfect. The public were most enthusiastic, yet carefully restrained everywhere. The road was closed to other traffic, making it possible to drive as we would in a European road race. We compared it often to our own famous "Mille Miglia."

We were not completely happy about the technical verification that all the entrants were 100% stock cars. Although we certainly have no alibis for not winning, we did feel that if the officials had been a little more strict we might have bettered our final positions and won a bit more of the prize money.

It was an excellent race and our Italian team enjoyed every mile of it.

Piero Taruffi (right) and Isidoro Ceroli, first to reach Tuxtla Gutierrez, by their Alfa after arrival. They were 7th in this leg and finally got fourth place in the entire race.

A California Photographer covers the Race

By BILL MARTIN

Bill Martin, a professional magazine cameraman, was assigned to cover the race for John Mantz and Sponsor Bob Estes. I thought his unusual story would add interest to the book.—Clymer.

It seemed like a dream coming true; I was going to cover the Mexican road race!

Things were tense a few days before the start in the Johnny Mantz garage in Southern California. On the last day before our departure for Juarez, everyone rushed around frantically to complete the last details on the Lincoln for which we had such high hopes.

We finally arrived at El Paso after a sleepless night. Like the days immediately preceding the Indianapolis 500-mile race, the enchanting race atmosphere completely engulfed El Paso. Circles of fans and mechanics were starting to form in the garages and cafes around the city. Most of us were curious to see who was supposed to have the fastest car. Rumors flew thick and fast, and soon not a single one of them could be trusted. Some drivers were taking trial spins down the Pan-American highway to get the feel of the course and to test their cars at the last minute. Others did their testing in and around El Paso.

A bad dust storm almost postponed the start of the race. It blanketed all that part of the country and ranged up in the sky as high as airliners fly. Texans said it was one of the worst in history. Our crew was rather worried because Bill Stroppe, our co-driver, was aboard a plane and couldn't land. Finally he arrived the morning of the start.

The cars had been impounded the night before the start and the engines were sealed. The impound area was completely dust-covered. I noticed everywhere that drivers were putting rags in the air cleaners and radiators to keep out the dust.

But the next morning we looked out from our fifth-story hotel room across the vast plains and saw nothing but clear blue sky! The day of the start had arrived, and it was a beauty.

I roamed around the impound area getting pictures and listening to the drivers' reactions and opinions in regard to each other. Most were calm and collected, but some were concerned over last-minute mechanical troubles. Lots of them were putting masking tape on the front of their shiny new cars to keep bugs and dust from damaging the brand-new paint jobs.

It seemed as though the whole city of Juarez had turned out for the great event. At 9 a.m. the cars were routed into their starting positions, forming a huge parade. Already it was impossible to find a place to see the start. As ten o'clock approached I noticed increasing impatience among the drivers to get started on their long trek. Finally I saw the first car getting the flag, and photographed it. Then the others departed one by one.

Finally, after the last car had left we proceded down the highway in our car carrying equipment. Our first and only taste of tragedy came when we saw the wreck of Car 112, the Guatemalan entry a Lincoln Cosmopolitan which had tried to take a turn too fast and had crashed, killing the driver. A few miles later we came upon Joel Thorne's wreck. He had missed a turn and plunged down a 25-foot enbankment. Luckily no one was hurt, but the car was out of the race.

Only a few minutes later we came to still another wreck, a Mexican Ford entry which also had left the road. The driver and co-driver already had the car back on the highway and were about to continue the race. The car was practically a total loss, except the engine still was running. Thus we proceded to Chihuahua, end of the first day's run.

The weather was ideal, but finding a room was quite a problem, especially since 260 drivers and co-drivers already had arrived. We had dinner at the Victoria hotel, by all means the best in town. Rumors were flying again at dinner. No one knew exactly what place he held at that time. I talked with the French drivers and they were rather coy about the whole thing. I was especially pleased to see them because it had been rumored that both had been killed that afternoon!

We thought that our boy Mantz had finished fourth or fifth, according to our unofficial timing. After several hours we were told a banquet was to be given by the City of Chihuahua, and at ten o'clock we were to meet in the dining room of the Hilton Hotel. The gang was promptly shuttled there by the mayor of Chihuahua in his radio-equipped car. Unfortunately he didn't speak English, but we certainly appreciated his hospitality. The dinner was superb, then the day's winners were announced. A dance followed, and finally the festivities ended.

We still were without a place to stay. We heard they had beds at the race track and we hurried to catch a ride there on the back of a truck. The quarters were large and blazing with lights, so immediately I visualized another sleepless night. We were awakened very early the next morning by the lights, which were still on. The showers were cold and shaving was practically impossible. Some of the drivers were out with their cars, giving them an early-morning warm-up. After breakfast we found the starting line. It seemed like cars were lined up for miles at the start. After about half the field had started I was about done for the day, and we still had a long drive ahead of us.

Once again we started after all the field had gotten away. This was the long drive to Durango. The day was hot and plenty of entrants had tire trouble on that leg. We saw several more accidents, the most spectacular of which was the one in which Cars 29 and 27 had piled up with the finish line in sight around a turn.

Durango was fun, although the city wasn't quite as clean as Chihuahua. We arrived long after dark but still found a nice hotel room. Then we went out to see the sights. Everyone was visiting the garages of the leaders, where necessary adjustments were being made and tires changed for the extra-long leg scheduled for the next day. The spirit of the drivers was good and a fine sportsmanship now was beginning to appear.

By this point I had decided to take some aerial shots of the race and to photograph the first cars coming into Mexico City the next day. I managed to get a flight the following morning. We came in at about 8,000 feet and there was picturesque Mexico City, in all her splendor. After driving to the official platform we had only a few minutes to wait before the first car would arrive.

We received the news that Mantz was leading the field. The crowds were terrific. People were jammed at every available window and in every possible space along the route of the speedsters. I could see police motorcycles driving close to the spectators to keep them back. Finally, when the cars arrived, it was like New Year's Eve in Times Square. The drivers were almost dropping from exhaustion from the long ordeal of 650 miles at top speed in the heat.

At last we could snatch a few hours' rest before dinner, although first there was quite a lot of work to do on Mantz's car. Later a dinner was given us by the courteous Mexicans and the city was ours. But having to get up early for the next day of racing made us turn in rather early instead of sampling the gay night life.

At the start of the fourth day all the cars drove past our hotel on the main street. This was to be still another day of hazardous driving, as we were getting into the high mountains of Mexico. The cliffs on this leg were quite steep and to go off one of them was almost certain death. By now the drivers were accustomed to the hazards of road racing in Mexico and took it rather cautiously. This leg also was a test of cars because of the high altitude and mountainous terrain. The roads so far had been perfect and adaptable to high speed. We left after the last car again and ran into all kinds of traffic because of the after-race crowd.

That night we arrived late again. Oaxaca was closed tight as a drum, but some of the larger hotels still showed some activity as the race talk went on into the night. The next morning we arose extremely early as usual. The weather was just right for racing.

Our next leg was to Tuxtla and a sort of tropical climate was setting in. We drove all night, for having got a late start out of Oaxaca due to some repairs on the car we were driving. Nearing Tuxtla at 4:30 a.m. we discovered the weather was quite balmy and sticky. Of course the town was completely asleep so we pulled up to the nearest park bench and napped until dawn.

It seemed as though many drivers were making last-minute repairs on their cars for the tortuous grind ahead. Not many appreciated the real difficulties ahead, either. Finally we took off after the last man again and headed high into the mountains, where it was raining. Blooming flowers and peaceful green grass made the trip pleasant. At San Cristobal, the natives gathered around our car and stared with utter amazement.

We now were running into some winding and extremely bad parts of what you might call a road. The last 100 miles to Guatemala was unpaved and the going was tough. From the constant beat of the race cars on the road, rocks were formed into two ruts on which we travelled in comfort and speed. We were on the downhill part now and almost could see the finish.

Finally it was in sight as darkness had fallen. Arriving at last, we talked to the winners about their hardships and troubles. Our man Mantz had had tire trouble and came in on the rims to capture ninth place.

I'm sure I learned lots, and so did all the rugged individualists who took part or were camp followers in such a great race. We are all looking forward to being back again next year.

Carrera Panamericana
Photos

GLOSSY PRINTS MADE TO YOUR ORDER.
PLEASE STATE SIZE AND QUANTITY WANTED.

— WRITE —

Bill Martin

3136 Norton Ave.   Lynwood, Calif.
NEwmark 1-7814

Full Page Race Publicity was Common in Mexico Papers

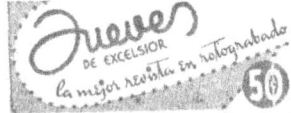

EXCELSIOR
EL PERIODICO DE LA VIDA NACIONAL
TERCERA PARTE DE LA PRIMERA SECCION
PAGINA VEINTICINCO

MEXICO, D. F.—MIERCOLES 10 DE MAYO DE 1950

Arrancó Aplausos el Carro México al Llegar en Décimo Lugar, Ayer

RODOLFO CASTAÑEDA, piloto del coche "México", que participa brillantemente en la carrera panamericana, revisando su motor en Oaxaca. Le acompañan su copiloto Palmieri y Celso Nájera.

EL PILOTO Pierre Taruffi, de Milán, Italia, llegando con su "Alfa Romeo" a la meta en la capital de Oaxaca, donde era esperado con gran ansiedad por la fama de estos carros en camino sinuoso.

EL CADILLAC número 3, de José Soto Beltrán, de Guanajuato, fotografiado por nuestro enviado especial Julio León, pocos metros antes de llegar a la meta, en la capital de Oaxaca, el día de ayer.

Resumen General de la Carrera, Hasta Tuxtla

Tremendo Aguacero Dificultó la Llegada de los Ultimos Automóviles

Por GUSTAVO DURAN DE HUERTA
enviado especial de EXCELSIOR

TUXTLA GUTIERREZ, Chis., mayo 9.—Al finalizar la quinta etapa, el Cadillac de Thomas A. Deal, número 113, de El Paso, Texas, que lleva como copiloto a Sam Cresap, se colocó a la cabeza en la carrera desde Ciudad Juárez hasta Tuxtla Gutiérrez, con un tiempo de 24 horas, 21 minutos, 7 segundos. En esta etapa de Oaxaca a Tuxtla Gutiérrez hizo 4 horas, 46 minutos, 33 segundos.

En cambio, Johnny Mantz pudiera dar la sorpresa en esta etapa ya que tiene un total de 24 horas, 49 minutos, 42 segundos.

Después están clasificados con mejores tiempos el número 32, Oldsmobile, tripulado por Hershel McGreef y copiloto Wright Ellis, el 31, Cadillac, de Al Rogers, y su hermano Ralph; el número 12, Oldsmobile, de Troy Lynn Tuttman, y copiloto John C. Balch; los tiempos de estos carros son, respectivamente: 24 horas, 29 minutos, 48 segundos; 24 horas, 48 minutos, 55 segundos y 24 horas, 53 minutos, 55 segundos.

Sigue el Nash 49, 1950, de Roy Pat Cunner y Robert Green, 24 horas, 54 minutos, 38 segundos; el 79, Oldsmobile, de Joe Littlejohnny y Luis Hawkins, con 24 horas, 54 minutos, y 57 segundos.

José Mantz Ganó la Etapa a Tuxtla Gutiérrez

En la jornada Oaxaca-Tuxtla Gutiérrez anotó mejor tiempo José Mantz, que a pesar de venir enfermo hizo 4 horas, 35 minutos, 56 segundos. Sigue el carro número 6 de Tommy L. Francis y Jimmie Crum, con 4 horas, 39 minutos, 7 segundos; después, el carro 113 de Hershel McGreef, con 4 horas, 40 minutos, 33 segundos; el 19, Delahaye, de Jean Trevoux y André Maricet, con 4 horas, 40 minutos, 54 segundos; carro 75, con 4 horas, 41 minutos, 39 segundos; carro 77, de Jesús Vales y Adolfo Dueñas, del Estado de México, con 4 horas, 42 minutos, 13 segundos; carro 80, tripulado por Pietro Taruffi e Isidoro Cerolli con 4 horas, 46 minutos, 18 segundos; y el 41, con 4 horas, 49 minutos, 24 segundos, tripulado por Edmund Kas y Cesare Contessoto.

En la meta estuvieron el gobernador del Estado, general Francisco J. Grajales, el oficial mayor de la Secretaría de Comunicaciones, licenciado Guillermo Ostos, y las autoridades locales.

Una multitud se congregó allí y estuvo aplaudiendo a los corredores que iban llegando a la meta. En otra tribuna estuvieron grupos de entusiastas muchachas que con sus gritos, porras y aplausos dieron chorrido al acto.

Los automóviles participantes en la carrera Ciudad Juárez-Ocotal llegaron a esta ciudad en el siguiente orden: 90, 32, 32, 79, 103, 39, 19, 71 y 46.

El Coche "México" Llegó en Décima Lugar

El coche "México" llegó en décima lugar y arrancó una verdadera ovación a su llegada.

El carro número 68, que había recuperado el liderazgo en la etapa anterior, quedó eliminado y llegó a la meta remolcado por una grúa, al final de la carrera.

Otros carros eliminados son: el 63, por fallas en el motor; el 45, por voladura de una llanta; el 44, por fallas del motor, el 25, por descompostura; el 81 por una voladura; en la más milagrosa de sus pilotos no resultaron es un precipicio. El 93 chocó contra un talud y quedó destrozado; al número 8 se le quemaron los frenos en Ciudad Ixtepec, Oax.

El presidente de la diputación local, señor Librado de la Torre Grajales, nos informó que por decreto de la Legislatura del Estado, El Ocotal se llamará, a partir de mañana, Ciudad Cuauhtémoc.

El gobernador del Estado descubrirá una placa y leerá el decreto respectivo, ya que el anhelo de los chiapanecos es seguir en plan mexicanista.

Averías en el Automóvil de Bennetto

Felice Bennetto, piloto del carro 103 nos dijo que al terminar la carrera irá en motocicleta hasta Comitán donde abordará un avión para la ciudad de México para continuar de allí a Nueva York y después a Londres a fin de participar en la carrera por el Gran Premio de Europa que se inicia el 13 de mayo. En este evento participan los mejores corredores del Viejo Continente. Indicó que el corredor mexicano Estrada Menocal tiene extraordinaria técnica para tomar las curvas y podría competir con buen éxito en Europa. Hizo elogios también para todos los demás corredores mexicanos.

Agregó Bennetto que el año entrante, si se organiza un evento similar volverá a competir, pues considera que esta carrera con más organización y técnica, será la más importante del mundo.

Para terminar dijo que difícilmente podría llegar a ocupar el primer lugar en la carrera debido a las muchas averías que ha tenido el carro que tripula, desde la salida de Ciudad Juárez.

Gesto Patriótico de Oscar López de Llergo

Oscar López de Llergo, piloto mexicano del carro número dos, pudiendo haber ganado una o dos etapas cuando menos, prefirió renunciar al triunfo y escoltar al destrozado carro "México" para auxiliarlo en caso de un nuevo accidente. Corre peligro el copiloto Peinado; Ruy se le zafó una rueda delantera y estuvo a punto de perecer en el accidente. Sin embargo, afirma que seguirá en la misión de ayer, que se ha impuesto.

De Oaxaca salieron 75 carros. El 48 no salió por falta de frenos y el 112 no se presentó. Quedaron eliminados diez más.

En breves palabras con los corredores: Mantz dijo que le gustaría correr el camino a El Ocotal que presenta grandes obstáculos por las lluvias; Sterling dijo que ha tenido una serie de averías frecuentemente en el embrague y en los frenos y reitero que es falso fundamentalmente en el cruce y en los frenos y reitero que es falso que tiene sus cámaras con gas especial, como se asegura. Hoy, se vió precisado a correr varios kilómetros con una mano en el freno; José Soto Beltrán del carro número 3 dijo: "Vamos haciendo lo posible por llegar a la meta". Luis Leal Solares, del carro número 45 que ocupa magnífico lugar, dijo haber sufrido tres accidentes de importancia a lo largo de la carretera. Dijo que no le importa ganar el premio sino clasificar en la tabla general.

Tormenta en Territorio de Oaxaca

Los pilotos Jesús Nava González, Octavio Anza, Leopoldo Almanza y otros mexicanos más, estuvieron de acuerdo en que el principal obstáculo que han tenido para desarrollar buenas velocidades es la mala calidad de las llantas.

Los pilotos sudamericanos dijeron que en su país, la carrera adolecía de defectos de organización técnica y que ello le restó calidad al evento.

Debido al vendaval que se ha desatado en esta región, los aviones al servicio de la Secretaría de Comunicaciones, que llevan a los corresponsales de la carrera y a periodistas, sufrieron desperfectos al ser arrojados un sobre otro por el viento. Por eso, las informaciones se ven precisadas a utilizar otros medios de transporte, para seguir los incidentes de la carrera.

Como medida preventiva para la seguridad de los corredores, la carrera, expidieron un boletín que se dió a conocer antes de la salida de Oaxaca, indicando que en un lugar denominado "Parcinla" (kilómetro 573) el camino tiene grandes acabamientos por las fuertes lluvias. Algunos de los deslaves tienen una extensión de cinco metros, y están marcados con piedras "fanlexpas" entre los kilómetros 820 al 860. También en los kilómetros 925 al 960 hay deslaves que se señalaron con banderas rojas.

La tormenta que azotó ayer en territorio de Oaxaca, interrumpió las líneas telefónicas y telegráficas.

OTRO ASPECTO del carro "México", piloteado por Rodolfo Castañeda y copiloteado por Palmieri, al llegar a Oaxaca, minutos después de haber traspuesto la meta, tras de un rápido viaje.

EL LICENCIADO José Vasconcelos, dando la salida al automóvil número 103, de Pierre Taruffi, de Milán, Italia, en la ciudad de Oaxaca, rumbo a Tuxtla Gutiérrez, Chis., el día de ayer.

UN ASPECTO de la salida de los primeros automóviles, en Oaxaca, Oax., rumbo a Tuxtla Gutiérrez, el día de ayer, para cubrir la penúltima etapa de la gran carrera panamericana, que hoy termina.

Censura la SCOP a los Propaladores de una Falsa Versión Acerca del Estado del Camino

TUXTLA GUTIERREZ, Chis. ... [text illegible] ...

Regreso Inmediato de El Ocotal, Pues no hay Gasolina, y Tendrán que ir Bien Abastecidos

TUXTLA GUTIERREZ, Chis., mayo 9.—Los competidores de la carrera se hallan disgustados por habérseles notificado que tendrán que cargar suficiente gasolina para ida y regreso hasta El Ocotal, en vista de que en este lugar no hay fuente de abastecimiento.

La opinión unánime de los corredores es que el carro número 19 de Francia es el triunfador más viable, en virtud de que se halla en magníficas condiciones y resistirá con buen éxito la última prueba.

...

AHORRE 5%
EN TODAS SUS COMPRAS
CON LOS CHEQUES QUE
NOVEDADES LE OBSEQUIA

NOVEDADES
EL MEJOR DIARIO DE MEXICO
CUARTA SECCION MIEMBRO DE LA PRENSA ASOCIADA VALE 25 CENTAVOS

Edición Especial de la Carretera Panamericana

Nº 3,813 - Año XV ★ PRESIDENTE Y GERENTE GENERAL: ROMULO O'FARRILL, SR. ★ MEXICO, D. F. LUNES 22 DE MAYO DE 1950 ★ DIRECTOR: Lic. Alejandro Quijano ★ Registrado como artículo de segunda clase el 21 de noviembre de 1935, en la Administración de Correos de México, D. F.

Significación Nacional e Internacional de la Gran Carretera Panamericana

Repercusiones Económico-Turísticas de las Carreteras Central y Cristóbal Colón.-La Obra del Comité Nacional de Caminos Vecinales.-Afirmación de la Unidad Nacional y Estímulo de la Amistad y Cooperación Internacional

Pasada la efervescencia de la Carrera Panamericana, que logro enajenar el interés y entusiasmo del pueblo de México y también del de Guatemala los Estados Unidos, es interesante analizar las repercusiones económicas que las dos nuevas rutas acarrearán a nuestro país.

A diferencia de la Carretera de Laredo, que al abrirse al tránsito no contaba sino con una Carretera de conexión, la de Saltillo, la Carretera Central Ciudad Juárez-México, surgen al servicio con grandes caminos alimentadores, algunos de primera clase. Estos caminos son los de Chihuahua-Cuauhtémoc, La Zarca-Reynosa, Durango-Mazatlán, Aguascalientes-Ojuelos, Silao-Guanajuato y Salamanca-Morelia. La Cristóbal Colón, a su vez, tiene ya en servicio ramales de alguna importancia como los constituidos por las Carreteras Huajuapan-Miahuatlán, Juchitán-Las Flores, Escopetazo-El Bosque. El Comité Nacional de Caminos Vecinales emprende la construcción de una red completa, tributaria de la Carretera Central, en la Zona Lagunera de Durango y otro sistema vial, de tipo complementario, en el Estado de Chiapas, y el cual quedara ligado a la Carretera Cristóbal Colón. Estos dos sistemas de Caminos Vecinales representan una inversión de $18.000,000.00 que permitirán estimular la economía regional de Durango y Chiapas, los cuales podrán mover su producción no solo dentro de los límites estatales, sino hacia el Norte y el Sur, aprovechando las rutas troncales nuevas. Esto es un factor muy importante puesto que, para que nuestra red troncal de Carreteras nacionales y estatales de 24,000 kilómetros pueda rendir los efectos económicos que justifiquen aun mas las fuertes inversiones que ha requerido, el país necesita cuando menos 100,000 kilómetros de caminos alimentadores o vecinales.

El efecto básico de los caminos, se cifra en la posibilidad de transportar mercancías de los centros de producción a los de consumo. Así, los focos industriales de Chihuahua, Torreón, Leon, Salamanca, México, y Puebla, situados de Norte a Sur a lo largo de las Carreteras Central y Cristóbal Colón, podrán surtir las necesidades de los centros de consumo situados a lo largo de las rutas, prolongándose la distribución al través de los caminos federales, estatales y vecinales que de ellas se proyectan. Como ejemplo para ilustrar este punto, baste señalar que Petróleos Mexicanos, al inaugurar proximamente su refinería de Salamanca, se propone distribuir por carretera gasolina y otros destilados hacia el Norte, hasta Torreon; al Sur, hasta Uruapan y Morelia; al Occidente, hasta Guadalajara y al Oriente hasta Dolores Hidalgo. Esto quiere decir que la nueva carretera permitirá, con sus ramales, distribuir productos petroleros en una distancia de 225 kilómetros del centro de producción, hacia los cuatro puntos cardinales, con notorio alivio para el sobrecargado sistema ferroviario; la escasez de gasolina quedara pues, resuelta dentro del área de servicio de la nueva carretera.

Un aspecto no menos importante es el aumento de las areas de cultivo agricola, lo que equivale al aumento de la producción. Todo este intercambio promovido por los caminos, representa a su vez un aumento considerable en la capacidad de compra del pueblo, pues es bien sabido que cerca de un 70 por ciento de nuestra capacidad agrícola e industrial, se desenvuelve en la vastísima porción de nuestro territorio ligado por las nuevas carreteras y las rutas de intercomunicación existentes.

El turismo presenta perspectivas igualmente prometedoras, sobre todo el de procedencia internacional. La Dirección General de Turismo estima, conservadoramente a nuestro juicio, que el año de 1951 será sin duda el año turístico cumbre de Mexico en su historia, con la visita de 400,000 turistas extranjeros, de los cuales 60 por ciento, cuando menos, harán el viaje por carretera.

En el año 1949, según fuentes insospechables, nos visitaron 314.000 turistas que dejaron en el país mil millones de pesos. Cuando solamente había una ruta carretera de acceso, el turista norteamericano no repetía el viaje frecuentemente, por conocer la ruta y no someterse a la tensión del camino montañoso de Laredo, una y otra vez. Las nuevas vias permiten establecer viajes de circuito; conocer diferentes y maravillosos paisajes y ciudades, extendiéndose la posibilidad de recreo turístico hacia regiones como las de Oaxaca, Tehuantepec y Chiapas, de excepcional fascinación para el turista, especialmente el norteamericano.

Con lo anterior queremos decir que no solamente aumentara el número de turistas que podríamos llamar "primerizos", sino que muchos de los que han hecho uno o dos viajes por carretera a la ciudad de México lo repetirán ahora inducidos por la novedad de los atractivos.

La publicidad que dió a México la Carrera Panamericana con su cauda de emociones y las cuantiosas inversiones que en publicidad desplegada y de gacetillas emprende ahora la Dirección General de Turismo en escala sin precedentes en los Estados Unidos, complementan el esfuerzo de nuestro país por desarrollar esta importante actividad económica.

Cuando Guatemala termine su tramo faltante de 40 kilómetros para entroncar con El Ocotal, quedarán unidos por carretera Alaska y Canadá con los Estados Unidos, México, Guatemala, El Salvador, Honduras y Nicaragua hasta la frontera con Costa Rica, pues sólo falta ese pequeño tramo para que quede establecido el tránsito en dicha vasta porción del Continente. Cuando ello ocurra no sería de extrañar que a Mexico viniesen, como meta de su viaje o en tránsito, unos dos millones de turistas, con lo que podríamos alcanzar y aun batir la marca del Canadá, que es el país extranjero que mas turistas norteamericanos recibe en el mundo.

Las repercusiones espirituales de nuestro sistema vial panamericano, podrían sintetizarse en esta premisa: Afirmación de la unidad nacional y estímulo del ideal panamericano de amistad y cooperación internacionales.

EL TRAZO PERFECTO de la Carretera Panamericana, en su tramo correspondiente a nuestro país, fué admiración de propios y extraños durante la Carrera Panamericana. Principalmente los participantes extranjeros, hicieron grandes elogios del camino, diciendo que era difícil que en cualquier otra parte del mundo pudiera existir camino tan bien hecho y de tanta belleza.

Una Madeja de Circunstancias Determinó el Resultado de la Gran Carrera Panamericana

Fallas Mecánicas e Inexperiencia, y un Gran Sentido Deportivo de los Mexicanos

"Mientras no se cuente con datos precisos acerca de la forma como se produjeron los más notables accidentes registrados durante la reciente gran Carrera Panamericana México, resulta lógico que no sea fácil señalar las causas más probables que los determinaron. Para poder hacerlo, será necesario esperar los reportes oficiales acerca de los accidentes que se produjeron", nos dijo al ser interrogado al respecto, don Rómulo O'Farrill, señor, gerente y presidente de NOVEDADES y, como es sabido, reconocida autoridad en materia automovilística. "En una competencia, como la que acabamos de presenciar, los accidentes pueden obedecer principalmente a tres factores: impericia del piloto; falla mecánica del carro, o imprudencia en los espectadores del evento", continuo.

Por lo que se refiere al último de estos tres aspectos, cabe subrayar que en Mexico, no obstante que puede considerarse al pueblo como impreparado para espectáculos de esta naturaleza, en los cuales un descuido aparentemente insignificante puede costar la vida del imprudente así como la de los pilotos que desafían el peligro en la competencia, resulta encomiable que no se haya producido ningun accidente fatal de este tipo.

Puede afirmarse que el pueblo mexicano —cosa impresionante— respondió ampliamente a las exhortaciones hechas para respetar los reglamentos formulados, los cuales fueron observados fielmente, con un alto sentido de responsabilidad popular.

En síntesis, los accidentes que surgieron, aunque trágicos y dolorosos, fueron insignificantes en su porcentaje con los que suelen producirse en condiciones semejantes, en otras partes del mundo.

FALLAS MECANICAS Y PROBABLES CAUSAS

De índole diversa y variada pueden ser las fallas mecánicas en competencias de esta clase. Desde una simple ponchadura de llantas hasta la descompostura total del motor, sin que se olvide que la suerte es factor determinante, ya que se trata en su mayoría de carros no construidos para alcanzar altas velocidades y sostenerlas durante mucho tiempo. La avería que en muchos años no se ha registrado, puede producirse en los momentos mismos de la competencia.

Con frecuencia aconteció, que las altas velocidades sostenidas causaran desperfectos irreparables. Así ocurrió con las llantas. Solamente cuando se utilizaron neumáticos especiales, los corredores no sufrieron reventones, con la consiguiente pérdida de tiempo, ocurriendo también que hubo competidores que por no disponer de suficientes llantas de refacción quedaron descalificados en determinada etapa.

ADITAMENTOS ESPECIALES

Positivamente, se puede afirmar que algunos de los carros que intervinieron tenían aditamentos especiales en sus motores que permitieron el desarrollo de mayores velocidades, consiguiendo así considerable ventaja.

Desde luego, como antes hemos asentado, la mayor parte de los carros no armados en el país, trajeron llantas especiales para gran velocidad, como las empleadas en los automóviles de carrera.

No obstante, nuestra opinión, es la de que no estamos en el momento oportuno para ahundar sobre el particular. Hay que reconocer que fué un sinnúmero de circunstancias que no se previeron debidamente, ya que es la primera vez que México se lanza a organizar justas deportivas de tal magnitud. La poca experiencia fué causa de los principales errores en que se incurrió.

Empero los yerros cometidos se empequeñecen y no restan brillantez a la magnitud del espectáculo ofrecido, que será inolvidable. La atención del mundo estuvo fija en nuestro país y la obra caminera del Gobierno de México está hoy ya fuera de toda discusión.

"La unión por carretera, de Ciudad Juárez a El Ocotal, es una realidad de unificación entre los pueblos de América, que se agigantó con la simbólica prueba automovilística corrida entre esos dos puntos limítrofes de la República Mexicana. Ello es suficiente para que a los triunfadores se les entregue sin reservas los premios ofrecidos, y para que se les reconozca su triunfo sin ambages".

CONTRASTE DE LOS TRIUNFADORES CON LOS PERDEDORES

Desde luego, admitiendo que el factor suerte fué determinante, y que es obvio esperar que un motor

SIGUE EN LA PAGINA 11, COL. 3.

EL "CHE" ESTRADA MENOCAL sorprendio a propios y extraños convirtiéndose en una de las figuras mas relevantes de la Carrera Panamericana México. Su técnica en el camino sinuoso, levantó los más calidos elogios de aquellos a quienes venció en el tramo mas difícil de la competencia: México a Oaxaca.

La Brillante Participación de los Pilotos Mexicanos en la Etapa Difícil de la Carrera

Entre los vericuetos de la montaña chiapaneca, estuvo a punto de encontrar la muerte un piloto norteamericano. Su vehículo había dado aparatosa voltereta y al ser transportado hacia el puesto de socorros de El Ocotal, todavía tuvo tiempo este automovilista, para expresar su admiración por los pilotos mexicanos. Dijo: Son verdaderos valientes del volante. Se trataba de Tommy Frances, tripulante del automóvil número seis.

Horas despues, tras la meta final otro piloto extranjero, el italiano Bonetto, dedicó los más cálidos elogios a la técnica de todos los pilotos mexicanos, particularmente en terreno sinuoso, y señalo a Estrada Menocal como auténtico as del volante, por la forma en que junto con su compañero, Fernando Razo Maciel, cubrió la etapa México-Puebla.

Y durante el desenvolvimiento de la parte más difícil de la carrera, el tramo de México a Oaxaca, se tuvo oportunidad de comprobar un hecho: los mexicanos ganaron terreno, arrebataron lugares y fijaron marcas de velocidad en los trechos más peligrosos, pero el tiempo ganado hubo de perderse en la reposición de un neumático que se volaba bajo la presión de la velocidad. Puede dividirse la actuación de los mexicanos en tres clasificaciones. Primeramente los que corrieron siempre al máximo de velocidad y realizaron maravillosas proezas sobre el pavimento. El "che" Estrada Menocal, Fernando del Razo, triunfadores de la etapa más difícil. Después los que como el camionero McGriff, calcularon punto por punto la trayectoria y terminaron el recorrido sin ningun accidente. Luis Leal Solares que conquistó un lugar de honor para México al calificar entre los diez primeros sitios. Y por ultimo, aquéllos que corrieron solo con el corazón: Rodolfo Castañeda a bordo del México, Oscar López Liergo y César Peinado, a bordo del número dos.

Por todos estos méritos, los valientes mexicanos merecen un lugar aparte en los anales de la carrera y al lado del triunfador McGriff cabe mencionar la técnica de Estrada Menocal que sorprendió a los pilotos italianos en el camino sinuoso y metiendo la nariz del automóvil por la parte interior de la curva al momento que su contrincante entraba por el carril exterior, logró rebasar a varios corredores precisamente en aquellos lugares donde el peligro era mayor.

Y al lado del cálculo preciso de Deal también debe ser mencionado Luis Leal Solares que llegó hasta El Ocotal en octavo lugar sin tener un solo accidente. El mérito de Leal Solares radica en que cubrió una carrera sin tener la experiencia de sus opositores en lo que toca al acondicionamiento mecánico de su automóvil, equipo de neumáticos apropiado y otros cien detalles que hacen posible un triunfo como el de McGriff o de Deal.

Fernando del Razo, tiene un lugar preponderante en esta carrera, el cual sólo se compara con el del agente de comercio Sterling que durante dos etapas se mantuvo en primer lugar. Fernando del Razo rompió el record de velocidad en el tramo de México a Puebla.

Y por ultimo Rodolfo Castañeda, luchó contra viento, lluvia, calor y frío, para hacer que el automóvil México llegara hasta la ansiada meta. Sus proezas ya fueron relatadas ampliamente por los diarios, pero NOVEDADES está en condiciones de asegurar, por haberlo seguido desde un automóvil de carrera, que en cada curva en cada tramo recto expuso la vida. Y también debemos mencionar al piloto Oscar Lopez Liergo, sin duda alguna una de las figuras de más colorido en esta sensacional competencia.

U. S. Newspapers gave daily Reports

Mexican Paces Road Race

CHIHUAHUA, Mexico, May 5. —(AP)—Gregorio Pirez of Puebla, Mexico, drove the first stock car to finish the starting lap of Mexico's road race tod...

Henry Bradley o... second to cross... here on the 228-m... Juarez on the frontie...

The first car to... not necessarily win th... they started one min... The shortest time will...

The official results p... Ruttman of South Gate... third to arrive, followed... Davalos of Mexico City, first car to start.

Another United States d... Lou Figaro of Inglewood, C... started fourteenth and finis... fifth. A Mexican car finish... sixth and Tommy Francis of S... Gabriel, Calif., was seventh.

Race headquarters reported... that the car entered by the... Mexican government turned over twice. The occupants were not injured. The car was righted and continued both times.

Two other Mexican cars turned over during the first lap, and two...

89 Drivers Racing Across Mexico Start Mountainous Lap

MEXICO CITY, May 8. (AP)—Tom Deal of El Paso, Texas, led 89 stock car racers into the mos... mountainous lap of Mexico's bor... der-to-border road race today.

Deal left the starting line... the road to Puebla promptly... 10:30 a.m. EST. A minute... hind him, Johnny Mantz of from... Beach, Calif., took off...

Deal started first be... won the second of yeste... two laps. Mantz, who le... the general classification, y... ond in the Sunday lap.

The racers have cove... kilometers (1295 miles)... U.S. frontier in three d... still have 1307 kilom... miles) to the finish Guatemalan border.

Italian Tops Mexico Race

TAPANATEPEC, Mex., May 9. —(AP)—An Italian driver was again in the lead as the Mexico road race cars passed Tapanatepec, 168 kilometers (112 miles) short of today's finish at Tuxtla Gutierrez.

Piero Taruffi, who started first this morning, lost the lead... Jose Estrada Menocal of Me... after about 200 kilometers (... miles). The Mexican led for a... other 320 kilometers (200 mile... before Taruffi again went in... the lead.

Estrada Menocal was secon... as the racers passed here, wit... another Italian, Felice Bonett... third. Mexicans were fourth, fift... and sixth.

The United States drivers who are still in the first five places in the general classification appeared to be driving more cautiously today and were well back.

The first American, Bill Sterling of El Paso, Tex., had a 40-minute advantage over the first Mexican in the general standings when they started this morning. Sterling was 12 minutes ahead of the second man, Herschel McGriff of Portland, Ore...

Sterling's tactics appeared to be to save his car by careful driving and rely on his accumulated advantage to win. A win in today's lap would give him only 2000 pesos ($231), whereas if he stays in the rac... has...

Sennett 5th, Mantz 9th after 4 laps

OAXACA, Mexico, May 9.-(U.P.)- William Sterling and Thomas Deal, two El Paso, Tex., drivers, led the unofficial general classifications in the Pan-American stock car race today after four laps of the 2178-mile grind.

Sterling, who lost time on the last two laps after setting a blistering pace at the start, led the unofficial classification with a time of 19 hours, 40 minutes, 43 seconds.

Hershel McGriff of Portland, Ore., was next with 19:41.01; Al Rogers of Colorado Springs, Colo., was fourth with 19:53.53; followed by Bud Sennett of Los ... th 19:58.07.

...rivers' positions: ... of Corsicana, ... Littlejohn of ... th; Johnny ...if., ninth; ...ater, Tex., ...loit, Wis., ...Manhattan ...and Bill ...ach, Fla.,

Mantz leads road race

MEXICO CITY, May 8.-(U.P.)- Veteran auto racer Johnny Mantz of Los Angeles, with the "luck of the road," held first place in the unofficial over-all classifications of the 2178 miles long Pan American auto race today.

Mantz negotiated the torturous winding mountain roads between Durango and Mexico City yesterday in 6 hours, 54 minutes, 47 seconds. His unofficial average speed for the 608 miles was 87 mph. It was a considerable drop from the 97 mph average for the first leg of the race. Driving a Lincoln, Mantz had a total time of 14 hours, 11 minutes.

William Sterling of El Paso, in a Cadillac, got a bad break today when, after starting out of order due to an official mix-up in Durango, he was flagged down by the federal highway police because of an accident ahead. He had been running in first place in time classifications.

Sterling was held up 32 minutes by the police while the wreckage was cleared from a narrow bridge. The committee restored the 32 minutes and calculated Sterling's time at 7 hours, 9 mins., 5 secs. for the day, to give him a total of 14:22.33 and, apparently, second place.

Sterling in Lead Again

MEXICO CITY, May 9.—William Sterling of El Paso, Texas, regained first place today in Mexico's... derby,... from... 19 hou... Ste... Mantz... held... fifth... City,... coln,... place...

He... Ore.,... Th... yest... Fre... Barto... ent j... nerta... accid... but... C. D... Dani... Figa... and... cuts.

Yanks win 1st 4 spots in stock race

EL OCOTAL, Mexico, May 11.- (UP).Four American drivers turned...

win-... the... of... n the... and... ough,... uarez... y of... riving... edged... , who... town... Griff... was...

mmy... ightly... south... is co-... Demo-... d As-... es, es-... d their... car, however, and resumed the race.

Bud Sennett led Southern California contenders by coming in sixth in 28:02.21; John Mantz of Inglewood finished in the first 10. Only 56 cars finished the race. One driver, Enrique Hachmeister of Guatemala, was killed.

McGriff Triumphs

EL OCOTAL, Mexico, May 10. —(AP)—Hershel McGriff of Portland, Ore., won the six-day 2178-mile Mexican race for stock cars today by a margin of one minute, 19 seconds.

Tommy Francis of San Gabriel, Calif., was reported badly injured when his Ford turned over on the final lap.

Observers along the route sent word ahead, however, that his co-driver, Jimmy Crum, was bringing the car into El Ocotal. This contradicted a previous radio report that both were killed.

BORDER TO BORDER

McGriff's 1950 Oldsmobile crossed the finish line here on the Guatemalan frontier with a time of 27 hours, 34 minutes, 25 seconds from the start at Ciudad Juarez on the United States border.

Tom Deal of El Paso, Tex., drove his Cadillac from border to border in 27:35.41. Ray Pat Connor of El Paso was third in a Nash. His time was 27:50.35.

McGriff wins $17,381. Deal's second prize is worth $11,570. Connor gets $5785.

McGriff's time averaged 89 miles per hour over flat, straight desert highway, curving mountain roads and a final tough lap of washed-out gravel.

Other Californians to finish were Johnny Mantz, Long Beach, seventh; Edmundo Kasold, Huntington Park, ninth, and Jack McAfee, Manhattan Beach, 10th.

Interesting Information

WHERE ENTRIES CAME FROM

From the UNITED STATES -- 59 from 42 towns in 15 states

CALIFORNIA -- 20, including 4 each from Los Angeles and Inglewood, 2 from Pomona, and 1 each from Alhambra, Bakersfield, Broderick, Hollywood, Huntington Park, Idyllwild, Manhattan Beach, North Hollywood, Norwalk, San Francisco

TEXAS -- 13, including 4 from El Paso, 2 each from Lubbock and San Antonio, and 1 each from Corsicana, Houston, Jacksonville, Port Isabel, Shallowater

ILLINOIS -- 4, including 2 from Chicago, and 1 each from Bensenville and Des Plaines

MICHIGAN -- 3, including 2 from Detroit and 1 from Grand Blanc

NEW MEXICO -- 3, including 1 each from Anthony, Carlsbad, Clovis

NEW YORK -- 3, with 1 each from Glen Aubry, New York, Schenectady

COLORADO -- 2, both from Colorado Springs

GEORGIA -- 2, both from Atlanta

OHIO -- 2, including 1 each from Columbus and Mount Gilead

OREGON -- 2, both from Portland

And 1 each from ARIZONA (Willcox); FLORIDA (Daytona Beach); NEVADA (Las Vegas); SOUTH CAROLINA (Spartanburg); WISCONSIN (Beloit)

From MEXICO -- 57 from 20 states

DISTRITO FEDERAL (Mexico City) -- 33

JALISCO (Guadalajara) -- 4

PUEBLA (Puebla) -- 2

GUANAJUATO (1 each from Celaya and Guanajuato) -- 2

And 1 each from BAJA CALIFORNIA (Lower California, Northern District); CAMPECHE; CHIAPAS; CHIHUAHUA; DURANGO; GUERRERO; MEXICO STATE; MICHOACAN; MORELOS; NUEVO LEON; QUERETARO; QUINTANA ROO; SAN LUIS POTOSI; TAMAULIPAS; VERACRUZ and ZACATECAS.

From other countries -- 16 from 8 countries

COLOMBIA -- 4; VENEZUELA -- 4; ITALY -- 2; PERU -- 2;

And 1 each from FRANCE; GUATEMALA; REPUBLIC of CHINA; EL SALVADOR

CARS ENTERED BY MAKE AND YEAR

Make	'37	'38	'39	'40	'41	'42	'43	'47	'48	'49	'50	Total	Finished a	b	c
GM															
Chevrolet	--	--	--	--	--	--	--	--	1	--	3	4	4	0	4
Oldsmobile	--	--	--	--	--	--	--	--	--	3	10	13	9	0	9
Buick	--	1	--	1	1	1	--	--	3	3	7	17*	3	3	6
Cadillac	--	1	1	--	1	1	--	1	1	8	8	22*	8	0	8
FORD															
Ford	--	1	--	--	--	--	--	--	--	3	4	8	3	2	5
Mercury	--	--	--	--	--	--	--	--	--	1	10	11	4	1	5
Lincoln	--	--	--	--	--	--	--	--	1	12	3	16	6	1	7
CHRYSLER															
De Soto	--	--	--	--	--	--	--	--	--	2	--	2*	0	1	1
Chrysler	--	--	--	--	--	--	--	--	1	--	2	3*	2	0	2
Other U.S.															
Hudson	1	--	--	--	--	--	--	1	--	2	4	9	1	0	1
Nash	--	--	--	--	--	--	--	--	--	2	6	8	2	2	4
Packard	--	--	--	--	--	--	--	--	2	5	--	7	0	0	0
Studebaker	--	--	--	--	--	--	--	--	--	--	4	4	2	1	3
Cord	1	--	--	--	--	--	--	--	--	--	--	1	0	0	0
EUROPEAN															
Alfa Romeo	--	--	--	--	--	--	--	--	--	--	2	2	2	0	2
Delahaye	--	--	--	--	--	--	--	--	--	1	--	1	1	0	1
Jaguar	--	--	--	--	--	--	--	--	1	--	--	1	0	0	0
Lago Talbot	--	1	--	--	--	--	--	--	--	--	--	1	0	0	0
Hotchkiss	--	--	--	--	--	--	--	--	--	1	--	1	0	0	0
Totals	2	3	2	1	2	1	--	5	8	42	64	131	47	11	58

* -- Two 1950 Cadillacs, a 1949 Buick, a 1949 De Soto and a 1950 Chrysler were entered but failed to start the race. One entry was paid but failed to inscribe a car or a crew, and of course did not start the race. Thus 126 cars actually set out from the starting line.

Under finished, 'a' refers to cars which finished within the legal time on every leg and were classified for the race as a whole; 'b' refers to cars which were disqualified in one or more legs, mostly for exceeding the legal time, and therefore were not classified for the race as a whole, but nevertheless finished the last leg under their own power; 'c' refers to the total number of cars which crossed the finish line under their own power.

Interesting Information

OFFICIAL AVERAGE SPEEDS OF WINNERS

IN MEXICAN PAN-AMERICAN RACE

	First		Second		Third	
	Car no. Speed		Car no. Speed		Car no. Speed	
Entire Race	52	78.421 Oldsmobile '50	113	77.362 Cadillac '50	21	76.440 Cadillac '49
First Leg	68	100.425 Cadillac '50	36	99.591 Cadillac '50	38	98.991 Lincoln '49
Second Leg	55	95.885 Cadillac '50	38	94.614 Lincoln '49	68	93.888 Cadillac '50
Third Leg	68	85.993 Cadillac '50	38	85.150 Lincoln '49	113	84.199 Cadillac '50
Fourth Leg	81	90.133 Cadillac '49	68	89.980 Cadillac '50	38	89.710 Lincoln '49
Fifth Leg	113	93.169 Cadillac '50	38	89.078 Lincoln '49	118	87.278 Cadillac '49
Sixth Leg	44	79.777 Packard '49	8	79.336 Packard '49	118	78.715 Cadillac '49
Seventh Leg	103	68.129 Alfa Romeo '50	8	67.584 Packard '49	32	66.873 Mercury '50
Eighth Leg	38	73.032 Lincoln '49	6	72.117 Ford '50	113	71.752 Cadillac '50
Ninth Leg	90	57.153 Alfa Romeo '50	103	56.664 Alfa Romeo '50	52	55.533 Oldsmobile '50

Speeds are given in miles and thousandths of a mile per hour.

HOW THEY DROPPED OUT

Leg	Number Legally in Race at Start	Number Disqualified for Prizes	Number Legally at the Finish	Disqualified Cars Still after Leg Prizes	Total of Cars at Finish of Leg
1	132	19	113	—	113
2	113	3	110	3	113
3	110	7	103	2	105
4	103	11	92	1	93
5	92	4	88	2	90
6	88	12	76	3	79
7	76	4	72	3	75
8	72	12	60	3	63
9	60	13	47	11	58

NUMBER FROM EACH COUNTRY IN RUNNING AFTER END OF EACH LEG

	U.S.	Mex.	Venez.	Colom.	Italy	Peru	Fran.	Salv.	China	Guat.
Start	59	57	4	4	2	2	1	1	1	1
Leg 1	53	46	4	4	2	2	1	0	1	0
Leg 2	50	46	4	4	2	2	1	0	1	0
Leg 3	48	41	4	4	2	2	1	0	1	0
Leg 4	42	38	3	4	2	1	1	0	1	0
Leg 5	38	38	3	4	2	1	1	0	1	0
Leg 6	31	33	3	4	2	1	1	0	1	0
Leg 7	28	32	3	4	2	1	1	0	1	0
Leg 8	22	27	3	3	2	1	1	0	1	0
Leg 9	13	23	3	3	2	1	1	0	1	0

(Plus 7 disqualified U.S. cars and 4 disqualified Mexican cars which crossed final finish line.)

Complete Leg-by-Leg Statistics

Leg One...

CAR No.	LEG TIME	POSITION IN LEG
68	2:19:12	1
36	2:20:22	2
38	2:21:13	3
12	2:24:33	4
55	2:24:47	5
111	2:24:49	6
52	2:24:59	7
45	2:25:05	8
89	2:25:16	9
49	2:25:22	10
88	2:25:55	11
37	2:26:04	12
71	2:26:26	13
79	2:26:28	14
49	2:26:50	15
63	2:27:17	16
78	2:28:04	17 (tie)
75	2:28:46	18 (tie)
5	2:28:46	18 (tie)
21	2:28:57	20
81	2:29:03	21
19	2:29:27	22
20	2:29:27	23
66	2:29:38	24
62	2:29:50	25
113	2:30:05	26
39	2:30:53	27
77	2:32:08	28
42	2:33:09	29
42	2:33:33	30
8	2:34:12	31
118	2:35:30	32
25	2:35:53	33
6	2:36:15	34
51	2:36:31	35
96	2:37:49	36
35	2:37:54	37
14	2:38:07	38
103	2:38:16	39
1	2:38:22	40
129	2:38:36	41 (tie)
110	2:38:50	42 (tie)
54	2:37:03	43
123	2:37:13	44
82	2:37:38	45
59	2:38:36	46 (tie)
58	2:39:12	47 (tie)
64	2:39:29	48
130	2:39:36	49
104	2:39:55	50
11	2:40:34	51
93	2:41:47	52
114	2:42:05	53
48	2:42:09	54
120	2:42:11	55
60	2:42:30	56
46	2:42:33	57
132	2:43:31	58
41	2:43:51	59
50	2:44:00	60

CAR No.	LEG TIME	POSITION IN LEG
125	2:44:48	61
84	2:44:59	62
35	2:45:29	63
75	2:45:42	64
128	2:45:56	65
102	2:46:15	66
95	2:46:54	67
53	2:49:04	68
121	2:49:56	69
18	2:50:04	70
13	2:50:06	71
92	2:51:04	72
86	2:51:28	73
116	2:52:44	74
74	2:53:12	75
26	2:55:24	76
29	2:55:11	77
72	2:55:22	78
115	2:57:23	79
16	2:57:55	80 (tie)
23	2:57:55	80 (tie)
31	2:58:11	82
119	2:59:14	83
127	3:00:27	84
107	3:00:42	85
106	3:02:31	86
124	3:03:50	87
94	3:04:27	88
33	3:07:33	89
17	3:07:33	90
9	3:08:28	91
131	3:08:44	92
2	3:09:31	93
87	3:10:10	94
109	3:12:23	95
24	3:12:57	96
73	3:13:04	97
105	3:14:40	98
83	3:22:19	99
17	3:22:34	100
80	3:26:51	101
40	3:29:45	102
70	3:29:56	103
96	3:30:17	104
101	3:34:55	105
57	3:35:58	106
27	3:46:38	107
44	3:54:34	108
108	4:02:07	109
61	4:19:17	110
34	4:22:45	111
10	4:45:58	112
4	5:32:03	113

Summary of Disqualifications

Cars which failed to appear for the start: 28, 53, 58, 67, 69, 117.

Cars which failed to arrive at finish line: 22, 30, 43, 47(accident) 51, 56 (accident 28 miles from start)(later competed for some leg prizes). 65 (tire trouble - arrived after deadline and later competed for some leg prizes), 99, 100, 112 (accident 19 miles from start, fatal to the driver), and #126.

Leg Two...

CAR No.	LEG TIME	CUMULATIVE TIME	POSITION IN LEG	POSITION IN RACE
55	1:56:38	4:21:25	1	1
38	1:58:12	4:19:25	2	2
68	1:59:08	4:18:25	3	3
81	2:00:16	4:24:19	4	12
19	2:00:25	4:29:52	5	13
37	2:01:22	4:27:45	6	7
12	2:01:33	4:26:06	7	4
52	2:01:42	4:26:41	8	5
45	2:01:36	4:26:52	9 (tie)	6
79	2:01:47	4:28:20	9 (tie)	10
88	2:02:11	4:28:06	11	9
89	2:02:58	4:27:48	12	8
71	2:03:24	4:31:55	13	26
118	2:03:12	4:37:42	14	15
14	2:03:19	4:28:41	15	11
66	2:04:13	4:33:51	16	16
29	2:04:58	4:47:31	17	25
5	2:04:58	4:33:44	18	36
42	2:05:14	4:38:47	19	28
8	2:05:14	4:39:26	20	28
111	2:05:23	4:30:12	21	14
39	2:05:11	4:35:43	22	23
113	2:06:04	4:36:09	23	22
62	2:06:07	4:35:57	24	21
6	2:06:54	4:34:11	25	17
78	2:07:00	4:35:46	26	19
5	2:07:16	4:35:49	27	20
90	2:07:30	4:44:05	28	30
20	2:07:39	4:37:07	29	24
123	2:07:46	4:46:02	30	32
103	2:08:14	4:45:27	31	31
49	2:08:10	4:35:07	32	18
26	2:08:23	5:02:47	33	59
65	2:08:07	4:50:30	34	45
114	2:08:30	4:48:44	35	35
64	2:08:32	4:47:44	36	37
73	2:09:17	4:48:29	37	47
3	2:09:32	5:13:22	38	64
98	2:09:20	4:50:30	39	34
95	2:09:44	4:58:38	40	33
1	2:10:28	4:48:06	41	38
59	2:10:30	4:49:06	42	41
91	2:10:44	4:50:20	43	34
2	2:10:50	5:00:17	44	74
121	2:10:50	5:00:46	45	58
6	2:10:58	4:47:13	46 (tie)	35
82	2:10:58	4:49:20	46 (tie)	42
101	2:12:32	5:47:27	48	92
7	2:12:30	5:40:37	49	29
32	2:12:16	5:49:24	50	43
48	2:12:48	5:28:27	51	82
41	2:12:46	5:54:53	52	48
54	2:12:49	4:56:40	53	52 (tie)
93	2:13:51	4:52:07	54	46
44	2:14:01	4:56:40	55	52 (tie)
65	2:14:53	4:00:59	56	102 (tie)
132	2:15:25	4:59:28	57	56
77	2:15:38	4:56:38	58	40
11	2:15:41	4:48:50	59	51
9	2:15:53	5:24:48	60	67
108	2:16:20	6:18:53	61	79
14	2:16:46	6:18:53	62	104

CAR No.	LEG TIME	CUMULATIVE TIME	POSITION IN LEG	POSITION IN RACE
73	2:16:55	5:29:59	63	83
128	2:17:06	5:03:02	64	61
120	2:17:14	4:59:25	65	55
129	2:17:16	4:55:05	66	49
110	2:17:21	4:55:28	67	50
60	2:17:56	5:00:26	68	57
125	2:18:08	5:02:56	69	60
92	2:19:18	5:10:22	70	63
72	2:19:43	5:15:05	71	70
84	2:20:20	5:05:01	72	62
87	2:21:24	5:31:34	73	85
31	2:21:31	5:19:42	74	73
116	2:21:33	5:14:17	75	67
86	2:22:30	5:14:30	76	68
106	2:22:07	5:24:38	77	78
71	2:23:34	4:50:00	78	44
57	2:23:42	5:59:45	79	98
70	2:24:04	5:54:00	80	97
15	2:24:23	5:13:34	81	66
18	2:24:31	5:14:35	82	69
97	2:25:25	5:20:36	83	75
74	2:27:41	5:38:23	84	91
34	2:26:08	6:46:53	85	106
119	2:26:16	5:25:30	86	80
23	2:26:31	5:24:24	87	77
33	2:26:36	5:34:09	88	87
74	2:27:41	5:20:53	89	76
127	2:27:46	5:28:13	90	81
35	2:28:13	5:13:25	91	65
27	2:28:47	6:15:25	92	103
102	2:31:44	5:17:59	93	71
94	2:31:50	5:38:17	94	90
107	2:32:17	5:32:59	95	86
40	2:32:55	6:01:40	96	99
124	2:33:41	5:37:39	97	89
50	2:35:19	5:19:19	98	72
131	2:37:25	5:48:25	99	93
105	2:37:29	5:51:32	100	94
61	2:39:02	5:35:23	101	88
10	2:39:22	7:38:19	102	109
17	2:40:17	6:02:51	103	100
131	2:40:56	5:52:40	104	96
130	2:50:46	5:30:22	105	84
16	2:51:57	7:11:14	106	108
14	2:53:53	5:51:48	107	95
80	2:59:47	6:26:38	108	105
85	3:01:00	6:09:09	109	101
75	3:23:27	6:54:06	110	107
4	4:32:00	10:04:03	111	111
#25	4:59:00	7:34:53	112	---

-- over maximum time

Summary of Disqualifications

Cars previously disqualified which continued running in competition for leg prizes: 65, 85.

Car disqualified in this leg for arriving after time limit: 25.

Car which failed to ppear for start: 96.

Car disqualified for failure to present Route Book and make compulsory half-hour stop between legs: 36.

Leg Three...

CAR No.	LEG TIME	CUMULATIVE TIME	POSITION IN LEG	POSITION IN RACE	CAR No.	LEG TIME	CUMULATIVE TIME	POSITION IN LEG	POSITION IN RACE
68	2:55:08	7:13:28	1	1	73	3:31:25	9:01:24	61	70
38	2:56:52	7:17:17	2	2	75	3:32:35	8:41:44	62	88
113	2:58:52	7:32:01	3	10	28	3:32:49	8:46:11	63	59
37	3:00:17	7:28:02	4	3	87	3:32:56	9:04:32	64	75
81	3:00:20	7:29:39	5	6	108	3:34:16	9:53:09	65	94
88	3:01:08	7:29:14	6	5	24	3:34:30	9:12:53	66	80
21	3:01:44	7:22:18	7	8	70	3:35:00	9:29:00	67	84
52	3:01:59	7:20:40	8	7	23	3:35:56	9:01:20	68	69
46	3:03:48	7:51:19	9	24 (tie)	110	3:37:07	8:42:35	69	53
49	3:04:21	7:39:28	10	12	125	3:38:32	8:41:28	70	56
7	3:04:39	7:45:16	11	16	106	3:39:14	9:03:52	71	73
2	3:05:20	8:25:37	12	46	25	3:39:45	8:44:38	72	49
114	3:05:34	7:56:04	13	27	91	3:40:43	8:27:14	73	-
12	3:05:56	7:52:02	14	8	18	3:41:34	8:56:09	74	65
63	3:06:05	7:40:16	15	13	97	3:43:27	9:04:03	75	74
14	3:06:43	7:35:24	16	11	102	3:43:54	8:57:22	76	67
36	3:07:06	7:33:41	17	15	16	3:44:19	9:36:07	77	85
26	3:07:06	8:03:52	18	36	105	3:44:55	9:49:36	78	86
90	3:07:08	7:51:21	19	30	92	3:49:34	9:49:36	79	92
118	3:08:13	7:45:55	20	17	127	3:43:16	9:14:24	80	75
66	3:08:26	7:42:17	21	14	102	3:47:22	9:07:28	81	76
42	3:08:32	7:47:39	22	19	17	3:47:23	8:28:34	82	93
6	3:09:15	7:50:50	23	28	57	3:47:35	9:49:36	83	-
55	3:10:10	7:51:21	24	7	65	3:49:51	9:26:02	84	83
32	3:10:14	7:55:38	25	31	131	3:50:24	9:14:24	85	89
5	3:11:03	7:46:52	26	18	116	3:53:11	9:07:28	86	78
20	3:11:18	7:54:25	27	20	19	3:54:42	8:28:34	87	40
98	3:12:08	7:58:58	28	30	109	3:55:03	10:48:24	88	90
1	3:12:23	8:11:01	29	37	107	3:56:03	9:26:02	89	83
123	3:12:48	7:58:50	30	29	71	3:56:12	8:14:24	90	60
44	3:13:09	9:23:08	31	82	124	3:59:27	9:37:06	91	87
82	3:13:12	8:03:03	32	32	45	4:01:46	8:28:38	92	52
62	3:13:47	10:02:40	33	96	40	4:05:23	9:05:50	93	77
4	3:14:00	8:03:03	34	22	120	4:06:25	9:05:50	94	77
77	3:14:22	8:03:12	35	33	94	4:07:30	9:45:47	95	91
101	3:14:36	9:02:03	36	71	54	4:10:54	9:23:01	96	72
78	3:17:08	7:52:23	37	25	61	4:13:20	11:24:37	97	102
48	3:17:08	8:12:01	38	38	104	4:17:55	9:11:51	98	79
121	3:18:40	8:15:49	39	33	33	4:26:18	10:00:27	99	95
103	3:19:00	8:04:27	40	34	89	4:27:25	8:55:13	100	63
111	3:19:04	7:49:16	41	21	10	4:35:12	12:13:31	101	103
93	3:19:10	8:15:50	42 (tie)	39	80	4:44:45	11:11:23	102	-
84	3:19:10	8:25:20	43 (tie)	48	119	5:22:15	10:48:24	103	99
122	3:21:02	8:09:31	44	35	50	5:33:06	10:52:25	104	100
31	3:21:29	8:41:11	45	55	8	6:12:58	10:22:24	105	98
41	3:21:18	8:18:14	46	41	124	3:59:27	9:37:06		
9	3:23:18	8:40:06	47	62					
128	3:25:10	8:38:13	48	45					
132	3:25:28	8:26:29	49	43					
74	3:25:33	8:26:26	50	61					
35	3:26:14	8:39:39	51	57					
72	3:26:35	8:41:40	52	57					
59	3:27:01	8:16:07	53	40					
79	3:27:11	7:55:31	54	26					
83	3:28:36	8:57:23	55	66					
130	3:29:13	8:59:35	56 (tie)	68					
129	3:30:38	8:44:58	57 (tie)	47					
86	3:30:38	8:34:58	58	58					
1	3:31:14	8:19:20	59	42					
11	3:31:20	8:27:47	60	50					

Summary of Disqualifications

Cars previously disqualified which continued running in competition for leg prizes: 25, 65.

Car previously disqualified which started in competition for leg prizes, then dropped out in this leg: 85 (engine trouble).

Cars which failed to arrive at finish line: 4 (transmission broke), 13 (engine trouble), 27 (accident 200 yards from finish line), 29 (accident 200 yards from finish line), 60 (engine trouble), 64 (accident 45 miles from Parral), 115 (engine trouble).

Leg Four...

CAR No.	LEG TIME	CUMULATIVE TIME	POSITION IN LEG	POSITION IN RACE	CAR No.	LEG TIME	CUMULATIVE TIME	POSITION IN LEG	POSITION IN RACE
81	3:46:14	11:15:53	1	3	102	4:28:03	14:33:24	61	71
68	3:46:37	11:00:05	2	1	15	4:29:05	13:21:33	62	57
38	3:47:18	11:03:05	3	2	24	3:31:40	13:44:33	63	64
21	3:51:25	11:23:06	4	5	106	4:32:31	13:36:05	64	61
113	3:51:37	11:26:41	5	6	116	4:32:51	13:40:19	65	63
26	3:53:03	12:02:55	6	22	77	4:36:00	12:39:12	66	38
52	3:53:46	14:36:06	7	81	104	4:31:08	13:48:55	67	67
70	3:53:46	11:22:26	8	4	109	4:37:47	14:20:57	68	75
23	3:54:07	11:49:26	9	14	38	4:39:14	14:39:41	69	83
46	3:54:31	11:45:50	10	13	86	4:40:07	13:25:05	70	58
12	3:56:13	11:28:15	11	7	70	4:40:46	14:05:46	71	72
71	3:56:30	12:43:42	12	40	97	4:43:16	13:46:44	72	65
44	3:56:36	13:25:44	13	77	10	4:44:06	16:55:37	73	92
14	3:56:38	11:32:02	14	9	105	4:46:13	14:24:04	74	76
19	3:54:31	12:23:57	15	30	74	4:51:06	13:37:32	75	62
63	3:59:23	11:39:41	16	10	131	4:52:51	14:35:19	76	80
114	4:00:25	11:56:29	17	18	127	4:52:51	14:07:15	77	78
66	4:01:09	11:42:24	18	12	124	4:53:43	13:46:16	78	78
72	4:01:09	11:42:49	19	15	40	4:54:10	14:30:42	79	87
42	4:02:32	11:50:11	20	15	17	4:55:59	14:45:59	80	85
49	4:02:41	11:30:45	21	11	94	5:01:17	14:41:34	81	84
37	4:02:52	12:21:28	22	8	25	5:00:00	16:07:15	82	-
103	4:04:52	12:08:58	23	28	50	5:05:00	15:54:25	83	89
5	4:04:56	12:08:50	24	26	18	5:08:44	14:04:25	84	70
-	4:05:31	11:52:23	25	16	107	5:10:13	14:38:15	85	82
35	4:06:33	12:46:12	26	44	55	5:14:42	12:45:32	86	43
90	4:07:23	12:07:01	27	20	61	5:15:42	16:40:49	87	90
101	4:09:04	12:08:32	28	25	20	5:19:07	13:07:32	88	52
1	4:09:18	11:50:11	29	33	2	5:20:00	11:55:19	89	51
101	4:10:45	13:12:48	30	50	80	5:39:34	16:50:57	90	91
9	4:11:07	12:59:06	31	53	123	5:48:30	13:47:20	91	66
39	4:11:10	11:54:48	32	51	125	6:10:36	14:52:04	92	86
111	4:11:11	12:00:37	33	17	83	6:32:00	15:29:03	93	88
45	4:11:20	12:41:20	34	21					
-	4:11:42	12:46:23	35	39					
3	4:12:54	12:59:05	36	50					
82	4:13:20	12:06:06	37	29					
6	4:13:02	12:09:37	38	27					
59	4:13:12	12:29:19	39	34					
31	4:13:30	12:54:41	40	49					
48	4:14:00	12:26:01	41	31					
118	4:14:03	11:57:09	42	74					
121	4:14:52	11:11:23	43	19					
36	4:14:58	10:52:25	44	36					
57	4:15:31	14:05:07	45	71					
91	4:16:40	12:53:51	46	48					
16	4:17:10	12:35:24	47	37					
62	4:17:30	13:15:18	48	68					
-	4:17:47	12:43:30	49	24					
129	4:17:47	12:43:30	50	42					
93	4:17:59	12:33:49	51	35					
122	4:18:07	12:27:38	52	32					
128	4:19:13	12:50:13	53	54					
73	4:22:28	13:23:52	54	47					
84	4:22:30	12:48:33	55	45					
132	4:21:26	12:21:56	56	-					
23	4:26:45	13:28:05	57	59					
92	4:22:45	13:22:09	58	55					
120	4:27:21	13:33:11	59	60					

Summary of Disqualifications

Car previously disqualified which continued running in competition for leg prizes: 25.

Car previously disqualified which started in competition for leg prizes, then dropped out in this leg: 65 (did not start).

Cars which failed to appear for start: 11, 54, 78, 89, 110, 119.

Cars which failed to arrive at finish line: 7 (accident at Rio Florido), 75, 87 (accident in Zacatecas, resumed running in later legs), 88 (accident at Rio Florido), 108 (broke piston).

CAMINO SINUOSO
WINDING ROAD

Complete Leg-by-Leg Statistics

Leg Five...

CAR NO.	LEG TIME	CUMULATIVE TIME	POSITION IN LEG	POSITION IN RACE	CAR NO.	LEG TIME	CUMULATIVE TIME	POSITION IN LEG	POSITION IN RACE
113	2:59:15	14:25:56	1	3	131	3:52:02	18:27:21	61	76
38	3:07:29	14:11:04	2	1	57	3:52:48	17:57:55	62	70
118	3:11:21	15:12:08	3	15	106	3:53:15	17:29:38	63	61
79	3:14:59	15:04:45	4	11	33	3:53:18	16:32:59	64	78
46	3:15:15	15:01:30	5	10	116	3:53:24	17:33:43	65	63
49	3:11:53	14:58:02	6	9	114	3:54:40	15:51:09	66	29
44	3:16:56	16:36:40	7	47	48	3:55:53	17:24:45	67	41
14	3:17:22	14:49:26	8	7	23	3:56:40	17:24:45	68	45
8	3:18:32	17:54:38	9	69	86	3:57:00	17:22:05	69	58
21	3:20:28	14:45:44	10	6	102	3:57:32	17:30:56	70	62
103	3:21:03	15:30:01	11	21	10	3:57:58	20:56:35	71	85
71	3:21:56	16:03:56	12	31	24	3:57:59	17:59:49	72	66
26	3:21:35	15:24:30	13	19	77	4:00:27	17:41:01	73	49
75	3:22:14	14:50:29	14	8	127	4:01:06	18:07:15	74	54
12	3:22:14	15:22:14	15	8	104	4:02:06	17:51:05	75	68
68	3:22:28	14:22:37	16	2	124	4:07:37	18:33:43	76	79
95	3:22:40	15:21:41	17	18	1	4:07:37	16:32:15	77	46
3	3:23:08	15:47:26	18	42	94	4:08:23	18:49:57	78	80
19	3:24:11	15:31:13	19	27	17	4:09:08	17:52:05	79	82
32	3:24:30	15:31:43	20	22	18	4:09:38	18:14:31	80	75
55	3:24:36	16:10:08	21	35	107	4:14:17	18:52:32	81	81
65	3:24:43	15:38:36	22	25	40	4:20:40	19:18:27	82	84
95	3:25:12	15:08:47	23	23	20	4:33:29	17:41:01	83	64
121	3:25:58	16:00:36	24	30	2	4:36:53	16:32:12	84	77
63	3:26:23	15:06:04	25	12	111	4:51:01	17:50:07	85	67
6	3:26:53	15:36:30	26	24	25	5:04:23	21:20:18	86	---
42	3:27:50	15:18:01	27	16	61	6:02:00	22:42:16	87	87
129	3:27:52	16:11:22	28	36	125	6:16:17	21:08:21	88	86
5	3:28:28	15:20:23	29	17	80	6:20:00	23:10:57	89	88
41	3:28:38	16:10:02	30	32					
81	3:29:00	14:44:53	31	5					
35	3:29:08	16:15:20	32	40					
72	3:29:31	15:23:10	33	37	Summary of Disqualifications				
39	3:29:44	15:25:59	34	20					
16	3:31:21	17:24:39	35	57					
82	3:31:39	15:47:45	36	28	Cars previously disqualified which continued running in competition for leg prizes; 25,26 - (arrived without Route Book and no official time was ever recorded).				
62	3:32:07	15:40:08	37	26					
29	3:32:11	16:05:58	38	33					
34	3:32:40	17:24:23	39	66					
111	3:34:59	15:33:08	40	23					
45	3:14:50	16:14:50	41	39	25				
84	3:34:19	16:22:52	42	43	Cars which failed to arrive at finish line: 50, 98, 123, 130 (had engine trouble - continued to run in subsequent legs, never presenting Route Book).				
101	3:36:53	19:05:17	43	51					
83	3:36:56	16:22:23	44	52					
91	3:39:05	16:22:56	45	44					
59	3:39:10	16:08:29	46	34					
37	3:39:41	16:21:57	47	53					
120	3:41:46	17:14:57	48	14					
73	3:42:23	17:06:15	49	55					
97	3:42:31	17:29:15	50	60					
31	3:43:12	16:37:53	51	50					
92	3:44:41	17:07:50	52	53					
128	3:45:29	16:35:42	53	38					
122	3:46:25	16:14:03	54	54					
15	3:47:38	17:14:11	55	54					
74	3:48:19	17:26:01	56	59					
132	3:48:39	16:37:32	57	48					
105	3:49:20	18:14:00	58	74					
70	3:50:58	18:00:03	59	71					
109	3:51:12	18:12:09	60	73					

Leg Six...

CAR NO.	LEG TIME	CUMULATIVE TIME	POSITION IN LEG	POSITION IN RACE	CAR NO.	LEG TIME	CUMULATIVE TIME	POSITION IN LEG	POSITION IN RACE
44	1:03:05	17:39:45	1	39	25	1:14:50	22:35:08	61	---
8	1:03:26	18:58:04	2	56	20	1:14:52	18:55:53	62	54
118	1:03:56	16:16:04	3	12	15	1:14:56	18:29:07	63	48
38	1:04:49	15:15:53	4	1	111	1:15:02	16:48:10	64	23
77	1:04:53	15:42:32	5	40	124	1:15:21	19:49:04	65	69
90	1:04:54	16:26:08	6	17	48	1:15:31	17:37:25	66	38
113	1:05:06	15:31:02	7	3	125	1:15:59	22:24:20	67	74
86	1:05:22	16:06:52	8	20	15	1:16:14	18:38:19	68	49
52	1:05:32	15:49:42	9	4	24	1:16:18	18:58:50	69	58
79	1:05:42	16:10:27	10	11	87	1:17:55	---	70	---
68	1:05:44	15:28:21	11	2	109	1:18:03	19:30:12	71	63
35	1:06:21	17:16:49	12 (tie)	32	131	1:18:23	19:24:44	72	68
14	1:06:21	15:55:47	12 (tie)	7	18	1:19:46	19:34:17	73	65
121	1:07:15	17:07:15	14	28	94	1:21:14	20:11:01	74	65
103	1:06:40	16:36:41	15	20	107	1:21:19	20:13:51	75	72
83	1:06:49	20:12:46	16	71	127	1:22:21	19:30:42	76	64
75	1:06:53	16:32:15	17	29	17	1:22:28	20:17:33	77	73
34	1:07:05	18:56:28	18	55	10	1:25:19	22:31:54	78	75
12	1:07:07	16:57:36	19 (tie)	8	80	1:25:35	24:36:32	79	76
26	1:07:07	17:13:37	19 (tie)	18					
6	1:07:12	16:43:42	21	22					
39	1:07:39	16:33:28	22	19	Summary of Disqualifications				
66	1:07:49	16:16:28	23	13					
21	1:07:50	15:53:34	24	5	Cars which failed to appear at starting line: 1, 23, 55, 61, 102.				
32	1:08:02	16:39:33	25	21					
19	1:08:03	16:55:29	26	25	Cars which failed to arrive at finish line: 5 - (clutch collapsed 55 miles from start), 16 (had accident 20 miles from start), 40 (tire trouble 20 miles from start), 59 (engine trouble), 95, 122, 129 (steering knuckle broke).				
9	1:08:09	18:58:16	27	57					
129	1:08:15	15:06:17	28	9					
49	1:08:19	16:26:20	29	16					
42	1:08:32	17:30:45	30	35					
3	1:09:19	18:38:57	31	50					
106	1:09:25	19:41:37	32	66					
2	1:09:32	17:21:52	33	33					
72	1:09:40	18:14:23	34	55					
116	1:09:41	16:20:13	35 (tie)	15					
37	1:09:41	17:13:43	35 (tie)	30					
41	1:09:44	17:32:36	37	36					
84	1:09:46	17:15:44	38	31					
93	1:09:52	17:47:45	39	41					
31	1:10:14	17:33:10	40	37					
91	1:10:16	17:01:25	41	27					
114	1:10:14	18:00:12	42	44					
101	1:10:35	15:55:32	43	6					
81	1:10:39	16:59:15	44	34					
45	1:10:38	17:25:28	45	60					
57	1:10:51	19:08:46	46	14					
63	1:10:57	16:17:01	47	45					
73	1:11:14	18:17:29	48	26					
82	1:11:30	16:59:15	49	52					
97	1:11:38	18:40:53	50	59					
62	1:11:52	16:52:00	51	24					
33	1:11:56	19:44:55	52	67					
104	1:11:58	19:25:58	53	62					
128	1:13:01	16:59:15	54	59					
120	1:13:20	17:49:02	55	42					
15	1:13:39	18:28:36	56	47					
74	1:13:48	16:39:49	57	56					
132	1:14:26	17:51:57	58	---					
56	1:14:30	19:15:14	59	61					
70	1:14:48	18:22:38	60	46					

146

Leg Seven...

CAR No.	LEG TIME	CUMULATIVE TIME	POSITION IN LEG	POSITION IN RACE		CAR No.	LEG TIME	CUMULATIVE TIME	POSITION IN LEG	POSITION IN RACE
103	3:45:26	20:22:07	1	14		20	4:39:31	23:35:24	61	56
8	3:47:15	22:45:29	2	43		109	4:40:33	24:10:45	62	61
32	3:49:40	20:33:13	3	18		125	4:43:01	27:07:21	64	69
90	3:50:32	20:16:40	4	12		92	4:44:42	23:03:20	64	50
52	3:51:19	19:41:01	5	3		107	4:50:41	25:03:45	65	65
71	3:53:22	21:04:11	6	24		83	4:51:10	25:03:56	66	66
3	3:54:58	21:25:43	7	29		94	4:53:07	25:04:18	67	67
35	3:55:50	21:17:31	8	27		124	4:58:57	24:47:01	68	64
46	3:56:30	20:03:27	9	6		38	4:58:10	24:58:03	69	9
68	3:56:46	19:25:07	10	1		17	5:06:46	25:24:19	70	68
44	3:58:04	21:38:49	11	32		127	5:10:20	24:41:02	71	63
66	3:58:20	20:14:48	12	11		10	5:13:03	27:36:57	72	70
5	3:58:40	22:56:26	13	46		80	5:38:55	30:15:21	73	
39	3:59:48	20:53:26	14	19		41	5:59:40	23:13:23	74	51
21	4:00:19	19:53:53	15	4		93	6:55:00	24:10:44	75	--
12	4:00:31	19:58:07	16	5						
34	4:01:01	22:57:29	17	47		Summary of Disqualifications				
97	4:01:53	20:28:13	18	16						
42	4:02:03	20:08:20	19	42		Car disqualified for failure to present Route Book at finish: #2.				
79	4:02:51	20:13:18	20							
82	4:03:04	21:02:19	21	23		Cars which failed to arrive at finish line: 14 (accident 18 miles after Puebla), 18 (accident), 114 (accident – returned later to compete for leg prizes).				
118	4:03:37	20:19:38	22	13						
97	4:03:37	22:44:30	23	42						
73	4:04:30	22:21:59	24	41						
91	4:05:29	21:38:19	25	30						
19	4:06:02	21:01:33	26	22						
121	4:06:18	20:50:00	27	20						
37	4:06:23	21:15:38	28	15						
56	4:07:41	out	29	--						
63	4:09:32	19:40:43	30	2						
72	4:11:28	22:09:29	31	36						
31	4:13:51	22:53:40	32	44						
62	4:13:34	21:19:24	33	34						
45	4:14:42	22:38:40	34	57						
81	4:14:44	20:31:45	36	17						
84	4:16:36	21:38:28	37	37						
33	4:16:44	22:06:29	38	30						
86	4:17:40	21:09:40	39	25						
101	4:18:34	22:21:40	40	33						
81	4:18:54	20:14:26	41 (tie)	10						
84	4:18:54	21:51:30	41 (tie)	34						
33	4:19:23	24:04:18	43	60						
86	4:19:51	22:58:10	44	48						
101	4:20:49	22:21:01	45	40						
24	4:20:58	23:19:48	46	53						
128	4:21:28	22:13:25	47	39						
104	4:23:28	23:43:16	48	55						
26	4:24:40	23:25:16	49	21						
120	4:27:14	22:55:50	50	45						
25	4:29:57	27:05:05	51	49						
15	4:30:12	22:59:19	52	49						
48	4:31:12	22:09:14	53	38						
70	4:32:56	23:49:10	54	58						
57	4:33:33	23:17:55	55	58						
111	4:37:02	21:25:12	56	28						
87	4:37:45	23:21:34	57	54						
116	4:38:11	24:24:30	58	62						
131	4:38:26	23:17:55	59	52						
106	4:38:58		60							

Eighth Leg...

CAR No.	TIME IN LEG	CUMULATIVE TIME	POSITION IN LEG	POSITION IN RACE
38	4:35:38	24:49:41	1	4
36	4:39:08	25:29:08	2	15
113	4:40:33	24:21:07	3	16
19	4:40:54	25:21:43	4	16
79	4:41:39	24:54:57	5	7
77	4:42:14	26:36:38	6	23
90	4:46:25	25:01:42	7	9
49	4:46:18	24:54:38	8	6
52	4:48:18	24:57:43	9	2
118	4:49:10	25:08:48	10	10
41	4:49:24	28:02:47	11	36
39	4:51:15	25:27:16	12	11
32	4:54:18	25:27:16	13	13
9	4:54:53	27:51:49	14 (tie)	30
21	4:55:02	24:48:55	15 (tie)	3
101	4:55:02	27:16:03	15	27
12	4:55:48	24:53:55	17	26
128	4:56:12	26:56:54	18	31
34	4:56:48	27:53:54	19	17
82	4:56:40	25:59:09	20	17
46	4:56:49	25:00:11	21	8
71	4:59:19	26:08:53	22	18
91	5:00:34	26:03:09	23	19
72	5:00:34	25:28:39	24	24
42	5:00:46	25:28:59	25	14
103	5:02:03	25:24:41	26	11 (tie)
74	5:03:32	27:57:12	27	34
62	5:05:00	26:24:14	28	21
83	5:06:04	30:10:00	29	50
121	5:08:20	26:21:58	30	22
70	5:21:12	27:34:27	31	43 (tie)
15	5:12:26	28:14:45	32	37
86	5:16:35	28:12:45	33	37 (tie)
92	5:19:19	28:26:05	34	39
105	5:19:26	29:00:06	35	42
132	5:21:12	27:34:27	36	28
97	5:22:38	26:47:11	37	35
109	5:24:44	28:13:08	38	38
87	5:35:08	29:15:29	39	46
			40	--
120	5:36:02	28:31:52	41	40
124	5:36:50	29:07:28	42	44
106	5:41:55	28:59:50	43	41
131	5:54:02	30:06:19	44	49
37	5:54:32	26:11:33	45	20
31	5:47:42	27:54:11	46	22
56	5:50:56	29:57:21	47	52
33	5:53:03	30:13:47	48	48
94	5:54:15	28:58:33	49	48
			50	54
24	5:58:41	29:18:29	51	45
80	6:01:06	36:16:27	52	60
127	6:03:48	30:13:47	53	53
17	6:08:48	31:33:07	54	57
20	6:11:11	29:29:47	55	47
107	6:14:36	31:18:17	56	56
125	6:23:38	33:30:59	57	58
26	7:01:47	30:23:19	58	33
116	7:01:45	27:37:46	59	31
10	7:01:49	34:33:46	60	59

Summary of Disqualifications

Cars previously disqualified which continued running in competition for leg prizes: 25, 56, 87.

Cars which failed to appear at starting line: 48, 111.

Cars which failed to arrive at finish line: 8 (engine trouble), 35 (engine trouble 194 miles out of Oaxaca), 44 (engine trouble 165 miles out of Oaxaca), 45 (tire trouble 30 miles from Oaxaca), 63 (engine trouble 15 miles out of Oaxaca), 66, 73 (engine trouble 278 miles from Oaxaca), 81 (accident 31 miles before Tuxtla Gutierrez), 84 (engine trouble 169 miles from Oaxaca), 93 (accident).

Complete Leg-by-Leg Statistics

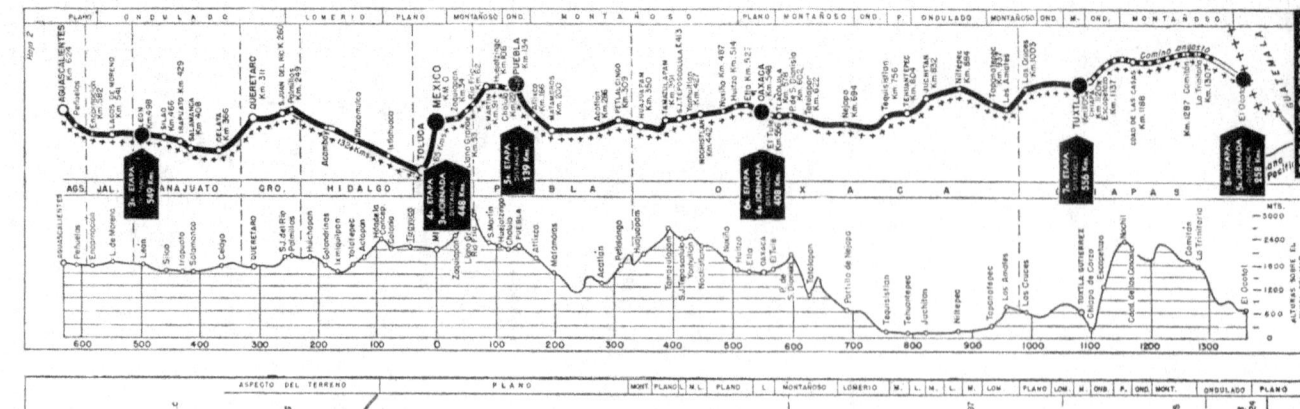

TRANSLATION OF MAP INSCRIPTIONS:
Camino Revestido: All-Weather Road
Camino Pavimentado: Paved Road

Aspecto de Terreno: Kind of Terrain
Plano, or P.: Level
Montañoso, Mont. or M.: Mountainous

Lomerio, Lom. or L.: Hilly
Ondulado, or Ond.: Rolling
Estados: States

Alturas Sobre el Nivel del Mar: Altitudes (in meters)
Etapa: A Leg of the Race (see text)
Jornada: A Day of the Race (see text)

Summary of Disqualifications

Cars previously disqualified which continued running in competition for leg prizes: 25, 56, 87, 114, 130.

Cars disqualified in this leg for arriving after time limit: 6, 15, 105, 107, 132.

Car disqualified in this leg for illegal change of crew: 49.

Cars which failed to arrive at finish line: 10, 26, 31, 32 (accident 5-1/2 miles from finish), 37 (broke radiator at Las Casas), 68 (did not start), 94 (turned over to race officials for inspection run over route).

CONDITIONS

Nearly all cars which were disqualified were so classified for failure to arrive at the finish line, or for failure to arrive within the maximum time permitted for a leg. Under the rules, such cars could continue and competing for leg prizes, but were disqualified for the over-all prizes. Those which continued under this condition were classified in the leg standings, but not in the over-all standings. In the above set of tables, total times are given for such cars when they are available.

Cars which were disqualified for violation of any rule except the maximum-time rule were barred from further competition, and were not classified in leg or over-all standings.

Since cars which dropped out of the race voluntarily were not required to report to the officials the reasons for their dropping out are not always known. When they are known, they are reported.

Cars otherwise qualified which did not appear for the start of a leg are counted among "cars in running for major prizes at start", and also among "cars disqualified during leg", since the disqualification was for nonappearance. The total and leg times were reported by the officials only for those cars which finished each leg, it is possible that cars which are listed as "failed to arrive at finish line", actually did not appear at the starting line.

Ninth Leg...

CAR NO.	TIME IN LEG	CUMULATIVE TIME	POSITION IN LEG	POSITION IN RACE
49			Disqualified	disqualified
90	2:55:57	27:50:35	1	4
103	2:59:22	28:01:04	2	8
52	3:03:55	28:25:36	3	16
21	3:04:24	27:34:25	4	1
12	3:05:29	27:52:39	5	3
	3:03:26	28:02:21		
41	3:08:30	31:11:17	6	26
19	3:08:39	28:51:04	7	12
51	3:14:00	31:03:17	8	25
9	3:14:18	31:07:07	9	24
118	3:11:15	27:35:41	10	2
97	3:11:34			
74	3:16:16	33:13:28	11	27
3	3:16:45	30:49:53	12	20
77	3:17:47	28:26:25	13	10
78	3:19:15	29:17:15	14	19
97	3:21:00	31:34:08	15	28
39	3:21:07	28:45:48	16	11
121	3:21:45	29:43:13	17	16
33	3:22:37	33:19:58	18	36
79	3:22:49	33:45:17	19	39
71	3:23:32	29:26:52	20	15
128	3:23:36	30:19:30	21 (tie)	22
86	3:23:36	31:38:28	22 (tie)	29
46	3:23:43	28:23:23	23	7
82	3:23:57	29:23:06	24	17
79	3:24:18	28:19:15	25	6
83	3:24:24	33:34:43	26	38
25	3:25:34	31:52:11	27	33
62	3:26:29	29:24:50	28	18
70	3:27:29	32:29:50	29	32
101	3:28:37	30:44:40	30	23
42	3:29:23	28:58:22	31	13
92	3:29:55	29:38:48	32	16
114	3:30:29	30:09:07	33	21
24	3:37:26	32:55:55	34	35
38	3:37:29	28:27:10	35	9
57	3:37:42	34:52:51	36	43
87	3:38:10	31:23:02	37	33
20	3:41:55	33:30:30	38	37
131	3:44:25	33:51:04	39	40
127	3:51:00	35:50:37	40	34
120	3:51:10	32:23:02	41	30
55	3:59:46	32:32:51	42	31
124	4:11:20	34:48:51	43	42
17	4:17:30	35:50:37	44	45
127	4:18:37		45	44
80	4:24:59	40:41:26	46	47
23	4:28:50	34:14:39	47	41
125	4:31:36	38:02:35	48	46

Over Maximum Time for Leg

107	4:42:00	34:26:27	51	
6	5:02:29	36:00:17	52	
105	7:22:58	34:11:35	53	
130	no time recorded	32:52:06		
132	no time recorded			
15	no time recorded			
56	no time recorded			

25	7:21:22	34:26:27	61	
57	7:31:50	34:11:35	62	55
68	8:22:18	27:47:25	63	29

148

Classic Auto Titles from - www.VelocePress.com

Le Mans 24

Author: Denne Petitclerc **Pages:** 196 **Dimensions:** 5" x 8"

Description: Subtitled: Ford Battles Ferrari, Men Race Against Time And Death. Fiction, originally published 1971, this is the VelocePress reprint. This book was originally written as the script for Steve McQueen's movie, Denne Petitclerc's "Le Mans 24" was born at the 1967 Le Mans, where it was Ferrari versus Ford, old-world craftsmanship versus machine-age efficiency. Petitclerc crafts a novel of action and suspense transporting the reader to the rain-swept Le Mans race course and the battle between man and machine. The story line of the movie and Petitclerc's novel are essentially the same. What Petitclerc does is flesh out the story, making the main character three-dimensional and perhaps more believable, giving him a life away from the circuit. He also creates a series of interesting characters for the protagonist to interact with. On one level, "Le Mans 24" works as a sort of guide to the movie. On another level, it is a sequel to the movie. Ultimately, "Le Mans 24" is what the movie could have been.

If Hemingway had Written a Racing Novel, The Best of Motor Racing Fiction: 1950-2000

Editor: Richard Nisley **Pages:** 200 **Dimensions:** 5" x 8"

Description: Sixteen short stories and excerpts from the best automotive racing fiction written between 1950 and 2000. "If Hemingway Had Written A Racing Novel" provides behind the scene accounts of the action, adventure and romance 'round the track. Richard Nisley has brought together, in a single book, the most significant automotive writers of the 20th century -- for a raucous ride to the checkered flag.

Dialed In - The Jan Opperman Story

Author: John Sawyer **Pages:** 144 **Dimensions:** 5 1/2" x 8 1/2"

Description: We are pleased to announce the VelocePress edition of a book that is acknowledged by many as being a classic auto-racing story. It is filled with passion and pathos, sometimes humorous, sometimes sad. The Jan Opperman Story is one of never giving up and having faith in a divine being. It provides the reader the rare opportunity to peer behind the glamorous facade of auto racing and meet the inner man. The friendship between narrator and author is evident and while much of the book is Jan's own words, John Sawyer has carefully authored them. There is something very special about this book, it almost demands the readers' attention and then refuses to let go! From a teenage street fighter, motorcycle flat track racer and California hippie to respected Sprint car driver and Indy 500 racer - Jan Opperman's story is remarkable, entertaining and difficult to put down. Unfortunately, I never got to meet Jan Opperman - I wish I had.

VelocePress "Books & Manuals"

We have included a sample listing, however, for the most up-to-date information please visit our website at www.VelocePress.com

- FERRARI GUIDE TO PERFORMANCE
- IF HEMINGWAY HAD WRITTEN A RACING NOVEL
- OBERT'S FIAT GUIDE
- LE MANS 24
- FERRARI SERIAL NUMBERS PART I
- FERRARI SERIAL NUMBERS PART II
- MASERATI BROCHURES AND SALES LITERATURE
- FERRARI TUNING TIPS & MAINTENANCE TECHNIQUES
- ABARTH BUYERS GUIDE
- BMW ISETTA FACTORY WS MANUAL
- MASERATI OWNER'S HANDBOOK
- FERRARI BERLINETTA LUSSO
- FERRARI OWNER'S HANDBOOK
- FERRARI 250/GT SERVICE AND MAINTENANCE
- DIALED IN - THE JAN OPPERMAN STORY
- FERRARI BROCHURES & SALES LITERATURE 1946-1967
- FERRARI OPP, MAINTENANCE & SERVICE H/BOOKS 1948-1963
- PERFORMANCE TUNING THE SUNBEAM TIGER
- TRIUMPH MOTORCYCLES WS MANUAL 1937-1951
- TRIUMPH MOTORCYCLES FACTORY WS MANUAL 1945-1955
- TRIUMPH MOTORCYCLES (BOOK OF) WS MANUAL 1935-1939
- BMW M/CYCLES FACTORY WS MANUAL R26 R27 (1956-1967)
- BMW M/CYCLES FACTORY WSM R50 R50S R60 R69S (1955-1969)
- NORTON MOTORCYCLES FACTORY WS MANUAL 1957-1970
- NORTON MOTORCYCLES WS MANUAL 1932-1939
- FERRARI 308 SERIES BUYER'S AND OWNER'S GUIDE
- ARIEL MOTORCYCLES WS MANUAL 1933-1951
- VINCENT MOTORCYCLES MAINTENANCE AND REPAIR 1935-1955
- FERRARI SPYDER CALIFORNIA
- AUSTIN-HEALEY 6-CYLINDER MAINTENANCE & REPAIR
- HONDA MOTORCYCLES WSM 250-305 TWINS C/CS/CB SERIES
- PORSCHE 356 OWNERS WORKSHOP MANUAL 1948-1965
- PORSCHE 912 WORKSHOP MANUAL
- VOLVO 1944-1968 WS MANUAL ALL MODELS
- HONDA MOTORCYCLES MANUAL: 1960-1966 50cc TO 305cc
- DUCATI FACTORY WSM: 160cc, 250cc & 350cc OHC MODELS.
- ROYAL ENFIELD FACTORY WS MANUAL: 736cc INTERCEPTOR
- FERRARI BROCHURES AND SALES LITERATURE 1968-1989

——————www.VelocePress.com——————

VelocePress "Autobooks" Service & Repair Manuals

Through our partnership with Brooklands Books Ltd, VelocePress is pleased to bring back these easy to read, concise repair manuals that have been out-of-print and unavailable for a number of years. The "Autobooks" series of manuals are guaranteed to become your close companion in the shop. We have included a sample listing, however, for the most up-to-date information please visit our website at **www.VelocePress.com**

Alfa Romeo Giulia 1300, 1600, 1750, 2000 1962-1978 WSM
Austin Healey Sprite, MG Midget 1958-1980 WSM
BMW 1600 1966-1973 WSM
Fiat 124 1966-1974 WSM
Fiat 124 Sport 1966-1975 WSM
Fiat 125, 125 Special 1967-1973 WSM
Fiat 126 / 650 1972-1982 WSM
Fiat 127, 900, 1050, 1971-81 W/S Manual
Fiat 128 1969-1982 WSM
Fiat 131 1975-1982 WSM
Fiat 132 1972-1982 WSM
Fiat 500 1957-1973 WSM
Fiat 600 & Multipla 1955-1969 WSM
Fiat 850 1964-1972 WSM
Fiat 1100 & 1200 1957-1969 WSM
Fiat 1300, 1500 1961-1967 WSM
Jaguar E-Type 1961-1972 WSM
Jaguar Mk 1, 2 1955-1969 WSM
Jaguar S Type 420 1963-1968 WSM
Jaguar XK 120, 140, 150 MK 7, 8, 9 1948-1961 WSM
Land-Rover 1, 2 1948-1961 WSM
Mercedes-Benz 190 1959-1968 WSM
Mercedes-Benz 230 1963-1968 WSM
Mercedes-Benz 250 1968-1972 WSM
MG Midget TA-TF 1936-1955 WSM
Mini 1959-1980 WSM
Morris Minor 1952-1971 WSM
Peugeot 404 1960-1975 WSM
Porsche 911 1964-1969 WSM
Porsche 911 1970-1977 WSM
Renault 16 1965-1979 WSM
Renault 8, 10 1100 1962-1971 WSM
Rover 3500, 3500S 1968-1976 WSM
Sunbeam Rapier, Alpine 1955-1965 WSM
Triumph Spitfire, GT6, Vitesse 1962-1968 WSM
Triumph TR2, TR3, TR3A 1952-1962 WSM
Triumph TR4, TR4A 1961-1967 WSM
Volkswagen Beetle 1968-77 WSM